Stendhal
and the
Age of Napoleon

Gita May

1977
COLUMBIA UNIVERSITY PRESS
NEW YORK

Library of Congress Cataloging in Publication Data

May, Gita.
Stendhal and the Age of Napoleon.

Bibliography: p.
Includes index.
1. Beyle, Marie Henri, 1783–1842.   2. Authors,
French—19th century—Biography.   I. Title.
PQ2436.M35   848'.7'09 [B]   77-8379
ISBN 0-231-04344-9

Columbia University Press
New York   Guildford, Surrey

Contents

Acknowledgments

IT IS A pleasure to express both personal and professional gratitude to those who have helped me in the preparation of this book.

I gratefully acknowledge the senior fellowship granted by the National Endowment for the Humanities, which enabled me to take a full year of sabbatical leave from Columbia University. I am also greatly indebted to Professor Jacques Barzun, the noted critic and cultural historian, for reading the book in manuscript and for offering valuable suggestions and useful counsel. For a kind, encouraging interest in my work through the years, special appreciation is due to Professor Jean Seznec, of All Souls College, Oxford University. And as always, I received from my husband, Irving May, sound advice, helpful editorial assistance, and unstinting moral support.

GITA MAY

Columbia University
December 1976

STENDHAL AND THE AGE OF NAPOLEON

Prologue

STENDHAL BELONGS TO that small and privileged group of writers whose work and personality form a consistent, integrated whole and whose modernity has grown with the passage of time. An eminently self-conscious and self-critical artist, he nevertheless did not consider art above or apart from the business of living. Endowed with a keen intellectual curiosity, wide-ranging interests, and a lifelong passion for reading, he is one of the most highly cultured and articulate men of letters in a country where writers with an imposing intellectual and ideological background are far from rare. Yet despite his eclectic tastes and the delight he took in playing the role of the sophisticated amateur and dilettante, Stendhal evolved a wholly original and personal philosophy of life and of art.

Stendhal's position among French Romantics is crucial by virtue of several factors. His life span embraced an era marked by swift and momentous changes, ranging from the French Revolution, through the Empire, the Bourbon Restoration, and the July Monarchy. He maintained strong intellectual and ideological ties with the eighteenth century, especially the Enlightenment and the republican and radical politics of the Jacobins. He was supremely conscious of the ambiguous yet essential nature of the creative man's relationship to contemporary society. In Stendhal one finds a frequent tension between antithetical tendencies, impulses and attitudes which can be partly explained by the fact that he was

1

born early enough to remain, in several essential ways, a man of the eighteenth century who felt most comfortable with the *philosophes*. He was also a perceptive and discriminating student and analyst of the French classical authors, especially the dramatists and moralists. Yet he did not hesitate to espouse the cause of the Romantics and play a key role in the battle against entrenched academicism and traditionalism.

Rebellious and non-conformist by nature and inclination, Stendhal readily welcomed a controversy or political struggle if his sense of justice was sufficiently aroused. Unlike a Flaubert, he accepted the challenges, absurdities, and contradictions of life and did not regard his calling as a writer as a sufficient reason for retiring to a safe and isolated ivory tower. He could, like a Voltaire, a Rousseau, or an André Gide, become deeply and intimately involved in the political events of his time. Yet something would always hold him back from total commitment. Intellectual lucidity, humor, a sense of the grotesque, skepticism which some contemporaries identified with cynicism would inevitably prevent him from becoming the docile follower of a cause, no matter how compelling. In this respect, as in so many others, Stendhal remains the supreme individualist. Hence his sense of alienation and his growing estrangement from his contemporaries.

There are many ways to approach Stendhal, and no single method can capture the multifarious aspects of his complex personality or of his innovative and subtle art. My purpose is not only to present Stendhal to the English-reading public in the light of the research accomplished in the last twenty years, much of which remains unavailable in English, but also to examine the tangled interplay of history and personality, for Stendhal's work is based largely upon actual experience.

Few are the writers whose lives constitute such an integral part of their literary creations. Each of Stendhal's works, however impersonal and theoretical in nature, contains the sum total of his human experience, of his rich sensibilities and intuition, of his loves and perpetual youthful enthusiasms, of his disappointments and failures, of his inexhaustible curiosity about everything concerning intellectual, literary, and artistic life as well as politics. For Stendhal the artist was far from disdainful of topicality and everyday reality, and he knew how to make the news of the day the stuff of his dreams and cogitations.

To reduce Stendhal's work to a standard biographical account would, of course, singularly impoverish the scope and depth of his originality as a writer. Several generations of commentators have, indeed, been guilty of this critical failing, and they have rightly been taken to task by modern proponents of textual analysis and structural criticism. But, on the other hand, to ignore those experiences and memories, traits and tics, obsessions and preoccupations that play such an important role in Stendhal's inner world and to concentrate, to the exclusion of everything else, on a textual analysis of the novels is to deny oneself the delights and insights of becoming acquainted with Stendhal's persona.

It might also be pointed out that, despite the considerable body of autobiographical information Stendhal himself left behind, his life and character are less transparent than might at first appear. To take at face value Stendhal's own revelations and interpretations of events is to neglect an important aspect of his character: his love of discretion and secrecy, his reluctance to dwell upon his innermost thoughts and feelings, his need to hide behind a mask of breezy and flippant light-heartedness.

Not that Stendhal deliberately or consciously concealed the real facts of his inner life behind a veil of fictionalized and embellished truth. As a thoughtful disciple of Rousseau, he was keenly aware of the exigencies of the truthful autobiographer and of the dangers that lurk in the writer's natural tendency to allow his imagination to dramatize and color facts or to fill in those episodes and details from the past that a faulty memory cannot resurrect. Stendhal harshly reproached Rousseau, who otherwise took such pride in his sincerity and candor, with being guilty of this kind of self-indulgence, which may enhance the literary and artistic merits of autobiographical writings, but which is fatal to their value as a historical and psychological document.

To uncover Stendhal the man behind Stendhal the writer is

not necessarily made less arduous by the fact that he wrote so extensively about himself. For Stendhal the world was a stage. From his earliest childhood years, he enjoyed playing roles and mystifying his elders. He looked upon the members of his family and entourage as protagonists and himself as the main character in a kind of tragi-comedy. This vision of life was only reinforced by his growing interest in the theater as a means of expression and as a desirable personal career. And as a timid and lonely adolescent, he soon came to believe that the man of superior talent and sensibilities had better learn to conceal his innermost thoughts and feelings if he was to survive the many traps laid by the maliciousness or indifference of society. Hence a complicated strategy of dissimulation and duplicity several aspects of which are reflected in Stendhal's fictional world.

Some of this attitude spills over in Stendhal's private writings, and if few authors have left such a complete record of their intellectual and emotional evolution and inner struggles in diaries, letters, and autobiographical essays, on the other hand few have evidenced a comparable capacity for what the French so aptly call *dédoublement*. But it is precisely Stendhal's frequently divided self, his ability to see himself from the outside, so to speak, to effect swift and unpredictable changes in plans and purpose—a tendency that often baffled his family and friends—which can largely account for the scope of his perceptions. The fact that Stendhal tirelessly spoke about himself does not automatically open the doors to his inner psyche. He was a man of many personalities and innumerable moods.

Yet this multi-faceted personality is present in every page Stendhal ever wrote. It is unmistakably imprinted in the tone and rhythm of every sentence, and of all the fascinating characters that sprang from his pen, his own real persona is probably the most compelling. And his opinions, attitudes, prejudices, obsessions remained remarkably constant through a succession of careers and professional endeavors.

To write a book about Stendhal therefore presents a special challenge: it requires not merely an account of his activities and evolution, but also a constant awareness of the apparently erratic yet steady progress of the man as a literary artist. And no one was more keenly aware than Stendhal himself of the role that chance and caprice play in shaping our destinies. He therefore always strove to remain available and open before the twists and turns that life offers us. Nothing was more alien to his temperament than a fixed, rigid course and set ways. The variegated and colorful pattern of his own life and career amply testifies to this openness of mind and heart: the rebellious and morose child of Grenoble, the bookish and solitary young philosopher, the enthusiastic yet shy and melancholy dragoon of Milan, the passionate and quixotic lover, the fearless soldier and capable administrator closely involved in Napoleon's campaigns across Europe, the avid theatergoer and witty conversationalist, the incisive and provocative critic, the tireless tourist, and, finally, the disillusioned yet tender-hearted middle-aged man turned novelist.

Through his peregrinations, literary endeavors, and amorous adventures and misadventures, Stendhal elaborated a set of principles which are not an abstract philosophical system, but rather an art of living that has come to be known as *beylism*. *Beylism* is an attitude, a pragmatic and practical combination of theories, reflections, maxims, and observations based on wide-ranging and critical reading and study as well as on direct experience and the trial and error learning method. *Beylism*, above all, demands rigor and lucidity in reasoning, and absolute devotion to truth and clear thinking. Stendhal had no patience with any form of self-indulgent sentimentalism or exhibitionism displayed by such Romantics as Chateaubriand or Victor Hugo.

For Stendhal the parading of one's inner turmoils and torments was tantamount to charlatanism. He would never exploit and exalt his feeling self in the name of sincerity. To be sure, his sensibility was no less acute and exquisite than that of a Rousseau or a Byron. But he recoiled from assuming heroic or sublime poses, for his perpetually alert critical faculties never failed to warn him that the marshaling of lofty sentiments in a noble, high-flown rhetoric can all too easily become an escape into the imaginative and subjective world of self-justification and self-delusion. Self-centered though he always was, Stendhal remained acutely wary of the dangers that lurk in a lyrical exaltation of the ego. The Rousseauistic and Romantic rhetoric of hyperbole frequently produced in him a real sense of embarrassment and dismay. As a reaction to the contemporary cult of telling all and of overstating one's case in the process, Stendhal, in order to preserve the veracity and authenticity of what he had to say, preferred to err in the direction of the understatement. This was especially true of his personal and autobiographical writings, where he invariably avowed less than what he had actually experienced in moments of intense emotion and high excitement. As a writer Stendhal strongly felt that the truth was best served in a simple, direct, unadorned style.

It is this respect for intellectual integrity and lucidity that can also go a long way toward explaining his abiding loyalty to Montesquieu and the *philosophes* in an age when it was becoming fashionable to reject the message of the Enlightenment as too narrowly rationalistic. Few nineteenth-century authors can be said to have shared his deep kinship with the novelists, memorialists, essayists, and *philosophes* of the eighteenth century. Skeptical in matters of religion and unremittingly hostile to the Church, striving for logic and consistency in his thinking, partial to a clear, concise, and straightforward style of writing as exemplified by the prose of a Voltaire, appreciative of a Laclos's pitiless lucidity and elegant cynicism, yet basically Rousseauistic in his esthetic and emotional responses to nature and matters of the heart, Stendhal early on made a lifelong commitment to the intellectual, ethical, and esthetic values of the Enlightenment. Despite his involvement with the Romantic controversies, his ideology, and more profoundly than that, his basic impulses and perceptions can best be understood as a natural outcome and continuation of the currents and forces unleashed by the preceding century, not as a rejection of the values heralded by the *philosophes* and their revolutionary disciples. In this respect, as in several others, he differs markedly from a Chateaubriand or a Balzac. This commitment to the political and intellectual ideals of the eighteenth century is repeatedly attested by Stendhal's steadfast devotion to libertarian principles, a democratic form of republicanism, and by the hostility and scorn he heaped on Restoration and Orleanist France.

To the aging and disillusioned Stendhal watching France revert to pre-Revolutionary ways, the Enlightenment, the Revolution, and the Napoleonic era glowed more brightly than ever, for they had galvanized the talents and energies of men of ability. Restoration France, on the other hand, stifled individual talent and initiative. After Waterloo, even the Old Regime, especially in its waning years when authority had sufficiently disintegrated to allow, through sheer ineptitude, critical thought to blossom, seemed preferable to the narrow conformism and hypocrisy fostered by legitimist France.

Stendhal was a great believer in the behavioristic and deterministic doctrines of Helvétius, Destutt de Tracy, and the Ideologists—whom he viewed as the worthy successors of Montesquieu. With them he held that man is an eminently malleable creature, a product of his environment and of the social forces that shaped and condition his intellect and sensibilities. Yet his own deepest impulses and those of his principal fictional protagonists belie this mechanistic psychology. Man's complexity and unpredictability, his irrepressible quest for freedom and for personal fulfilment and self-expression constitute some of the most central themes of Stendhal's thought and works.

It is in this light that one can best comprehend Stendhal's lifelong fascination with Napoleon. As we shall see, he was no blind follower or disciple. Far from it. But he viewed Bonaparte as a child of the Revolution, as a man who had managed to impose his will upon Europe through sheer daring and determination. That the Emperor Napoleon had betrayed some of the ideals and purposes of the young General Bonaparte did not escape him, but the Bourbon Restoration made him long all the more nostalgically for those days that had brought forth from among the ranks of young Frenchmen vigorous personalities and leaders of genius and imagination. From his lonely, defiant days as a restless youth rebelling against the values that his family and milieu tried to impose upon him in his native Grenoble, he had an almost instinctive dislike for the unquestioned acceptance of authority. It was Napoleon's Italian campaign that gave young Stendhal his first taste of real freedom and adventure. He would never quite recover from this heady experience.

History is determined both by events of a violent and traumatic nature—such as wars and revolutions—and by the slow, sometimes imperceptible, evolution of ideas, attitudes, and beliefs. The interrelation between these two sets of events is of course crucial as well as immensely complex and frustratingly difficult to trace and interpret by historians. Events of an immediately portentous nature and with a sudden and profound impact certainly played a decisive role in Stendhal's life: the beheading of Louis XVI, the coup of 18 Brumaire, the fall of Moscow and the crossing of the Berezina, Waterloo and the July Revolution, to name some of the cataclysmic events which directly affected Stendhal and some of which he personally witnessed as a direct participant. But he was no less a participant in the transformation of ideas and values marked by the end of the Enlightenment and the rise of Romanticism.

To envisage the French Revolution as a watershed between eighteenth-century rationalism and skepticism on the one hand and nineteenth-century Romanticism on the other is to establish a highly oversimplified division. In reality, changes took place in a far less orderly way. There is no doubt, of course, that the Revolution had an enormous impact on all intellectual movements, literary schools, and artistic trends. But to divide thinkers, writers, and artists neatly into two separate categories amounts to betraying historical truth for the sake of logical clarity.

Stendhal's role in the history of ideas and of literature is of special importance in that it demonstrates so clearly that Romanticism—like most "isms" of the nineteenth century—cannot be understood without an awareness that the eighteenth century was far more diverse than is generally acknowledged and that no dividing wall separates it from the intellectual, literary, and artistic movements of the post-Revolutionary era.

No personality springs out of nowhere. Although Stendhal frequently strikes us as a writer who drew the principal elements of his thought and art from his own inner resources and, from the outset, rebelled against the beliefs and attitudes evidenced by his elders, the impact of these early surroundings can hardly be discounted, if only because the future novelist reacted so strongly against the provincial and bourgeois milieu in which he grew up. The bourgeoisie he knew, mainly incarnated by his father, the dour Chérubin Beyle, was not the class that had struggled for the humanitarian principles of 1789. If young Beyle broke away so rapidly and so completely from his father's heavy-handed authority, it was, to no small extent, because he identified, as soon as he gained access to books, with the forward-looking liberalism of Montesquieu, the progressive social and political philosophy of the Encyclopedists, the aggressive anti-clericalism of Voltaire, the radical individualism of Rousseau. The historical timing of Stendhal's birth and formative years had undoubtedly a great deal to do with his ability to transcend the traditions and class prejudices that were pounded into him from an early age. The ideas of the Enlightenment had reached out and penetrated into all corners of France, and even conservative Grenoble. Henri Beyle's grandfather on his mother's side, moreover, the cultured Dr. Henri Gagnon, as a beloved mentor and favorite relative, imparted to him his own admiration for the *philosophes*, if not his reverence for Voltaire, with whose ideas Stendhal would remain in sympathy but whose personality and character he judged severely.[1]

On the whole, Stendhal occupies a fairly solitary position among his immediate contemporaries.[2] By 1783, the year of his birth, the principal figures of the Enlightenment had already died or were about to disappear from the scene (Montesquieu as early as 1755, both Voltaire and Rousseau in 1778, Diderot in 1784, and Buffon in 1788). His knowledge of the *philosophes* and writers of the eighteenth century would—with very few exceptions, notably that of Laclos whom he was to meet in person in Milan—be second-hand and through their works. But his curiosity about their personalities and character traits was to be a lively one and he would endlessly question those who—like his grandfather who had met Voltaire in person—had come into direct contact with these by then legendary figures.

Stendhal was born too late to be able to play—as he would have loved to—a direct role in the great drama of the Revolution. He was a remarkably precocious and politically-minded ten-year-old boy in 1793 and had already by then, at least according to his autobiography, formed his own ideas on the situation. Whereas his family, and especially his father, mourned the fall of the monarchy and execution of Louis XVI, he hero-worshiped the Jacobin leaders, but could only secretly rejoice over their successes and achievements. Once again he felt cheated by Fate. He was too young to enact the kind of part he dreamed of, and his sense of frustration sometimes exploded into fits of rage and temper, especially when he found himself at odds with his relatives over the latest political developments. All his revolutionary heroes were born in the 1750's: Vergniaud and Brissot in 1753, Mme Roland in 1754, Robespierre in 1758, and Danton in 1759. The political figure he ultimately most admired, Napoleon, was born in 1769.

As for the first great precursors of Romanticism, they were his seniors by a whole generation: André Chénier (born in 1762), Mme de Staël (in 1766), Benjamin Constant (in 1767), Chateaubriand (in 1768), Senancour (in 1770). On the other hand, the Romantics proper were all his juniors: Lamartine, the first Romantic poet, by seven years, Alfred de Vigny by fourteen, Balzac by sixteen, Victor Hugo by nineteen, and Mérimée by twenty.

Interestingly enough, few men or women of note in politics or the arts were born in the 1780s, Stendhal's decade.[3] No wonder he had to find his own role and identity outside the usual framework of literary schools, coteries, or cenacles. His experience as a voluntary exile in Milan would only reinforce this sense of isolation. Whether in his native Grenoble, where he did not take long in rebelling against his highly conservative family and milieu, in Paris, where at first his timidity and then his outspoken views and idiosyncratic mannerisms frequently baffled the people with whom he came into contact, or in his beloved Italy, where he

always remained a foreigner, Stendhal was all his life the quintessential stranger and outsider. In this respect, as in several others,
he must be regarded as a true spiritual son of Rousseau. As stubbornly as Jean-Jacques, Stendhal set out to live his own life and to
follow only the dictates of his conscience and his heart. And, like
Rousseau, it was ultimately through his writings that he was able
to define his identity.[4]

For someone who never personally experienced the intellectual excitement and sense of common purpose shared by the Encyclopedists, it is remarkable how close Stendhal would remain to
their ideological outlook and how tenaciously he would cling to
the main tenets of their philosophy.[5] His scientific turn of mind,
his love of clarity and precision of thought and expression, his
emotional self-control, his religious skepticism and political liberalism, his natural antipathy for all forms of mental vagueness, mys-
ticism, and abstract idealism are all typical of the pre-Revolutionary French intelligentsia. Furthermore, his cosmopolitism, his
devotion to all matters intellectual and cultural, his abiding faith
in man's powers of reason and thought would have made him feel
at ease in the company of a Voltaire or a Buffon. And his brilliance as a conversationalist and wit, his enthusiastic appreciation
of intelligent and independent-minded women would have endeared him to such demanding and critical eighteenth-century
salonnières as Mme Du Deffand, Mme Geoffrin, or Mme Necker.

With mischievous delight, Stendhal would never miss an opportunity to satirize and ridicule the blind spots and shortcomings
of the literary heroes of the day, especially their monumental egotism and vanity and their total lack of humor and aptitude for self-
criticism. That among his own faults he may have been guilty of a
hyper-critical propensity, both with regard to himself and to others, is something that he readily admits, and that it had complicated his existence and earned him enemies is an inevitable consequence of this character trait of which he was fully aware. Yet
Stendhal remained an unrepentant admirer of men endowed with
sharp wit and acute critical faculties. The decline of this once
much-esteemed intellectual trait left him disconsolate, and that

public opinion was largely determined by such men as the immensely popular Alphonse de Lamartine made him muse ruefully:
"How would M. de Lamartine be a judge of wit? . . . He does
not have any." [6]

To be sure, Stendhal would join in the demand for the aboli-
tion of the famous rules of classical dramaturgy, which were applied too obediently and indiscriminately by neo-classical authors
lacking the genius and originality of the great seventeenth-century
playwrights, and he scorned La Harpe, the immensely successful
and popular upholder of classicism. And in the battle that was to
oppose the defenders of tradition and the innovators, he unhesitatingly sided with the latter. But a non-conformist in this as in many
other respects, Stendhal remained his own man.

Stendhal belongs to a period of transition and lightning
change on the political scene, a period that is hardly favorable to
the arts and letters, for the dramatic events of the French Revolution and Napoleonic wars left no one untouched. Stendhal
came upon the scene in a moment of history when the impe-
tus created by the Enlightenment had spent itself, to be followed
by a succession of political upheavals and traumas that left little
time or energy for purely cultural pursuits. No wonder Stendhal's
own generation is not particularly fruitful in transcendent names
in the fields of arts and letters! It is not in times of revolutions and
wars that literature and art flourish.

Interestingly, Stendhal's loyalty to the ideals of the Enlightenment produced among many of his contemporaries the misleading
impression that he was not moving with the times. Perhaps because he was too young in 1793 and was furthermore spared the
spectacle of violence and persecution on a mass scale, Stendhal
emerged from the Reign of Terror with his belief in the Revolutionary cause untouched. Unlike many of his elders and contemporaries, he envisioned the Revolution and the Napoleonic era as
a natural outcome and continuation of the Age of Enlightenment.

Any biographical or critical study, no matter how objective or
impartial, evidences some point of view. Since I regard Stendhal
as a direct and logical heir of the eighteenth century, especially of

the Enlightenment, and feel that his special brand of Romanticism cannot be understood without a proper comprehension of this background, I shall focus on the early, formative years, which were crucial in determining his lifelong attitudes, prejudices, and preoccupations. At the same time, while I don't intend to apply directly the psychoanalytical methods or terminology of the Freudian or post-Freudian schools, I am keenly aware that in many ways Stendhal's case presents an exemplary illustration of some of the most heatedly debated problems concerning creativity and personality. Hence my special interest in the young Stendhal struggling to find his own identity.

No destiny, especially that of a first-rate thinker, artist, or writer is pre-ordained. It is therefore imperative to go back to the origins of the man, to observe the child awakening to a world of sensations, impressions, and feelings, to follow his first hesitant steps as a thinking, questioning being. Stendhal would no doubt agree that the initial and most vital clues must be traced to the heredity, moment, and milieu. No wonder Taine, the leading nineteenth-century exponent and inheritor of the deterministic school of psychology, was such an admirer of Stendhal.

But if Stendhal had a profound impact upon the positivist thinkers of the nineteenth century and is also frequently referred to as one of the first practitioners of the "realist" novel, he defies all attempts at classification. To approach him from a positivistic angle and to study him merely as a product of a certain milieu and historical moment is to rob him of his uniqueness as a man and artist. Neither the conventional, external biographical approach, which dutifully follows a chronological sequence of facts and events, nor the fictionalized recreation of some of the more dramatic circumstances of Stendhal's experience can provide us with the key to a full understanding of the meanings and events which constitute his destiny.

A more experiential approach is in order. That Stendhal was the architect of his own destiny, that at every crucial point in his life he made deliberate choices which went counter to the wishes of his family and sometimes thwarted his own carefully laid-out

plans, must be kept in mind if one is to probe below the testimony
of biographical data. Like Rousseau, with whom he had a far
greater affinity than he was willing to admit, Stendhal liked to
keep his options open. Hence, the element of unpredictability, or
even apparent capriciousness, in some of the most portentous decisions he made in the course of his lifetime.

   But a thoughtful—if not exhaustive—reconstruction of the
conditions within which Stendhal made his choices is necessary in
order to gain an understanding of his inner world. This involves a
search for vital clues within the framework of the family structure,
the social situation, the school milieu, and the historical moment.
Let us therefore begin with Grenoble, Stendhal's starting point.

I

Beginnings

GRENOBLE, AN ANCIENT and picturesque town stands out against a spectacular, sometimes grandiose landscape. Situated on the banks of the Isère, at the foot of the Alps, it is the major city of the old Dauphiné province in the southeast of France. It boasts a famous university founded in the Middle Ages, Gothic churches, and a Renaissance palace (now serving as courthouse), and today an art museum of some note as well as a museum devoted to its most famous native son, Stendhal, pseudonym of Marie-Henri Beyle.

The city proper nestles between two mountain ranges, the Chartreuse to the north, and the Vercors to the south. It was in the Chartreuse that St. Bruno founded in 1084 the famous monastery of the Grande Chartreuse. The Vercors, on the other hand, acquired its own fame much later, in World War II, under the German occupation, as a center for the *maquis*, the underground Resistance movement.

All his life Stendhal was to love mountains and miss them sorely whenever he found himself in a city such as Paris. There is no doubt that the magnificent vistas which, as a young boy, he could admire from the medieval ramparts of Grenoble, with the snow-crested Alps visible in the distance, had a great deal to do with this predilection. For while he would detest and loathe the pettiness and provincialism of his native town, he would always cherish its mountainous setting and vast horizons and panoramas.

Like Rousseau, Stendhal could find even unhappiness less unbearable when his eyes could feast upon those regions of France,
and later Lombardy, which are favored by nature in all its loveliness and grandeur.

Admittedly, unlike Rousseau and the Romantics, Stendhal
was to refrain from describing at length and rhapsodizing over
soaring mountain ranges or shimmering lakes, but his references
to natural sites that had affected him, albeit sober and restrained,
bespeak an intensity of feeling commensurate with that expressed
by more verbose writers. To describe an intimate, powerful emotion was, in Stendhal's eyes, tantamount to betraying it, not to
mention the fact that overwhelming emotions had the temporary
effect of paralyzing his pen. And undoubtedly he felt that to depict
in scrupulous detail the particulars of a landscape was to shatter its
enchantment and mystery. Hence one would seek in vain for the
kind of sumptuous and richly-orchestrated prose passage describing
nature in all its glory that so frequently occurs in the works of the
Romantics. As we shall see, Stendhal's feeling for nature was of a
different kind and it would find its literary expression in a more
subtle, symbolic way in his works of fiction. In his more personal
writings, such as his autobiographical and unfinished essay, *The
Life of Henry Brulard,* his allusions to nature are always discreet
and deliberately matter-of-fact. It is as though Stendhal was consciously avoiding the flights of lyrical inspiration and rhetoric characteristic of Rousseau and his Romantic followers. Yet the authenticity of his response to the beauties of nature is evidenced by a
remark like the following: "I have searched for beautiful landscapes, with an exquisite sensibility; it is for that reason alone that
I have traveled." [1] A lovely landscape "played" on his soul like the
bow of a violin on the strings of a well-tuned instrument.

Grenoble itself was always far from attractive, especially at the
end of the eighteenth century. With its gloomy streets and alley-
ways, open and foul-smelling sewers, and generally nondescript architecture, the city was a perfect example of haphazard urban con-
glomeration and ugliness. Around 1800, Grenoble, whose origins
go back to the Roman times, was a somber, depressing place,

compressed within the ancient fortifications and forced to develop upward. Numerous Grenoble houses were four or five stories high in Stendhal's time. Tiny courtyards, dark and humid and where the sun never penetrated, separated the houses. Although two rivers, the Isère and the Drac, crossed the town, their beds carried only yellow, foul-smelling waters.

The close proximity in which the Grenoble inhabitants had to live, in addition to the usual gossipy mentality characteristic of life in the French provinces, created an atmosphere of suspiciousness and watchful curiosity which was the very air young Henri Beyle breathed. Stendhal had few good words for his native city: "Everything that is petty and common in the bourgeois manner reminds me of Grenoble, everything that reminds me of Gr[enoble] fills me with horror, no, *horror* is too noble, with *loathing*." [2] The joylessness of his childhood still rankled the aging Stendhal writing *The Life of Henry Brulard.*

Snuggled within its ancient man-made ramparts and natural boundaries, Grenoble, at the end of the eighteenth century, was not entirely the dull town smothered by provincialism and traditionalism which Stendhal describes in his autobiographical essays. It had an active social life and its women were both charming and not exceedingly virtuous. This particular aspect of Grenoble is indirectly portrayed in a famous novel, *Les Liaisons dangereuses*, whose author, Choderlos de Laclos had been stationed for six years in Grenoble, from 1769 to 1775, as an officer in the French artillery and knew its covertly scandalous mores at first-hand. [3]

But it was only through the testimony of his elders that Stendhal was to find out that Grenoble, for some, had been quite a different town from what he himself remembered. In his *Henry Brulard* he recalls with amusement that, as a young boy, he had personally known Mme de Montmaur, the woman who, according to local tradition, had been the original model of the notorious heroine of the *Liaisons dangereuses*, Mme de Merteuil. [4] But by then, Mme de Montmaur was an elderly lady walking with a pronounced limp and long past the time for intrigues and amorous machinations. A neighbor of young Beyle's grandfather, she was kindly to the boy and regaled him with candied nuts. He noticed, however, that members of his family always spoke in whispers when referring to her, and this both mystified him and piqued his curiosity; but it was only many years later that he found out the reason for all this secrecy.

That Grenoble, the seat of a *Parlement* (a court of justice) and the historic, administrative, and intellectual heart of the Dauphiné province, was also its social center where elegant and pleasure-loving young men and women could savor the famous *"douceur de vivre"* that Talleyrand associated with the Old Regime, was an aspect of his native city that Stendhal never experienced personally. For him Grenoble would forever symbolize those bourgeois and provincial values he held in greatest abhorrence. The peculiar circumstances of the novelist's early years account for this lifelong aversion.

Grenoble, at the end of the eighteenth century, was governed by a rigid caste system. The city numbered about twenty-five thousand inhabitants, and by the time young Henri Beyle came upon the scene the high-spirited men and women who frequented the more fashionable salons of Grenoble under the Old Regime had either been dispersed during the Revolution or had settled down to a more sedate way of life. Stendhal's own contacts with Grenoble society were circumscribed by the devout, middle-class circles with which his family associated.

The traditions governing the nobility and upper bourgeoisie were especially strict, for this is where most of the jostling occurred. Stendhal's family, especially on his father's side, was a perfect example of this mentality, and in *Henry Brulard* there are several anecdotes illustrating the possessiveness and passion with which class privileges were guarded.

Members of the legal profession, to which Stendhal's father belonged, were particularly conscious of the subtlest class distinctions. Any breach of etiquette was sternly frowned upon. Henri Beyle was brought up in an atmosphere of reverence for nobility and wealth, and it was his father's most cherished dream to become sufficiently influential and rich to gain admittance for his family into the prestigious circles of the well-born and the titled.

The typical Grenoble bourgeois was motivated by two passions: to penetrate into the world of the aristocracy, but even more to acquire as much real estate as possible. And thus, he connived, schemed, and devoted all his energies to the acquisition of land and houses. As Stendhal caustically remarked: "A bourgeois in Grenoble is esteemed only to the extent that he is a man of property." [5] That his own father had eventually allowed himself to become involved in financially disastrous speculations was in no small measure due to this monomania. [6]

Henri Beyle was born on January 23, 1783, in a house on the rue des Vieux-Jésuites which still stands today (it is number 14 of the renamed rue Jean-Jacques Rousseau). Both the house and the street are in the heart of the old part of Grenoble. The street is narrow and dark, the building itself is fairly tall, and its rooms are deprived of direct sunlight.

Fortunately for young Henri, he could always take refuge in the opulent and cheerful home of his maternal grandfather, Henri Gagnon, a doctor in medicine and one of those charming, sophisticated, and immensely cultured and erudite men not too uncommon in the Age of Enlightenment. Dr. Ganon's elegant residence was well situated on the Place Grenette and the corner of the Grand-Rue. It had a southern exposure and directly faced the animated Place Grenette, the main square of Grenoble, at a point where the oblong square met the Grand-Rue, the principal street of the city. Its tall windows afforded a clear, sweeping view of the spacious square. With its two "rival cafés," perennial hangers-on, and regularly-scheduled arrivals and departures of stagecoaches, the Place Grenette was the very heart of Grenoble. [7]

Dr. Gagnon's house was among the most substantial in Grenoble. It boasted an imposing entrance hallway with an arched ceiling, a fine staircase leading to a large drawing room in the Italian style, and a well-stocked library, as well as several other spacious, well-lighted rooms. The view from the tall windows extended beyond the Place Grenette, to the city's shingled rooftops and, in the distance, to the mountains.

One of the most respected members of the professional and social community, Dr. Gagnon had also been in his heyday a man of not inconsiderable means, as was attested by an ambitious and costly program of renovation and embellishment of his house. He had a spacious terrace built which connected with the library and which was a favorite place of his because of the splendid panorama it afforded across the Public Garden of Grenoble, where elegant men and women congregated on tree-lined alleys. The terrace was broad, drenched in sunlight, lined with plants and flowers, and decorated with an open structure of latticework covered with vine. There Stendhal spent some of the happiest hours of his childhood watching his grandfather lovingly water his flowers or listening to him expound on botany or astronomy.[8] The aging but intellectually alert doctor, feeling his rheumatism, would sometimes pace stiffly up and down, peering at the panorama while explaining to his only grandson some of the mysteries of botany or astronomy. Stendhal had a specially fond recollection of the summer evenings on his grandfather's terrace. The air was mild and charged with exotic fragrances, the sky was a deep blue, and as the sun would slowly set behind the Vercors mountain range the firmament would light up with myriad stars. And all the while young Henri would listen intently to his grandfather's cultured voice and learn about Pliny the Elder, the Roman naturalist, Linnaeus, the Swedish founder of the modern system of designating plants and animals, or about the configuration of the Great and Little Bears. There is no doubt that the good doctor's love of learning and fondness for books had a profound and lifelong impact upon his only grandson.

Just as Chérubin Beyle's somber, depressing house reflected the dry and unappealing personality of the provincial lawyer, Dr. Gagnon's handsome residence mirrored the intellectual interests and refined taste of a man who was conversant with the ideas of Montesquieu and proudly proclaimed himself a disciple of Voltaire.

In Henri Beyle, the future Stendhal, two opposing strains of the French ethnic family converged into an uneasy alliance. The Gagnons, on his mother's side, originally hailed from the south of France, from Provence and the region of Avignon. The Gagnons possessed a fertile imagination, a lively curiosity, and an artistic temperament. On the other hand, the Beyles, on Stendhal's father's side, were of Dauphiné peasant stock and slowly rose through dogged, persistent effort.[9] Stendhal himself liked to believe that he had inherited all his best attributes from the Gagnons: sensibility, imagination, tenderness. Yet, more than he himself realized, he was also a true offspring of the Beyles: stubbornness, singleness of purpose, patience, reticence, and a sense of the realities.

While the Provençal is gay, voluble, and light-hearted, the Dauphinois is morose, stubborn, and silently obstinate. The Provençal is broad-minded and generous; the Dauphinois, petty and vindictive. The Provençal is a dreamer; the Dauphinois, a down-to-earth realist.

It is a major fact of Stendhal's personal experience that he loved and revered the engaging qualities of the Gagnons, passionately adored his charming, cultured, and vivacious mother and detested his somber, parsimonious, and authoritarian father. That he was the offspring of an ill-assorted matrimonial union becomes evident when one examines somewhat more closely the contrasting personalities of Chérubin Beyle and Henriette Gagnon.

Chérubin Beyle descended from an old Dauphinois family of peasant origins that had come down from the mountains surrounding Grenoble. The Beyles hailed from the mountainous Vercors regions, made famous, as has already been indicated, during World War II by the French underground and *maquisards* and by the Resistance writer Jean Bruller who, under the *nom de plume* Jean Vercors, wrote *The Silence of the Sea* and other eloquent denunciations of the German occupant. The Vercors mountains form one of the natural bulwarks of the Dauphiné, a harsh and desolate region whose inhabitants reflect, in their deliberate, obstinate ways, the rugged character of their surroundings.

In the seventeenth century, a branch of the Beyles started veering toward the bourgeoisie. A Jean Beyle, son of Ambroise, merchant draper in Lans toward 1650, had two sons the youngest of whom, named Joseph, appears on the list of attorneys to the Parlement and fulfilled, moreover, the duties of treasurer-syndic.[10] His son Pierre, born in 1699, also became a lawyer. By then the Beyles had acquired the house on the rue des Vieux-Jésuites in which Stendhal would be born and raised, as well as the attractive country domain of Claix, among other properties and real estate. Pierre Beyle married well (his wife, Jeanne Dupéron, was the daughter of a Grenoble banker). This Pierre Beyle is Stendhal's paternal grandfather. He died in 1760, after having fathered thirteen children.

Chérubin Beyle, the writer's father, was born in 1747. Orphaned before he reached his eighteenth birthday, he became, by virtue of being the eldest of a large brood of ten sisters and two brothers, the head of the family. These family responsibilities must have been a heavy burden for an adolescent barely on the threshold of manhood, and Chérubin Beyle quickly lost, if indeed he ever possessed them in the first place, the insouciance and gaiety characteristic of youth. Very early in life, he acquired, both by temperament and by force of circumstance, a keen sense of his duties. His demeanor was grave and solemn, with a touch of sadness and melancholy. The habit of exercising moral authority and of deciding upon financial family matters gave him a taste of power which he never relinquished. On the contrary, with growing age he became more heavy-handed and, at least in the eyes of the young Henri Beyle, arbitrary and dictatorial.

Stendhal's harsh indictment of his father, however, requires a corrective. Too many biographers and critics have been content to reproduce the negative portrait of Chérubin Beyle as presented by his famous son. To be sure, he was a highly representative member of the French provincial bourgeoisie, and as such harbored all the beliefs and prejudices of his class. He might well have sprung out of a novel by Balzac, for like most Balzacian characters, he valued, above all else, money and the acquisition of property, and his very greed was to be the cause of his eventual demise.

But Chérubin Beyle's youth must have been an unhappy one. It was no easy task for a young man to assure the future of ten sisters under the Old Regime! Four made solid, respectable marriages with members of the Grenoble bourgeoisie, five entered various convents and became nuns, and one died an old maid. At long last, at the age of thirty-five, Chérubin Beyle could turn his thoughts to his own establishment.

In 1782 he married the vivacious Henriette Gagnon, ten years his junior, and in temperament and outlook as different from him as one human being can possibly be from another. When, after eight years of marriage, she died in childbed, his world came to an end. With this single cruel stroke of fate, his own chance for happiness, hard-won after years of toil and worry, was destroyed. His ways, always stern and gruff, became harsh and positively overbearing. He concentrated more and more the considerable energies of his basically passionate character on the quixotic dream of amassing wealth through real estate speculation and agricultural experimentation. That his only son, the sole bearer of his name, rebelled with increasing boldness against his admonitions and injunctions had also a great deal to do with the growing surliness of his naturally somber and atrabilious character.

Stendhal introduces him in *Henry Brulard* in the most unflattering terms, portraying him as an extremely "unlikeable" man, who was constantly preoccupied with the acquisition and sale of property, who was excessively cunning, who always dealt with peasants—in short an "arch-Dauphinois," who, moreover, was very wrinkled and homely, gauche and silent with women. Ironically, however, women had an irresistible appeal for him. This gallant and romantic propensity, unexpected in a grubbing small-town lawyer and real estate speculator, enabled him, despite his ideological opposition to the writers of the Enlightenment, to value and cherish the finer nuances of Rousseau's tormented sensibility. Stendhal speaks of his father's admiration for Rousseau in terms that betray his grudging recognition of Chérubin Beyle's aptitude for love and tenderness: "This latter quality had made him appreciate *La Nouvelle Héloïse* and the other works of Rousseau, of whom he spoke only with adoration, while cursing him as an infidel." [11] Since Stendhal's main intermediary with the eighteenth century, Dr. Henri Gagnon, his maternal grandfather, was an enthusiastic Voltairean and had very little interest in Rousseau, one is free to surmise that young Henri's early discovery of Jean-Jacques and his intimate and lifelong involvement with this writer's works had something to do with his father's entirely emotional predilection.

Everything in Chérubin Beyle's obscure existence seems to indicate that, while he was a staunch upholder of authority and the establishment, and held a firm belief in Providence, monarchy, tradition, and family, he also had in him rich and largely unused treasures of affection and devotion. He was, of course, a typical Dauphinois, timorous, prudent, and enamored with a vision of his only son following the law and consolidating the family patrimony. "He did not love me as a person," Stendhal states bitterly in *Henry Brulard*, "but as the son who was to perpetuate the family." And he asserts, not without a touch of malice, that "Fate has probably never brought together two beings more basically unsympathetic to one another than my father and me." [12]

Yet Chérubin Beyle cherished his son. That he looked upon him as the heir to the Beyle name is undeniable. But he undoubtedly reasoned that the best mark of a good father was his firmness and severity. Chérubin Beyle, staunch traditionalist and legal adviser to the provincial Parlement, naturally conjured up visions of his son following the law, consolidating the family patrimony, gaining respect in his parish, and marrying the right sort of girl. As a hard-working and ambitious lawyer, Chérubin Beyle shared the typical aspirations of his class. To see his only son not only inherit his position in society and in the legal profession, but also rise above him and enlarge the family fortune and add luster to its name was his fondest dream.

By its very proximity to the nobility, the bourgeoisie of the robe, to which the elder Beyle proudly belonged, aspired to obtain many of the prized traditional privileges of the local aristocracy. To acquire the legal right to add the magic *de* to his name was therefore Chérubin Beyle's desire and the next logical step in the process of climbing the social ladder. His position as a consistorial lawyer of the Grenoble Parlement earned him several privileges generally reserved for the nobility, and he liked to think that he could, both through inherited rights and personal accomplishments, decorate without any impropriety his personal stationery with a seal bearing an elaborate family coat of arms. This claim was not entirely without foundation for, according to a family tradition as well as local history, Joseph Beyle, Stendhal's paternal great-grandfather, had not only occupied several important positions in the legal profession and judiciary and administrative hierarchy of Grenoble, he had also been ennobled.[13] Chérubin Beyle liked to show his son what he proudly insisted was a legitimate family coat of arms. On official family documents such as the baptismal act of his son, Chérubin Beyle identified himself as a nobleman.

With typical unfairness, Stendhal always spoke disparagingly of his father's nobiliary ambitions. Yet some of the greatest men of letters of the eighteenth and even the nineteenth centuries—notably Voltaire and Balzac—evidenced the same irresistible desire for self-ennoblement. And Stendhal himself, as we shall see, was not entirely immune to this form of vanity.

Stendhal's unrelenting hostility prevented him from giving us a fair and impartial account of his father. Yet, in his own narrow-minded and rigid way, Chérubin Beyle was nothing if not sincere in his beliefs. He was willing to pay the consequences for his convictions, even when these were unpopular or even dangerous. At the height of the Terror he figured on the list of suspects and enemies of the new order of things. His royalist sympathies were notorious and he made no effort to hide them. He sheltered the abbé Raillane, a refractory priest, in his home. Fortunately for him, the Grenoblois, a shrewd, pragmatic, and independent-minded lot, refused to go along with the ideological excesses of the

Terror and their consequences. Stendhal probably overstates the case when he writes: "The Terror, then, was very mild, and I will fearlessly add, very reasonable, in Grenoble." [14] The fact remains, however, that Chérubin Beyle had to go repeatedly into hiding, that he even spent some time in prison, in 1793 and in 1794, and that his house was searched, his property inventoried for an eventual confiscation, and that only the unexpected events of Thermidor probably saved him from further persecution and reprisals. [15] A stubborn, unbending man, Chérubin Beyle scorned compromise, a character trait which Stendhal, under different circumstances, would also evidence.

In his *Henry Brulard*, Stendhal speaks rather lightly of the dangers his father incurred as an anti-revolutionary. That in his own references to Chérubin Beyle's bouts with the Jacobins he stresses the reasonableness of the latter in the face of the recalcitrant and blatant behavior of his father is probably due both to his unwillingness to give his hated father any credit for courage and to the fact that at the height of the Terror he was only ten years old and therefore, despite his keen and precocious intelligence, unaware of the seriousness of the situation. No doubt, in order not to alarm the child, efforts were made in the Beyle household to mention these things in a rather casual, light-hearted way. Hence Chérubin Beyle's announcement, whenever he had to disappear for a while in order to place himself outside the reaches of the authorities, that he was off to visit and stay a while with a relative. [16]

Stendhal's own subsequent political republicanism undoubtedly greatly colored his reminiscences, as he himself is willing to admit. [17] After asserting that the White Terror of 1815, following the fall of Napoleon and marking the Bourbon Restoration, was, at least to his mind, far more cruel than that of the Jacobins in 1793, he added that, lest he be accused of partiality, he had to warn his reader that the extreme repulsion he felt for everything 1815 symbolized had perhaps made him forget some of the facts and that a more objective and detached historian, not personally involved in these events, might view them in quite a different light.

Chérubin Beyle was an eminently representative Dauphinois, a particularly tenacious as well as taciturn breed of Frenchman. Unlike the extrovert, outgoing, and volatile native of Provence or the witty, articulate Parisian, the Dauphinois is silently resolute and steadfast. Chérubin Beyle was patient, secretive, obstinate, parsimonious, calculating, and utterly lacking in charm or graciousness. Had his charming and beloved wife not died prematurely, she might have softened and humanized him and brought out the tender, sentimental sensibilities that had been repressed by a bleak existence totally devoted to stern, puritanical values and the relentless pursuit of riches. Prematurely aged by sorrow and worry, he had a deeply-lined face and an ungainly, stiff countenance. Portraiture shows us a man with wizened features, thin lips, a self-contained expression, cold inward-looking eyes, and a long, pinched nose.

Despite his hearty dislike of his father, Stendhal inherited not only some of his mental and emotional traits but also some physical characteristics of the Beyle side of the family and its peasant ancestry. Persevering and tenacious like his father, he also evidenced, from an early age onward, an aptitude for stubborn patience and an inner confidence in his own abilities. His lifelong passion for secrecy and dissimulation, his obsession with pseudonyms and acronyms, false identities and elaborate games of deception, fostered to be sure by circumstances, nevertheless had their inception in the Beyle household where adults generally spoke in whispers whenever anything serious or remotely controversial was brought up in the course of a conversation. These characteristics of the author of *The Red and the Black* and *The Charterhouse of Parma* can, at least to a certain extent, be traced to his Dauphinois lineage and to the impact of his father upon subconscious attitudes. His respect for facts and the practical, down-to-earth side of his nature which led him to reject the more extravagant manifestations of the Romantic sensibility, his stubborn, uncompromising pursuit of the truth as he saw it, his reluctance to elaborate upon the most intimate and intense feelings and emotions—whether they be his own or those of his fictional char-

acters—for fear of sacrificing in the process the demands of veracity and artistic honesty, all these are part of a profoundly ingrained
outlook on life which goes back to his Grenoble roots and upbringing and to his antagonistic relationship with his father.

Stendhal himself hardly ever acknowledged any affinities with
the Beyle side of his ancestry and preferred to dwell at length on
the traits he felt his mother had passed on to him. In reality, however, while he liked to view himself as a Gagnon first and foremost
in his temperamental and emotional tendencies, he was also,
more than he was willing to recognize it, a Beyle and a Dauphinois. It excited his imagination and flattered his ego that his nature
corresponded with his ideal of generosity, sensibility, and tenderness, what he was fond of calling his *espagnolisme,* and that he
owed these qualities to his adored mother, whose premature disappearance from his life had had the result of endowing her with a
poetic and mysterious aura of feminine loveliness and spiritual
perfection. While his father came to symbolize all the materialistic
values he despised, his mother, on the other hand, embodied for
him an ideal of beauty and artistic sensitivity that he would identify with the loftiest and noblest in mankind. No wonder he would
never admit that he was a Beyle, that the name itself would be dis-
tasteful to him, and that he saw himself only as a Gagnon, a free
spirit like his mother, unjustly and cruelly imprisoned by fate in
the somber Beyle household.

Stendhal, who in his checkered career came to look upon
Italy as his spiritual motherland, liked to think that through his
mother's ancestors Italian blood coursed through his veins, a notion which was fostered in him by his Great-Aunt Elisabeth Gagnon, a spinster who lived with her brother, the good doctor, and
who behind the stern and reserved exterior of the provincial old
maid hid a tender soul and a romantic imagination. She liked to
talk to young Henri about his ancestors on his mother's side and
told him, among other things, that his great-grandfather was born
at Avignon, in sunny, lavender-scented Provence, *"where oranges
came from."* And she mysteriously added that the Gagnons had
originally come from a land even more beautiful than Provence,

"that her grandfather's grandfather, as a result of some dark circumstance, had sought refuge in Avignon in the retinue of a Pope; that there he had been obliged to change his name somewhat and to hide, and that then he had made his livelihood as a surgeon." [18]

Stendhal's imagination, no less fertile than that of his relative, interpreted these "facts" in a manner worthy of the most romantic novel: "With what I know of Italy today, I would translate as follows: that a certain M. Guadagni or Guadaniamo, having committed a small murder in Italy, had come to Avignon, around 1650, in the train of some legate." Stendhal was all the more eager to subscribe to this rather fanciful family genealogy since it conformed so perfectly with his own concept of Italy as a place where strong passions and energetic personalities are not hampered by the petty rules and paralyzing customs of over-refined and sophisticated societies. That he himself was a descendant of one of those bold, ruthless Italians of the Renaissance greatly appealed to his personal mythology about the Italian character and mores. This, he felt, could go a long way toward explaining his own temperament and the fact that he had always felt so estranged in the strict, strait-laced Beyle household. He was eager to find data that would corroborate his great-aunt's assertions, and the notion of his Italian origin was borne out, he decided, by the fact that the Italian language was held in great esteem in his family, "a rather remarkable thing in a bourgeois family of 1780," [19] and that his mother could read Dante in the original.

How delightful for the author of the *Charterhouse of Parma* and of the dramatic tales of Italian passion, jealousy, murder, and revenge making up the *Italian Chronicles*, to dream, in the twilight of his own adventurous life, that, among his ancestors he could count one of those brigands capable of committing "a slight murder," as he humorously puts it in his autobiography, which forced him to seek exile in the hospitable and tolerant papal town and center of the great Schism of Avignon! "What impressed me greatly then was that we had come (for I regarded myself a Gagnon and thought of the Beyles with a repugnance which still persists in 1835) from a land where orange-trees grow in the open. What a land of happiness, I thought!"[20] In point of fact, Henriette Gagnon's linguistic accomplishment was not as unusual as Stendhal liked to think. Italian was the most popular foreign language in France since the Renaissance. Cultured men and women who read Italian fluently were not at all rare in the eighteenth century. Grenoble, furthermore, by its geographic location, favored this interest since it stands on one of the principal routes leading to Italy.

Stendhal's somewhat fanciful notions concerning the Italian origins of his family on his mother's side had a great deal to do with his preference for the artistic, sensitive, cultured Gagnons at the expense of the money-grubbing Beyles. Whether the Gagnons were really descendants of Italian immigrants remains a matter of conjecture. What is certain, however, is that the Gagnons were not Grenoblois but hailed from Provence, from the town of Bédarrides, which still exists and counts about 2,600 inhabitants and which is located in the near vicinity of Avignon, the papal see from 1309 to 1376. A prosperous commercial center where papal rule was tolerant, it was a haven for Jews and also harbored a substantial Italian colony, among whom, as records show, there was a Johannes Gaignoni as early as 1477.[21] A hundred years later, the name of Gaignoni had become Gaignon and, by the beginning of the seventeenth century, Gagnon. After that, the archives of Bédarrides lists scores of Gagnons, all farmers and small landowners.

Stendhal's own genealogy on his mother's side begins with a Jean Gagnon, born in 1653, who was the first in the line to give up tilling the soil and who, leaving the village of Bédarrides, settled in Avignon, where he became a master weaver of silk, a major industry of the region by that time. He married and had a son, baptized Antoine on December 14, 1677. In all likelihood, Jean Gagnon, who owned his own shop, was none too successful in business and, hoping to do better in the more northern town of Grenoble, where competition in his line of work would be less keen, moved to that city where he died in 1733. His son Antoine stayed in Grenoble, where he became a master surgeon and surgeon major in the artillery of the city. Antoine Gagnon was evidently successful in his calling and, in 1718, he married Elisabeth Senterre, daughter of a merchant and notable of Grenoble. He also acquired the handsome house on the corner of the Place Grenette and the Grand-Rue which would have such pleasant associations for Stendhal. He appears to have been an upright, hardworking man with both drive and a strong sense of honor and professional responsibility. He was Stendhal's great-grandfather.

Antoine Gagnon had two children: Elisabeth, born October 30, 1721, who never married and who stirred young Beyle's imagination by recounting to him the adventures of his "Italian" ancestors; and Henri, born October 6, 1728, who, following in his father's footsteps, also became a physician, one moreover who achieved success and social prominence. He it was who, for all practical purposes, became Stendhal's principal mentor.

A few more words about Elisabeth Gagnon, Stendhal's great-aunt whom he more simply called Aunt Elisabeth, are in order. Living as she did in her brother's house, she was a frequent and cherished companion to young Henri. It was she who instilled in him her taste for things chivalrous and heroic and to whose influence Stendhal attributed what he fondly called his *espagnolisme*, by which he meant his idealistic and romantic streak that could wreak havoc in his life and that he tried in vain to extirpate with massive doses of *logic* and cool-hearted self-analysis. If the eventual consequences of this early exposure of an already naturally imaginative and sensitive child to intoxicating stories of great deeds and noble feelings sometimes turned out to be disastrous for Stendhal's later plans and ambitions, their immediate impact was exhilarating. It was only when his own emotions and adolescent dreams clashed with the hard world of reality that he learned a painful lesson: men and women like Aunt Elisabeth are destined for a life of unhappiness or loneliness, for their delusions and impractical high-mindedness make them unfit to cope with the harsh exigencies of life. For the time being, however, young Henri eagerly sought out Aunt Elisabeth who, like her brother the good doctor, had great personal charm and the kind of refinement and exquisite courtesy more typical of the old regime than of the revolutionary decade that was about to begin. That such a handsome, cultured, and well-to-do woman should have ended up as an old maid was due, it was rumored in the family, to a disappointment in love, a quite credible explanation for the situation of the inordinately proud, romantic, and fastidious Elisabeth Gagnon, whose favorite literary works were Corneille's heroic dramas, especially *Le Cid*.[22]

It was largely through his almost daily contact with his grandfather and especially his great-aunt that Henri Beyle acquired the heady but dangerous habit of admiring acts of generosity and valor and, by the same token, learned to regard with scorn those innumerable compromises that one is forced to accept as a price for worldly success. Young Henri's first models were those men and women in history and literature who followed, not the dictates of cold, practical reason and narrow self-interest, but the exalted visions, noble dreams, and fiery passions.

Finally, like her brother, Elisabeth Gagnon detested imprecision, incorrectness, and vulgarity in verbal expression. The Gagnons spoke in that uniquely elegant yet unaffected, natural, and unadorned French characteristic of the best eighteenth-century authors. Their models, in that respect, were Fontenelle, Montesquieu, and Voltaire, those masters of the French tongue at its purest and most elegant and before the pre-Romantic effusions invaded the language. Young Henri was mercilessly chided whenever he was found guilty of resorting to a vague, vulgar, or inappropriate word or turn of phrase. At an early age, therefore, he acquired the salutary habit of seeking accuracy and felicity in speech, a training that was to stand him in good stead in his later apprenticeship as writer and novelist. Always he would prize clarity and correctness in the use of words and, loyal to the teachings of his early mentors, continued to regard aptness and concision as the highest stylistic qualities, even after the Romantics had given currency to a more inflated kind of rhetoric. The art of understatement and of leaving certain things unsaid was a lesson Stendhal learned early in life, and it is no doubt the verbal *pudeur* and the immense respect for language, accompanied by self-discipline, which he observed in the household of Dr. Gagnon that first made the future author of *The Red and the Black* singularly wary of the power of words and careful not to abuse it.

In 1756, Dr. Gagnon had married Thérèse-Félise Rey, daughter of a respectable bourgeois and granddaughter of a notary from the Grenoble region. She died young, having presented her husband with one son and two daughters. The eldest, Henriette-Adélaïde-Charlotte, born October 2, 1757, was Dr. Gagnon's favorite and Stendhal's mother. We shall presently have more to say about her. Félix-Romain, born one year later, grew up to be a handsome, light-hearted *bon vivant*, irresistible to the ladies and rather disdained by his more scholarly and serious-minded father for his laziness, indifference to intellectual effort and good authors, and predilection for salacious and erotic novels so much in demand by a whole sector of the eighteenth-century reading public.

Young Henri could not help but be fascinated by his frivolous, egotistical, but charming and witty uncle. The most notorious Don Juan in Grenoble, Romain Gagnon was a lawyer by profession, but devoted his energies to more agreeable pursuits. He liked to make fun of Chérubin Beyle's gravity of demeanor and dourness of temperament. On the other hand, the elder Beyle very strongly disapproved of his brother-in-law's light-heartedness and profligate ways. An avid theatergoer, Romain Gagnon decided to acquaint his nephew, then about six years of age, with the magic of the stage by taking him to a performance of Corneille's *Le Cid*.[23] That evening was one of the high points in Stendhal's childhood and, despite the objections of the family, which felt that this initiation to the theater was premature, Romain Gagnon now and then repeated the experience, to the child's utter delight and great excitement. He thus discovered an enchanted world of illusion and make-believe whose spell over him would grow stronger with the passing years. To be sure, the boy could hardly grasp the meaning of what he saw and heard, but he was dazzled by the spectacle. Provincial audiences especially appreciated energy and bravura in the acting style of the leading members of the touring companies. The reforms toward greater subtlety and naturalness instituted by the best Paris performers had not yet had a widespread impact, and young Beyle therefore dutifully aped his elders in their noisy approval of an actor or actress who could gesticulate with special ferocity or shout dramatic lines with unusual pulmonary vigor.

Surrounded as he was by dignified, right-minded adults, Henri Beyle looked upon his rake of an uncle with both admiration and wonderment. He could not help but notice that he was never bored in the company of his uncle, and by furtively borrowing volumes from the latter's library he became acquainted with those racy novels, the *romans galants,* that depict the relations between the sexes in terms of seductions, betrayals, and cynical, light-hearted banter.

Eventually, Romain Gagnon married and settled down to a more respectable existence, at least in outward appearance. He moved to the picturesque Savoyard village of Les Echelles, a small market town inhabited mainly by farmers who had grown rich and whose principal pastime was hunting. Now and then, Romain Gagnon would come to Grenoble for a secret escapade and assignation. His house at Les Echelles was a center of good cheer, and for young Beyle it was always a cause for celebration when his uncle would invite him to spend a few days with him. A sevenhours' drive in a light gig brought Henri to the river Guiers, which divided France from Savoy. The duchy of Savoy, part of the successive kingdoms of Burgundy, had not yet been annexed by France before the Revolution (this was to take place in 1792). To take long, leisurely walks in the country with his uncle, whose conversation was unfailingly amusing, if not instructive, to go fishing with him and contemplate at length the swift waters of the Guiers river, all this was like being transported to an enchanted, carefree land. It is on these visits that Stendhal had his first taste of the sense of freedom and exhilaration that comes with traveling and visiting new places, an experience he would never forget, he who one day would practically invent tourism as it has since been practiced, as the expression of our modern, restless sensibility and need for the unknown and the exotic.

The third and youngest offspring of Dr. Gagnon's marriage was Marie-Françoise-Séraphie, born in 1760, who remained unmarried and continued to live under her father's roof. She was to earn the dubious distinction of becoming Henri's most detested relative. Aunt Séraphie and Aunt Elisabeth, both spinsters and both living in the same house, could not be more dissimilar in temperament and outlook on life. Aunt Séraphie was the typical old maid found in families of a certain time and milieu. As ill-tempered and meddlesome as she was pious, she was disliked by most members of her family, yet managed to impose her will and enjoyed great authority in the Gagnon household. Far more aggressive and argumentative than Dr. Gagnon and Aunt Elisabeth, she succeeded, more often than not, in having things her own way thanks to her aptitude for making scenes. Others would give in to her merely to avoid disagreeable quarrels and confrontations. She was the only member of the Gagnon clan who openly sided with Chérubin Beyle in the latter's frequent disputes with his son. In his autobiography, Stendhal describes her as the evil genius throughout his entire childhood, a hated and feared figure that always loomed threateningly over all his activities, making him miserable with her constant scolding and tattling. That she and his father seemed to enjoy each other's company made him even more suspicious of her. That an affinity drew together the assertive old maid and the lonely Chérubin Beyle—especially after the latter was widowed—did not escape the observant boy's notice, and in his *Henry Brulard*, Stendhal even goes so far as to insinuate (probably by way of retaliation against the two principal "tyrants" of his early years) that his father and aunt entertained amorous feelings for each other.[24]

II

First Traumas
and Conflicts

STENDHAL WAS ONLY seven when he lost his mother, a painful emotional experience and shock which cast a pall over his
childhood and adolescence and which produced a psychic wound
that never completely healed. All the circumstances surrounding
this death conspired to make it the most traumatic and terrifying
event of Stendhal's formative years, if not of his entire life. The
brutal suddenness of it, its mysterious and incomprehensible nature for a seven-year-old boy, its accompanying religious rituals,
all this is recounted in greater detail in Stendhal's autobiography
than most other occurrences that affected him profoundly and had
a lasting effect on his psyche.[1]

Stendhal's recollection of his mother is tinged with nostalgia
and permeated with tenderness and sensuous adoration: "My
mother, Madame Henriette Gagnon, was a charming woman and
I was in love with my mother . . . I wanted to cover my mother
with kisses and that there should be no clothes. She loved me passionately and often kissed me; I returned her kisses with such ardor
that she was often forced to go away. I abhorred my father when
he came to interrupt our kisses. I always wanted to kiss her on the
breast . . . She was plump, with a perfect freshness of complexion, she was very pretty, only I think not quite tall enough. She
had a nobility and perfect serenity in her features; very lively, she

preferred to run and do anything for herself rather than order about her three maids, and finally she often read Dante's *Divine Comedy* in the original."[2]

This passage in *Henry Brulard* is, of course, one of the most crucial and extraordinary in the autobiography. That it presents one of the most striking examples of a classical Oedipus complex cannot be denied.[3] With Stendhal, however, nothing is clear-cut and simple. That there is a touch of exhibitionism and deliberate provocation in the mature writer's description of his love for his mother is also quite evident. Stendhal liked nothing better than to shock his reader and challenge his prejudices and preconceptions. Always the showman and mystifier, he found it difficult to refrain from assuming attitudes which he knew would be judged outrageous. Unlike Rousseau, however, Stendhal does not embellish his most startling revelations with rhetorical effects. His disclosures are direct and unadorned, and deliberately so. To lessen the impact of his self-avowals through stylistic beauty was, he strongly felt, a betrayal of the truth as he saw it. And no author has been more keenly aware of the decisive role played by his early childhood in forming his character. Hence the great importance he attached to his feelings toward his mother and father and the lucidity with which he viewed, long before the advent of Freudian psychology, his relationship with these two key figures in his childhood.

That his hatred for his father was of a most tenacious kind is once more demonstrated by the deliberately blunt and dramatic way he describes his passionate, sensual love for his mother, and contrasts it, in diptych fashion, with the physical repulsion he always felt when in close contact with his father. The antithesis is also of a spiritual nature. To young Beyle his deceased mother soon came to embody everything he admired, yearned for, and felt so cruelly deprived of: generosity of soul, tenderness of heart, and an appreciation for the finer, more artistic things in life. His father, on the other hand, stood for those bourgeois values—respect for wealth and position, conformity to social and religious customs and rules—against which he would rebel with increasing vehemence. To be sure, all this was not consciously perceived by the boy Beyle. But there is no doubt that, at a very early age, he loved his mother and disliked his father. These feelings were to become exacerbated by such circumstances as Mrs. Beyle's premature and tragic death, which endowed her with a quasi-mythical aura, and by Chérubin Beyle's singular ineptness in dealing with his son. Until his dying day, Stendhal would look upon his mother as the artist and idealist, his father as the social climber and unimaginative drudge. In his novels, too, the two sets of values are in perpetual and irreconcilable conflict.

That Stendhal depicted his mother as a lovely, desirable woman is hardly surprising in view of what we know of his own affectionate, amorous nature and his lifelong passionate involvement with women. And in his autobiography he intentionally underscored the fact that it was she who unwittingly aroused his childish sexuality: "She cannot take offense at the liberty I am taking with her in revealing that I loved her; if I ever meet her again, I shall once more tell her about it. Besides, she took no part whatsoever in this love. . . . As for me, I was as criminal as possible, I loved her charms with passion." [4]

A recent Rousseau biographer has pointed out that the writer's lifelong feeling of guilt was due to the fact that his very existence "had been bought at the price of his mother's life." [5] Whereas the death of the mother for Rousseau coincided with the beginning of life itself, for Stendhal, as he twice repeats in his autobiography, it meant "the beginning of my spiritual life." [6]

Like Rousseau's mother, Stendhal's died in childbirth. Although young Henri was kept in the dark at the time as to this circumstance, when he somewhat later found out about it, it only reinforced his hostility against his father. His mother had succumbed apparently as a result of the incompetent ministrations of an *accoucheur* selected by Chérubin Beyle. On the other hand, the generally undemonstrative Beyle was obviously grief-stricken by his wife's untimely death. But his sorrow awakened no sympathy in his seven-year-old son: "I found that my father looked quite ugly, he had swollen eyes and they constantly filled with tears." [7]

The disconsolate widower gave express orders that his wife's room be left exactly as it had been and permitted no one to enter the sacred shrine: "Her room remained locked for ten years after her death. Only reluctantly did my father permit me . . . to study mathematics there in 1798. But no servant was allowed to go in, . . . I alone had the key. This sentiment on my father's part does him great credit in my eyes, now that I reflect upon it." [8]

That young Henri was unable to grasp the meaning of the event that had taken place so suddenly and that plunged the household in an uproar is understandable. When he failed, upon being told that his mother had died, to demonstrate his sorrow in the proper fashion, he was sternly reproached by his Aunt Séraphie for having no heart and for being a monstrous child. Confronted with death for the first time, Henri Beyle, quite normally for a child his age, could scarcely be expected to fathom its finality: "It seemed to me that I would see her again the next day; I did not comprehend death." [9]

From bewilderment, Henri passed into a state of numbing uneasiness, and finally shock, terror, and sheer panic when he was made to participate in the funeral mass and burial ceremony with all the members of the family present and dressed in their Sunday best: "I went wild . . . It seems that I did not want them to throw earth on my mother's coffin, saying that they would hurt her." Inevitably, this association between some of the most somber rituals of the Catholic religion and the first great traumatic experience in his life lingered on in the boy's consciousness, and as he tells us, he could never thereafter look at the church where the Mass had been held or even hear the sound of its bells without experiencing an intense and disagreeable emotion akin to anger and despair. His resentment and rage had been heightened by the fact that, on the eve of the funeral, he had overheard a priest say, in manner of consolation, to the distraught Chérubin Beyle: "My friend, it is God's will." This remark made young Henri ponder deeply. Who was this God who, in such an arbitrary manner, took his mother away from him? It seemed to him that, if this was God's doing, then He was not to be trusted. He soon thereafter revealed his sacrilegious thought to the scandalized servants: "I started to speak ill of God."[10] It occurred to the middle-aged Stendhal, setting down these painful memories, that his lifelong antipathy to religion could be traced, at least in part, to this callous explanation, overheard at a highly impressionable age, and interpreted with impeccable if surprising logic.

Henriette Beyle's presence had enlivened and illumined the otherwise cheerless old house on the rue des Vieux-Jésuites. In addition to her not inconsiderable intellectual and artistic accomplishments, she had a lively and lovable disposition. No overweening bluestocking, she was gay and full of life and something of her zest for life, charm, warmth, and tenderness passed on to Stendhal's most appealing fictional heroines and can also be recognized in those women with whom he fell in love. After her death, light and joy seemed to have gone forever from the Beyle household. Chérubin Beyle withdrew completely within himself and in his world of business schemes and real estate deals. Increasingly, young Henri turned to his maternal grandfather for companionship and affection. But even Dr. Gagnon was all too frequently powerless in his efforts to protect his grandson against Chérubin Beyle's authoritarianism or the formidable Aunt Séraphie's neurotic outbursts. With Henriette Beyle's death the delights of childhood ended for Stendhal. Until then, the world had been a cosy, comfortable place where an inquisitive, active child could live happily through his senses and be secure in the knowledge that he could always find a haven in his mother's love. He was now on his own, forced to defend his rights in a world filled with uncomprehending, indifferent, or hostile adults.

Chérubin Beyle never felt at ease in the house of Dr. Gagnon, where it was expected that he dine at regular intervals. The only member of the family to whom he could freely speak his mind and who was sympathetic to him was Aunt Séraphie. Dr. Gagnon, for his part, was always extremely courteous to his son-in-law, but Henri could not fail to notice that there was no real sympathy between the two men. And another favorite relative of the boy, Aunt Elisabeth, had little liking for the dour widower and, despite her elaborate politeness, could not help but betray her real feelings to the observant Henri. More and more, therefore, Chérubin Beyle took to spending his days away from his family and to leaving his son in the care of his in-laws.

Although Dr. Gagnon gave the outward impression of being a skeptical, genteel, and somewhat cold-blooded disciple of the *philosophes*, he was capable of strong, lasting feelings, and therefore of suffering. The premature loss of his favorite daughter affected him deeply, for, as Stendhal states: "The only ones he loved in the world were that daughter and myself." [11] He had little affinity with his other daughter, Séraphie. She bored him and got on his nerves. He loved nothing better than peace and quiet, and she was always making scenes. Into his only grandchild he poured his treasures of knowledge, and, in so doing, imparted to him many of his beliefs and attitudes.

And no ordinary man was he. A leading physician of Grenoble in his day, he continued to be highly regarded and well liked long after his retirement from active practice. Once greatly in favor with the ladies, he still wore a powdered wig in the Old Regime style, with three neat rows of curls, walked with an elegant cane, and carried in his hand, but never actually wore, a little tricorn hat. Whenever he passed in the street, townspeople saluted him in a manner both amicable and deferential, and he never failed to return the greeting with a cordial little wave of the hand. Dr. Gagnon had willingly given of his time and energy, without any remuneration, to the poor people of Grenoble. Hence the respect and affection in which he was held by all alike. A portrait of him (which now hangs in the Stendhal Museum in Grenoble), executed by an anonymous but competent artist, shows him in his prime, attired in stylish but tastefully simple clothes, as befits a man in his position. The face is full, a bit heavy, and the dimpled double chin rests comfortably on a vigorous neck. The features are obviously those of a man who enjoyed good food and wine; the nose is somewhat longish and aquiline (Stendhal liked to think that it was typically Italian, thereby disclosing the ultramontane origins of the Gagnons); the mouth is that of a refined epicurean,

well-delineated and enlivened by a discreet smile; but it is the
eyes, penetrating and sensitive, that strike and retain our attention.
Those brown eyes sparkle with intelligence, yet are tempered with
gentle humor and benevolence. The doctor is standing, his robust
frame leaning slightly backward, his left hand resting, in a gesture
of quiet authority, under the embroidered waistcoat. The whole
solid yet sophisticated countenance bespeaks the more engaging
and affable aspects of an age of reason and optimism, of which Dr.
Gagnon, with his faith in science and knowledge, his easy-going
tolerance and smiling skepticism, was a slightly anachronistic representative and, during the clamorous years of the Revolution, a
melancholy and isolated survivor. For Dr. Gagnon belonged, at
least spiritually, to the more mundane half of the eighteenth century, to the generation of Fontenelle, Montesquieu, and the
young Voltaire. Like these writers, who were his idols, he was
both an intellectual and a man of the world. In an age of rapidly
changing values, he remained stubbornly yet discreetly loyal to
those thinkers and writers who could say profound things in a
witty, light-hearted way. When Rousseau burst upon the scene,
hypnotizing the younger generation, he continued to venerate
Voltaire. He had even made a personal pilgrimage to Ferney in
order to see and converse with the famed Patriarch himself. A
small bust of Voltaire occupied a place of honor in his study, and
his library was stacked with the works of the *philosophe*.

Philanthropist, discriminating amateur of literature and art,
enlightened leader of the Grenoble intelligentsia, sympathetic
friend of the common folk, Dr. Gagnon had one defect. He was
not only tolerant, he was too detached from the world around
him. Even after 1789, he managed to continue observing events
from afar, from the vantage point of his terrace where, surrounded
by his beloved plants, he would sip good coffee and read one of his
favorite authors. Political activism would have meant for the good
doctor an unworthy distraction from more spiritually and personally rewarding pursuits. In his way, he was an egotist and an
unashamed epicurean. In a world engulfed by ideological passions, he continued to live according to the dictates of a more aris-

tocratic, elegant, and hedonistic age. And just as he had determined to steer clear of Revolutionary politics, he refrained from
raising his voice against the authority of his son-in-law in the latter's disputes with the rebellious Henri. And while he did not
agree with Chérubin Beyle's pedagogical principles and with his
outlook on life in general, he remained a sympathetic but silent
bystander, rather than an active ally, throughout Stendhal's strife-
ridden childhood. Young Henri could not but sense the repressed
conflict between the two sides of his family and, unconsciously
perhaps, played on that enmity. But to his constant chagrin, he
found himself isolated and unsupported, for while his adversaries
in the persons of his father and Aunt Séraphie, were aggressive and
dogmatic, his allies, his grandfather and Aunt Elisabeth, rightly or
wrongly, felt obligated to stay in the background and to remain
silently forbearing.

Stendhal had two sisters, both younger than himself: Pauline-
Eléonore, born March 21, 1786, and Marie-Zénaïde-Caroline,
born October 10, 1788. He loved his sister Pauline, his confidante, ally, and accomplice in his epic battles against the tyrannical forces of authority embodied in his father and Aunt Séraphie. Dr. Gagnon used to tease Pauline gently by saying that she
believed in her brother as one would in God. Zénaïde, on the
other hand, perhaps because she was the youngest child so soon
deprived of a mother, seemed to have a special hold on her father's
affections. Every night, Chérubin Beyle would rock her to sleep
on his knees. As she grew older, Zénaïde sided with her father and
dutifully reported to him her brother's pranks or suspicious activities. Using his artistic talents, Henri would retaliate by drawing
caricatures of his younger sister on the whitewashed hallway wall
of his grandfather's house with the words, "Caroline-Zénaïde
Beyle, informer."
      On the whole, however, young Henri spent a great deal of his
time alone, and his sisters were only occasional play companions.
Despite his affection for Pauline, which was to deepen later in life
into a warm friendship, sustained by a voluminous corre-

spondence, she was too young and immature to be a real companion to the precocious, restless boy. His naturally expansive and affectionate nature early stiffened into rebelliousness and contentious belligerence. His father aroused in him the desire to argue and contradict. He also soon acquired the ability to disguise his true feelings and learned the art of concealment, that ultimate weapon of the weak and the oppressed.

Nothing is better suited to destroy a child's respect for his elders than the spectacle of uncontrolled temper or the arbitrary use of parental authority. Chérubin Beyle's rigidity and outbursts of anger were doubtless the expression of his helplessness in the face of his son's antagonism. Originating in personal differences, the conflict between father and son developed into an encounter between the old and the new: Chérubin Beyle represented the traditional, monarchical values, and his son eagerly espoused the new values and ideals of post-Enlightenment and revolutionary France. Chérubin Beyle failed completely in his obstinate and awkward attempts to mold his son according to the tenets that governed his own life. Henri soon learned to take mischievous delight in thwarting, at every step of the way, his father's will and in asserting his own, and his aptitude for resistance to outside pressure and entreaty grew stronger with every small victory or stalemate. When, upon several occasions, he managed to hide successfully what was going on in his head, he felt encouraged to defy more openly his adult adversaries. But the consequences of such overt resistance were so invariably disagreeable that the boy retreated into a strategy of seeming submission. To blurt out plain truths, he quickly found out, is a costly luxury in a world that prizes, above all, unquestioning obedience to authority. This lesson was to be reinforced by his later experience in the world. Frankness and sincerity, qualities so highly extolled by Rousseau and his followers, could only lead to personal disappointment or even disaster in a society which blithely and cynically condones flattery, hypocrisy, and dissemblance.

Even Henri's affectionate bond with his sister Pauline could not alleviate his sense of isolation and loneliness. She looked up to him, but she was an enthusiastic disciple and follower, not an equal. His early deprivation of the tender, reassuring presence of a mother was the one event that, more than any other, marked his inner being in an indelible way. Whenever he mentions her, the reader cannot but feel how profoundly Stendhal's childhood was affected by his mother's premature death. It left a void that no one could fill and a lifelong yearning for feminine affection, for that warmth and gentleness he first experienced when, as a little boy, he would seek solace and security in her comforting embrace and in the contact with her soft skin and rounded forms. Her sudden, brutal disappearance constituted an experience for young Henri comparable to the expulsion from the Garden of Eden. It marked the end of the serene dawn of life and the beginning of the struggle for survival, the shock that came with the realization that in this world he would have to walk alone and unaided.

In the absence of a mother, it was decided that Henri should have a private tutor. The man appointed for that important task was the abbé Jean-François Raillane, a Jesuit priest who, in Stendhal's autobiography, appears as an arch-villain and veritable rascal: "I don't mean that he had committed crimes, but it would be hard to find a more unfeeling soul, more hostile to all that is honest, more devoid of all sentiment of humanity." [12]

A refractory priest who had refused to swear allegiance to the Revolution and a fanatical royalist, the abbé Raillane had been invited by Chérubin Beyle in December of 1792 to live under his roof and take charge of his son. To give shelter to a non-juring priest could hardly improve Chérubin Beyle's own precarious situation with the revolutionary authorities. For periods of time, whenever it was deemed necessary, the abbé would leave the Beyle household and go into hiding. On the whole, his tutorship of young Beyle lasted approximately two years, a relatively short period of time, but one that was crucial in the emotional development of Stendhal and the disagreeable memory of which remained with him for the rest of his life. [13]

A great believer in discipline and unquestioning obedience, the abbé was the staunch ally of Henri's other two "tyrants," his father and Aunt Séraphie, and was forever chiding and scolding his recalcitrant charge. Chérubin Beyle's selection of the abbé as his only son's preceptor doubtless was an important factor in further alienating the boy from him.

Short of stature, the abbé Raillane was lean, with a sallow, swarthy complexion, and, as is revealed by a contemporary portrait, with a hard-featured face. The lips are thin and tightly pressed together, the eyes look out at the world with a cold, expressionless stare, the nose is sharp and aquiline. When his mouth managed to open into a smile, which happened only on rare occasions, it was, Stendhal informs us, "abominable." [14]

Authoritarian, narrow-minded, pedantic and stiff in manner and speech, and a staunch upholder of dogma, the abbé was, according to Stendhal, whether by cunning, education, or priestly instinct, "a sworn enemy of logic and all sound reasoning." [15] He taught his pupils according to old-fashioned rules that stressed rote and memorization and that completely disregarded the child's ability to reason for himself. It is primarily the abbé that Stendhal blames for having become a rabid unbeliever and for having turned into, at least for a while, a sullen, secretive youth. Fortunately, his naturally affectionate, outgoing, and optimistic temperament eventually had the upper hand. Both Chérubin Beyle and the abbé Raillane were great believers in the value of learning facts by heart, something Henri, with his inquisitive and restless intelligence, thoroughly loathed.

One day, Grandfather Gagnon said to the abbé: "But, monsieur, why teach this child the celestial system of Ptolemy, which you know to be wrong?" "Monsieur, it explains everything and, besides, is approved by the Church." [16] The good doctor could not stomach this answer, but instead of pursuing the discussion and voicing his protest, he thereafter quoted the abbé's reply with a laugh. Grandfather Gagnon's main weakness, at least where Henri was concerned, was his mildness of temperament, his detached and disabused outlook on life, and his quiet determination not to get involved in family matters which he considered outside his purview.

Much later, Stendhal admitted that he could hardly be fair in evaluating the abbé Raillane's character, just as he could not be objective when speaking of his father. The writer provides no particulars as to the exact time and manner in which his unhappy association with his tutor came to an end. It seems that the abbé merely vanished from the scene, probably in 1794, after several absences due to the need to go into hiding in order to escape from the revolutionary authorities. With the Thermidorean reaction he was able to resume his professional pursuits and, from 1799 until 1840, he ran a boarding school in Grenoble whose distinguishing feature was a set of Draconian rules regulating every aspect of the life of its unfortunate pupils.[17] One cannot but wonder how Henri, mutinous though he was during what he calls the Raillane "tyranny," would have reacted had he been entrusted to the abbé, not in the security and relative freedom of his own home, but far from his family, within the cold, impersonal institution. His hyper-sensitive nature, ruffled though it was by the constant frictions with the abbé, would have suffered far more had he not been reassured by the presence of such kind and enlightened adults as Grandfather Gagnon and Aunt Elisabeth. The dreadful abbé was, after all, an employee in the pay of Chérubin Beyle, one occupying a fairly lowly position in the family and barely above that of the servants. Whenever Henri found the abbé's authoritarian ways intolerable, he could seek a measure of consolation in the thought that this hated master was no more than a subordinate who had been hired by the socially ambitious Chérubin Beyle so that he could boast to the other bourgeois of Grenoble that his son had a private tutor.

Another major cause for unhappiness was due to the fact that he was isolated from boys his own age. As a proper young scion of a respectable family, he was forbidden to play with the children in his neighborhood. Following his mother's death, his family socialized very little. Partly out of boredom, they focused most of their attention and energies on him. To be the constant subject of conversation and preoccupation on the part of over-solicitous and fastidious relatives was a perpetual source of irritation. As a result, all those little spontaneous acts and impulses that go into making a happy and normal childhood were so thoroughly scrutinized and criticized as to become a virtual impossibility.

Brief moments of freedom and uninhibited play had to be snatched surreptitiously and guarded by an elaborate system of deceptions and half-truths. At a time when he should have been allowed to be carefree, Beyle, by his own later admission, became sullen and hypocritical, "a *slave* in one word, the worst sense of the word." Gradually he assumed the attitudes and feelings of a slave. His tyrants spoke to him with gently condescending words, or, when provoked, in darkly threatening tones. Willy-nilly, the recalcitrant boy had to submit to tiresome homilies on the duties of children. Reminiscing about the trials and tribulations of his difficult childhood, the aging Stendhal marveled that this early experience had not turned him into an ill-natured hypocrite for the rest of his life, but only an irreconcilable enemy of the bourgeois and their values.[18] That his character and sensibilities were not warped by his unhappy and lonely childhood he attributes to his lively spirit and stubborn pride which enabled him to resist his father's repeated efforts to mold him into a docile, right-thinking conformist.

Despite his isolation, young Henri did manage to find one true friend in the person of a handsome, bright, and sensitive young manservant of Dr. Gagnon, Vincent Lambert. Neither Henri's age nor of his social class, Lambert nevertheless became his trusted confidant in a way that his grandfather or sister could not be. His grandfather was, as he later put it in his autobiography, a "serious, respectable companion," and his sister was a docile, admiring disciple. To Lambert the boy could freely speak his mind. Furthermore, despite their disparity in age and social status, they shared a strong common bond: both were dissatisfied with their lot. Henri felt oppressed by his family and dreamed of freedom and adventure, and Lambert chafed under his menial tasks and dreamed of achieving financial independence by breeding silkworms. Lambert treated his younger friend with an affectionate, comradely authority and sympathetically listened to his little stories and complaints against his elders. When the boy's incessant chatter sometimes got on his nerves, he would give him a good-natured but firm tap on the cheek: "I only loved him more for it." Unaccustomed to such chummy familiarity, Henri responded to it eagerly. He felt happy in Lambert's company and liked to watch him perform duties that displayed the young man's strength and skill, such as chop and saw wood and prepare logs for grandfather Gagnon's fireplace.[19]

In 1793, when Henri was ten, he lost his friend just as suddenly and tragically as he had lost his mother three years previously. Lambert fell from a mulberry tree where he was working with his silkworms and was brought back to the house on a ladder used as a make-shift stretcher. He died after three days of delirium and despite the devoted efforts of Dr. Gagnon, who nursed him like a son. For the second time, death entered Henri's life. The loss of his mother had been an unfathomable event the portent of which had at first largely escaped him. When Lambert died, he experienced real, numbing grief and witnessed the actual, terrifying event, since he was allowed into his friend's room. In mute horror, he gazed at Lambert's handsome young face and was struck by the almost supernatural air of strength that delirium brought upon his features. He watched the repeated bleedings, as was the custom of the time, and saw a shining light being brought to his eyes and his pupils fail to respond to it.[20]

A week after Lambert's death, Henri upon recognizing a chipped little earthenware bowl which had been used in the bleedings broke into violent, uncontrollable sobs. Aunt Séraphie, with typical insensitivity, gave him a scolding for weeping over one who was not even a kin and had been a mere servant. The boy ran off to the kitchen muttering a word of protest and outrage he had recently learned from Voltaire: "Infamous, infamous!"[21]

Many years later, in Italy, Stendhal saw a painting representing St. John sadly watching the crucifixion of his friend Jesus, and it suddenly reminded him of what he had experienced at the sight of his first real friend's agony. The memory of Lambert's heightened beauty and nobility of face was perhaps also still present in his mind, at least subconsciously, when in *The Red and the Black* he described Julien Sorel's features as being particularly handsome and expressive on the eve of his execution: "Never had that head such poetic beauty as at the moment when it was about to fall." [22]

Death had successively robbed Henri Beyle of his beloved young mother and of his cherished friend. Thereafter, death would invariably be associated in his mind with youth and beauty, and in his fictional world would endow his heroes and heroines with a poetic and exalted aura.

Several other episodes in *Henry Brulard* are less crucial than the early demise of Lambert but are obviously related in order to underscore the impact of certain events upon Stendhal's character. Some incidents can be rapidly summarized and grouped together, since they obviously serve to illustrate the boy's conflicts with his elders, especially with his father, Aunt Séraphie and the abbé Raillane. There is the story of the thrush, which the boy had adopted and tamed. It had lost a leg, but valiantly hopped around the house. When it suddenly disappeared, having probably been killed accidentally by someone in the household, Henri immediately suspected his father of having done away with the bird deliberately. When Chérubin Beyle undertook to clear himself, Henri gloated over his father's air of distress and embarrassment. For once the tables had been turned, and it was Beyle *père* who stood accused and in the role of the guilty party awkwardly attempting to disculpate himself, while Beyle *fils* listened in a cold, dignified silence! [23]

There is also the tragi-comic and definitely Freudian episode of the bite: young Beyle one day had the irresistible urge to sink his sharp little teeth into the rouged cheek of a plump young aunt who was a frequent visitor and who liked to fondle the boy. The ensuing family scene was a memorable one and the outraged Aunt Séraphie promptly called him a "monster." And, as if to confirm this dire judgment, another incident which caused consternation took place soon thereafter. As Henri was arranging flowers on the balcony, the knife he was using slipped from his hands and fell into the street, missing by a hair a passerby, who by an unfortunate coincidence happened to be a lady friend of Aunt Séraphie. Henri was not only severely scolded, even by his generally indulgent grandfather, but also accused by his hysterical aunt of trying to kill people and of having "an atrocious character." [24]

Henri rebelled against this unfair accusation and for the first time felt the sharp sting of injustice, an anguishing experience that remained deeply etched in his consciousness and that brings to mind the similarly portentous episode of the broken comb related in Rousseau's Confessions. Young Jean-Jacques had also protested in vain and had been blamed for a misdeed of which he was innocent. [25] Like Rousseau, but with less rhetoric, Stendhal stresses the significance of this childhood incident and the role it played in shocking him into an awareness of the existence of injustice. From that time, when he could not have been more than five years of age, Stendhal dates his unalterable wariness of all forms of authority, notwithstanding the respectable guises it might assume. [26]

The obvious tenderness, concern, and nostalgia with which the mature writer went back in time and scrutinized his far-off childhood, seeking in its events big and small those prophetic signs that might help him gain a clearer insight into his self are comparable to similar efforts by a great many modern writers, beginning, of course, with Rousseau. Chateaubriand and Proust, to name but two famous French authors, have also evoked their early years in an attempt to trace the origins of their sensibilities, attitudes, and beliefs.

As one who had lived through the great upheaval that was the French Revolution, as well as the Napoleonic wars and the Bourbon Restoration and July Monarchy, the aging Stendhal understandably felt the need to take stock of himself and establish some unity and coherence in his own self in the face of a baffling and ever-changing world. That he should have been tempted to find in his childish sorrows, pranks, and misadventures an inner logic and consistency that portended his subsequent behavior and illumined the profound reasons for his most basic existential choices should not surprise us. Stendhal had this in common with Rousseau, among other things, that life had buffeted him about and exposed him to an uncommonly wide range of experience which left him, at the threshold of old age, without any reassuring sense of continuity and identity: "What have I been? I would not know. From what friend, however enlightened, can I expect an answer?" Asking himself what manner of a man he had been, tender-hearted or unfeeling, talented or mediocre, intelligent or witless, he had to admit to himself that he was far from having achieved the kind of self-knowledge which he considered a prerequisite for a meaningful understanding of the workings of his psyche: "I am going on fifty, it is high time I knew myself. What have I been, what am I? In truth, I would find it quite hard to say." It is therefore in the hope of unlocking the door to his inner self that he undertook to write his autobiography: "I should write my life, perhaps I shall know at last, when it's finished, in two or three years' time, what I have been." [27] That this self-portrait, however, remained uncompleted, stopping short with the year 1800 and the author's overwhelming happiness upon discovering Italy, does not preclude the fact that it provides essential clues, in its fragmentary, rambling form, to our perception of some of the most fundamental and distinctive traits of his nature. It is a mark of the modern sensibility that an individual, however introspective he may be (and Stendhal is doubtless among the most keenly self-aware writers in Western literature), no longer sees his inner self as a unified, consistent whole, but rather as a baffling aggregate of frequently contradictory tendencies, passions, and impulses. Hence Stendhal's special preoccupation with his childhood. By probing not only those momentous occurrences—such as the death of his mother—which are in a private life what cataclysmic events—such as wars and revolutions—are in human history, but also less dramatic but equally revealing happenings that punctuate a child's daily experience, he hoped to gain a clearer understanding of his character.

Doubtless one of the reasons why Stendhal left his vivid self-portrait unfinished was his very real fear, as he himself tells us, of becoming overly self-centered and bombastic, of writing about himself in a flowery style which would embellish and therefore veil the hard truths he wanted to uncover. Both Rousseau and Chateaubriand, he felt, had succumbed to the temptation of writing about themselves in a poetical, lyrical way, with the result that, perhaps unconsciously, they ended by mingling truth and fiction, adorning the bare and fragmentary facts furnished by a frequently faulty memory with beautiful stylistic effects and imagined narrative details in order to excite and retain the reader's attention. His own purpose would remain more modest and limited: "To tell the truth, I am not at all certain that I have enough talent to get myself read. I sometimes greatly enjoy writing, that is all." [28] In his concept of the autobiography, as in so many other things, Stendhal was in advance of his times, which very much relished the rhetorical flourishes and emotional displays of the Romantic confessional style of writing. He was determined to seek the truth about himself without allowing himself to indulge in any form of self-aggrandizement and without surrendering his critical faculties to the pleasures and gratifications of the imagination. When in doubt, he would rather remain on this side of self-avowal. Sincerity prescribes not only the courage to tell all, but, even more importantly, the self-discipline to be selective and discriminating and the will to avoid wrapping oneself in the mantle of self-righteousness. In this instance, a sense of humor could act as a salutary corrective, and Stendhal, unlike most Romantics, was endowed with a keen sense of the comic and the absurd. Whereas a Rousseau completely identified with Molière's Alceste, the hero of *Le Misanthrope* and the embodiment of sincerity misunderstood and ridiculed, and in his famous *Lettre à d'Alembert sur les spectacles* denounced Molière for having presented this virtuous character in a demeaning light, Stendhal understood that not all truths are of equal interest to the reader or spectator and that nothing is more pathetic and absurd than the spectacle of a man so preoccupied with himself that he is constantly proclaiming what he considers to be earth-shaking verities. As a loyal disciple of the eighteenth century, Stendhal shared with Montesquieu and Voltaire the belief that a writer's primordial duty is not to bore his reader.

The story of his life, he feared, might be tedious: "What a dreadful quantity of *I*'s and *me*'s! enough to put out of humor the most benevolent reader." Chateaubriand, thanks to his immense talent and enormous self-confidence, could perform this tour de force, Stendhal grudgingly admitted.[29] But he felt only uncertainty as to his own chances of offering a personal and intimate self-portrait that would have lasting appeal and interest. He therefore gave up the idea of emulating a Rousseau or a Chateaubriand and leaving a complete and detailed history of his life. What he did leave, however, is sufficiently vivid and compelling to make us regret that he did not persevere in his project.

What caused the mature novelist probing his early years to marvel at was that everything in his background seemed to conspire to make of him a typical bourgeois and that he was nevertheless able to overcome the fears, prejudices, traditions, conventions, and taboos which his family so persistently tried to inculcate in him. After all, he was the offspring of an eminently middle-class family and grew up in a provincial milieu, the kind that frequently proves permanently stifling to individual originality and the burgeoning of talent and genius. That he was somehow successful in breaking through the rigid code his family was attempting to impose upon him he later attributed to three principal factors: his own intelligence and will, which stubbornly resisted all efforts at indoctrination; the liberating impact of the eighteenth-century *philosophes* and Encyclopedists whom he read avidly early in life thanks to surreptitious forays into the libraries of his father and grandfather; the prodigious effect of the French Revolution and the enthusiasm with which he greeted its every triumph.

Stendhal's childhood was, in many ways, like a battleground, with the two armies struggling for his young soul: on the one hand, the malevolent forces of obscurantism in the ogre-like persons of his father, Aunt Séraphie and the abbé Raillane; on the other hand, the beneficent forces of love and enlightenment in the noble and poetic figures of his mother, his grandfather, Aunt Elisabeth, and Lambert. That it was precisely those members of his entourage whom he looked upon as his adversaries who preached the sacredness of Catholicism and monarchism undoubtedly had a great deal to do with his lifelong sympathy for revolutionary and republican causes and his irreligiosity and anticlericalism.

III

Revolutionary Fervor

FROM THE VANTAGE point of the windows of Dr. Gagnon's house which faced, it will be remembered, the Place Grenette, center and heart of Grenoble, Henri watched, as from a theater loge, the events and ceremonies of the Revolution. Some of these spectacles were bloody and terrifying, others imposing and soul-stirring in their colorful pageantry. All had a profound impact on the boy's sensibilities.

In ordinary times, the main square of a provincial town like Grenoble was the stage of regularly reenacted activities. With the advent of the Revolution, however, the Place Grenette witnessed some tragic as well as inspiring episodes. The fact that young Beyle personally saw these events endowed them with an immediacy and force that engraved them forever in his memory. All his life, Stendhal was to stress what he had actually witnessed. Epoch-making events, not as recounted by detached and omniscient historians and chroniclers, but as experienced in all their chaotic and bewildering impact. The quite precocious awakening of young Beyle's mind and sensibility coincided with the explosive events of the Revolution. It is remarkable how Stendhal's intellectual education and reading are similar to those of the revolutionary leaders, although a generation separated the latter from the future novelist.

While the Beyle family remained loyal monarchists and abhorred the Jacobins, young Beyle felt irresistibly drawn to the revolutionary cause. His father, in part because of his well-known anti-

revolutionary opinions and also because of an old rivalry with
another lawyer, André Amar, who had in the meantime become a
deputy to the Convention and hence an influential local politician, was placed on the list of suspects for twenty-two months and
even imprisoned at the height of the Terror (he was saved by the
demise of Robespierre).[1]

When the family discussed in discreet whispers revolutionary
events and commented upon Amar's action against Chérubin
Beyle, young Henri remarked loudly to his father: "Amar put you
on the list as notoriously *suspect* of not loving the Republic, and it
seems *certain* to me that you don't love it."[2] Such outrageous
words inevitably provoked anger, and everyone, especially Aunt
Séraphie, was convinced once more, on the basis of "*facts*," that
he was showing an "atrocious character." And yet, the logic of
what he said appeared irrefutable to Henri. While his family
prayed and wept over the sad fate of Louis XVI and Marie-An-
toinette, young Beyle sympathized with the revolutionary leaders,
including the Jacobins, and wholeheartedly detested the fugitives
and refractory priests whom his father housed and fed.

Grenoble, despite its provinciality, felt the impact of the Revolution from its beginnings. As early as June 7, 1788, a riot broke
out on the Place Grenette as a result of a large popular gathering.
The commander in charge of the Dauphiné province, M. de Cler-
mont-Tonnerre, gave orders to send in his two regiments in order
to disperse the crowd. The soldiers sent in to control the mob were
assailed with tiles thrown at them from the rooftops, whence the
name: Day of the Tiles.

Henri was having dinner in his grandfather's house when the
commotion outside caused everyone to leave the table and run to
the windows facing the square. Henri first caught sight of an old
woman, with her worn shoes in her hands, shouting with all her
might and running in the direction of the soldiers. But he was
quickly distracted by an even more shocking scene. A young
worker (it was later established that he was a journeyman hatter
named Alexis Geay), fatally wounded by a soldier's bayonet thrust
in his back, was painfully making his way, his arms draped over

the shoulders of two companions who were supporting him, toward a nearby house. Because of the warm weather, he wore no coat, and his shirt and trousers were soaked with blood. Henri was scolded and taken away from the window by his relatives. He later learned that the young man expired when he finally reached his room. This was the future novelist's first encounter with violence, and while the Napoleonic era would bring him face to face with many a spectacle of bloodshed and battle, this initial experience had a profound impact upon his sensibilities and the sight of the young worker, blood pouring from his wound, remained engraved in his memory: "This recollection, as is natural, is the clearest I have retained from those times." [3] It is important to remember that Stendhal lived in an age of upheaval and violence and that his imagination, as a novelist, would be directly affected by his firsthand knowledge of the more irrational and unpredictable aspects of human character and behavior.

After 1789, a mood of enthusiasm and exaltation, verging on religious fervor, swept over the capital as well as the provinces of France. Even the usually staid inhabitants of Grenoble shared in this new climate of popular rejoicing. Either on the Place Grenette or on the terrace of the Jardin de Ville, corteges and open-air banquets, enlivened with music and lighted with Chinese lanterns and girandoles, greeted the important events and victories of the Revolution. Through the windows of Dr. Gagnon's house, Henri eagerly took in the sights and sounds of the Revolution.

With the triumph of the revolutionary cause, celebrations took on a more official, solemn air. On October 16, 1791, an imposing procession, comprising the municipality, the national guard, and the gendarmerie, paraded in great pomp a copy of the new constitution. The following year, 1792, the pillory, detested symbol of the iniquities of the judiciary system of the Old Regime, was removed from the Place Grenette, and a Tree of Liberty, surmounted by the Phrygian cap, was planted in its stead. Henceforth, the Place Grenette was renamed Place de la Liberté. In 1794, the streets of the whole neighborhood familiar to Henri

Beyle were renamed: the rue des Vieux-Jéuites, where Chérubin
Beyle's house stood, was baptized rue Jean-Jacques Rousseau, after
the hero of the revolutionaries, a name it retains to this day.

At the foot of the freshly planted Tree of Liberty, there were
solemn commemorations, fiery speeches, lively farandoles, and,
on August 10, 1793, a Goddess of Liberty was erected on an altar
and a bonfire made of all the archives of the Dauphiné province.
At the end of that summer, Henri Beyle, who heard constant talk
of the siege of Lyons by the allied armies, went every evening to
his grandfather's terrace in the hope of catching the distant sound
of the republican cannons firing at the enemy.

As the Revolution followed its irreversible leftward course and
found itself facing formidable obstacles within, as well as the constant pressure of the allied armies on the borders, the popular
manifestations on the Place Grenette took on a more ominous and
sinister character. On January 21, 1794, the first anniversary of
Louis XVI's execution, a rather lurid ceremony marked that event.
Three huge mannikins, representing the late Louis XVI, the Pope,
and the nobility were erected, jeered at, decapitated, and dragged
through the streets while the carmagnole, the song and dance popular after 1793, celebrated the triumph of the people against its
enemies. And thus, in one way or another, the tumult of the Revolution surrounded the only son of Chérubin Beyle, despite the
latter's desperate attempts to insulate his offspring and heir. Henri
was too young to comprehend the full meaning of the momentous
events which were then shaping the future of France, and, indeed
that of Europe, but if the symbolic, psychological, or political intent of these fetes and demonstrations on the Place Grenette
eluded him, their dramatic impact profoundly and lastingly
marked his sensibilities and imagination. It did not occur to young
Beyle that there was some merit, at least of a moral kind, to his father's determination to harbor monarchical sympathies under the
Terror and to have the courage of his convictions. Chérubin Beyle
could have, as so many Frenchmen did during those dangerous
and volatile times, concealed his political sympathies. But the

elder Beyle scorned compromise as hypocrisy unworthy of an honest man, a resolutely individualistic attitude Stendhal himself, under different circumstances, was also to adopt.

On the whole, the Dauphinois, shrewd, pragmatic, and independent-minded, refused to go along with the excesses of the Terror. Stendhal himself asserted in *Henry Brulard* that it was far milder than the White Terror of 1815. To be sure, the novelist's testimony is not that of an objective and detached observer or historian and in his autobiography he is obviously intent upon proving that the White Terror which followed the fall of Napoleon was more cruel and ruthless than that of 1793.[4] But, lest he be accused of partiality, he hastens to add that the extreme repulsion he felt for everything that the Bourbon Restoration represented had perhaps made him overlook some of the facts.

One such unpleasant fact Stendhal could hardly overlook was the guillotining of two priests on the Place Grenette on June 26, 1794. This public execution, which drove Aunt Séraphie into a paroxysm of fury and intensified the proud reticence of Aunt Elisabeth, provoked, at least according to *Henry Brulard*, another reaction on the part of Henri that horrified his family. He blithely said: "My granddaddy has told me that twenty years ago they hanged two Protestant ministers in the same square. . . . The Parlement condemned the first two for their religion; the Criminal Court has just condemned these two for having betrayed their country." [5] Henri was given a terrible scolding and his father flew into one of the worst rages against him that he would ever witness. Aunt Séraphie, of course, was triumphant. Luckily, Grandfather Gagnon, while appalled by this execution, did not join Henri's enemies and privately agreed that the death of the two Protestant ministers was just as blameworthy as that of the two priests. It should be pointed out that this execution constituted, at least from all extant documentation, the only bloodshed in Grenoble during the Terror.

When a para-military "Battalion of Hope" was created by the local branch of the Society of Jacobins, comprising boys Henri's age, as the grandson of the popular Dr. Gagnon he was also nominally enlisted. But his father, not too surprisingly, objected to actual participation, and Henri enviously watched the Battalion marching proudly and in perfect formation, banners fluttering in the wind, under the windows of Dr. Gagnon. In his eagerness to join the Battalion, he decided to resort to deceit in order to obtain the necessary permission from his father. He falsified a letter, signed by Gardon, one of the most fanatical and feared Jacobins of Grenoble, sternly enjoining Chérubin Beyle to enlist his son in the Battalion. The reaction, as expected, was one of panic and outrage.[6]

The Revolution became sacred in young Beyle's eyes because it exalted those generous traits in men that he associated with the highest deeds of valor he so admired in books. A love of heroism, gallantry, and patriotism, fostered by his readings and encouraged by Aunt Elisabeth, found an outlet in the unfolding events of the Revolution. The newly-found notion of a motherland, worthy of the greatest sacrifices, was an exhilarating one for a solitary, imaginative, and sensitive boy like Henri Beyle. Regiments of dragoons paraded under the windows of his grandfather's house and soldiers were constantly billeted in his father's home.

Next to these young and dashing warriors the priests, who were perpetual guests in the Beyle household, appeared all the more paltry, and Henri looked with contempt upon these dark, fugitive, and cheerless figures as the enemies of the Revolution. One of his greatest joys was to watch from his grandfather's windows the multicolor regiments march past on the Place Grenette to the sound of drums on their way to Italy. The stirring sight of these gallant, high-spirited soldiers heading for the unknown and ready to sacrifice their young lives for France awoke in Henri a patriotic fervor and enthusiasm which, in the main, would persist, despite his growing cosmopolitanism, for many years to come. To some extent, his somewhat later admiration for Bonaparte and the latter's exploits directly resulted from these first memorable impressions of valiant young men going off to war to defend a besieged *patrie* that the counterrevolutionaries were plotting to give over to the Austrians. Such a naïve and emotional concept of events, reinforced by the child's revolt against his father, was the basis of much of his political outlook. But then, many of Stendhal's ideological principles can be traced to personal experiences and subjective reactions to events.

Even Henri's childish games acquired a patriotic character. He sewed a little tricolor flag, symbol of the Revolution, which he proudly paraded through the rooms of his grandfather's house to celebrate the latest republican victories. But the flag was confiscated and torn up, and he found a measure of consolation and pride in the thought that he too, in a small way, was a martyr of freedom and a defender of the Revolution.

Dr. Gagnon subscribed to Parisian newspapers and gazettes, and with every morning post, the family would gather and listen to the doctor read the latest military dispatches. The journals to which Dr. Gagnon subscribed covered the whole political spectrum, from the *Journal des Hommes Libres*, which was Jacobin in its political outlook, to the *Journal des Débats*, which was moderate and non-committal. Dr. Gagnon's attitude after 1789 was entirely consistent with his philosophy of skepticism and non-involvement. Of his beloved grandfather's political outlook, Stendhal writes that "Patriotism [which at the time meant a commitment to the revolutionary cause] for my grandfather would have meant an unpleasant distraction from his elegant and literary ideas." [7] By that affectionately ironical remark, Stendhal meant, in his typical elliptical and understated style, that Dr. Gagnon refused to be swept off his feet by the wave of emotionalism and revolutionary enthusiasm that overtook so many French intellectuals and disciples of the *philosophes* and especially of Rousseau after the storming of the Bastille.[8] Dr. Gagnon, in the middle of the revolutionary upheaval, remained an exquisitely courtly-mannered and supremely detached observer, a cosmopolitan and polished man of letters who, in his heart of hearts, intensely disliked popular passions as coarse and vulgar and continued to worship Voltaire's ideal of progress through reform and reason. Always the belletrist, who prized above all else correct, precise, and elegant language, he disapproved of the rhetoric favored by Rousseau and by the latter's revolutionary admirers.

As for young Beyle, his own rebellion against his family made him especially receptive to the inflamed rhetoric of the Jacobins: this new kind of eloquence unleashed in him heretofore unsuspected sources of enthusiasm and passion. It was with some consternation that Dr. Gagnon discovered in his shy and solitary grandson the fanatical soul of a would-be terrorist. The reaction of the other members of the family, however, was much more violent than that of the discreet Dr. Gagnon whenever Henri allowed himself to voice his radical opinions openly.

One cold evening at dusk, Henri mustered enough courage to venture into the Jacobins' Club which held its meetings in the church of Saint-André. His mind filled with visions of the heroes of Roman history, and his sense of excitement heightened by the awareness of the row that would ensue should his family find out about this last escapade, he entered the church and began listening intently to the speeches. His grandfather had made light-hearted fun of the inflated rhetoric of the Jacobins. Dr. Gagnon, whose own high standards of speech were those of an elegant and bygone era, disliked the bombastic eloquence and inflammatory slogans favored by the revolutionaries. It immediately struck the young spectator that his grandfather was right: "These people I so wanted to love appeared to me horribly vulgar." If Henri was fearlessly democratic in his ideals, his tastes remained more bourgeois than he was willing to admit. The audience was noisy, ragged, and disorderly; people clamored for the right to be heard and, when given the floor, spoke emotionally and in stereotyped phrases. This experience, to which he had looked forward with such eager anticipation, turned out to be a great disappointment. Henceforth, Stendhal assures us, he would be a sincere friend of the common people, but would always feel ill at ease in their company: "In short I was then as I am now; I love the people, I detest their oppressors, but it would be for me a constant torture to live among them." [9]

That first direct contact with the working classes of Grenoble had the unexpected effect of shaking Beyle's bookish notion of what a republican assembly of ordinary men engaged in heated political discussions would be like. Whereas he had imagined a dignified gathering of citizens striking noble attitudes and speaking in measured and beautiful cadences, a picture wholly inspired by his admiration, shared by his elders and contemporaries, for the republics of ancient Athens and Rome, he was confronted with an unruly, undisciplined crowd of vociferous men, a sight that ruffled his delicate sensibilities. Beyond the mass of gesticulating, shouting figures, barely perceptible in the dark dampness of the narrow nave of the church, he sensed dimly powerful, irrational forces at work. Upset and frightened, he quickly withdrew and hurriedly made his way through the deserted streets to rejoin his family.

A revolutionary by political conviction and an aristocrat by temperament and esthetic affinity, Stendhal would constantly waver between these two poles. His own fierce love of freedom made him the natural ally of all those who are oppressed and persecuted. But he much preferred the company of educated, elegant, and witty men and women, morally corrupt and cynical though they might be, to that of uncouth artisans or peasants. In this respect, he was never able to overcome the prejudices of his class. Rousseau, on the other hand, a man Stendhal so greatly respected for his stern individualism and simple, democratic tastes, fully trusted only those who earned their living with their hands. It must be added, however, to the credit of the young Beyle, that he did not linger on the less appealing aspects of the popular gathering he had secretly witnessed. His continuing difficulties with his family quickly made him fall back on his revolutionary sympathies. But never again would he be able to deify the Jacobins and imagine them fondly in the guise of the ancient heroes of Athens and Rome. Having at last observed real revolutionaries at close range, he had to recognize that his feelings for them were quite ambiguous and not unmingled with a certain fear and even repulsion. What he had fully expected to be an exhilarating, liberating experience that would lift his spirits and inspire him in his own battle against arbitrary authority left him strangely uneasy. This confrontation was only one of many between dream and reality that would teach him a lesson that was to become one of the major themes of his writings: reality rarely lives up to our impatient expectations. It is noteworthy that even his plebeian heroes, such as Julien Sorel, are endowed, not unlike their creator, with aristocratic tastes and predilections that set them apart from the common herd.

Stendhal was too lucid and self-aware not to realize, from an early age, that probably because of the influence of his family and the prejudices imparted to him during his impressionable childhood years, he could never identify unreservedly with the ordinary working folk. He passionately wished for their happiness and firmly believed in the basic principles of political democracy. But he could not help but recoil whenever he was brought into direct contact with unattractive outward manifestations of poverty and ignorance. The only city where he would not experience this feeling of revulsion when walking through the poor sections was Rome: but this was because here dirt and misery could not conceal, as he would later reason, the passionate nature of the populace. And Stendhal was an ardent admirer of that vital, boundless force that may be the cause of crimes, but without which nothing great in art, science, politics, or love can be possible. It was only when he discovered Italy that he became esthetically reconciled with the underprivileged inhabitants of the slums. In the ragged Roman urchins roaming the streets of the city he sensed that irrepressible passion and psychic energy, albeit in raw form, that he admired in Italian opera, art, and mores. The slums of Rome and their denizens therefore were to assume a romantic, picturesque aura in his eyes which made him overlook the ugliness of these surroundings. He would never have such sympathy for the poor of Grenoble or Paris.

IV
Widening Horizons

HENRI'S MOTHER HAD had a talent for drawing, and Dr. Gagnon, in memory of his favorite daughter, decided that his grandson should take drawing lessons. Before the Revolution, drawing used to be taught in the French provinces as a matter of course, like Latin. The student was supposed to become accomplished in making neat parallel hatchings in red chalk in imitation of engravings. Little attention was paid to other aspects of composition, such as outline, perspective, expression. In short, it was the kind of mechanical style long prevalent in French academic schools of fine arts.

The person selected to impart to Henri the rudiments of drawing was an elderly artist from Paris who had settled in Grenoble, where he earned his living by painting portraits and giving lessons in art. His name was Joseph Le Roy, which under the Terror he wisely decided to change to the less subversive form of Roley.[1] With the Thermidorean reaction, however, he hastened to have his original name restored.

While M. Le Roy's house, where Henri took his lessons, was hardly a stone's throw from Grandfather Gagnon's on the Place Grenette, and the boy's goings and comings were closely watched, especially by the indefatigable Aunt Séraphie, he soon found means to elude his family's vigilance and, for the first time in his life, began wandering in the streets by himself. He generally hastened to the inviting and tree-shaded lanes of the Jardin de Ville and enviously observed the lower-class urchins boisterously engaged in fun and games, a privilege which he, a proper bourgeois child, was denied. Before long, however, M. Le Roy was asked to come to the Beyle household in order to give his lessons.

M. Le Roy was a typically polite and sophisticated Parisian who, though wizened and weakened by age, retained a worldly charm and courtliness of manner reminiscent of the Old Regime. Eking out a meager living, he was hard hit by the spiraling cost of living and the precipitous devaluation of the *assignat*, the revolutionary paper currency: "Monsieur," he would sometimes say to Henri at the end of a lesson, "tell your *dear* father that I can no longer come for thirty-five or forty-five francs a month." [2] Despite his academic and conventional methods, M. Le Roy awakened young Beyle's imagination and sensibility to the plastic arts—no small accomplishment in view of Stendhal's later activity as an art critic and connoisseur.

In the art teacher's studio there was a large landscape which made an enormous impression on Henri. It represented a steep mountain near the foreground, adorned with tall trees; at the foot of this mountain a shallow but wide and limpid stream flowed, in which three nude women bathed and frolicked. This landscape, quite aside from its artistic merits, which may well have been nil, embodied for the young art student the absolute ideal of beauty and voluptuous felicity: "To bathe like this with lovely women!" [3] Stendhal's approach to art would always be of this subjective and subject-oriented nature. [4] Art, for him, would always retain a basically hedonistic, literary, or psychological message. A painting would fascinate him to the extent that it engaged his thoughts and feelings, often independently of the purely pictorial merits of the work itself. The more a composition had the power to make him meditate or dream, the more likely he was to praise it: hence his predilection for a pictorial art that stresses formal beauty, elegance, and psychological symbolism. His lifelong preference for the masters of the High Italian Renaissance and his almost total indifference to the more realistic and down-to-earth Northern Schools of

Germany and the Netherlands can readily be understood in the light of his admiration for a kind of painting that idealizes reality and invites the spectator into a romantic dream world. The fact that in his *Life of Henry Brulard* he speaks at such length about the landscape in his art teacher's studio is significant of his concept of art as a delightful escape into fantasy, wish-fulfilment, beauty, and love.

Henri did his homework at a little table near one of the windows of the large Italian-style drawing room in his grandfather's house on the Place Grenette. While translating Virgil he could, by merely lifting his head, see the never-ending stream of human activity on the large, animated square. Dr. Gagnon's library contained vast riches through which Henri eagerly rummaged. He was attracted to a pile of paper-bound volumes, untidily flung together in a corner of the library. They were those spicy novels, so popular in the eighteenth century, which Uncle Romain had left in Grenoble when he settled in Les Echelles. Henri opened a few of these books, and for him they represented the discovery of sensual delight. Grandfather Gagnon had forbidden him to touch them, but he kept watch for propitious moments to borrow them surreptitiously and take them to his room.

Chérubin Beyle also possessed a not inconsiderable collection of books. Most of these were dull legal treatises or technical volumes dealing with agriculture, but he also owned a complete set of Diderot's and d'Alembert's *Encyclopedia,* many articles of which Henri read with keen interest. But what were all these discoveries compared with the enchantment experienced when the boy got hold of Rousseau's impassioned and romantic novel, *La Nouvelle Héloïse,* snatched from the top shelf of his father's bookcase in his summer house at Claix? Henri read it after locking himself in his room, and the impact on his imagination and sensibility of a book that, by then, had hypnotized a whole generation of men and women, was immeasurable.[5] Stealing forbidden books from the libraries of his father and grandfather and reading them on the sly had become Henri's favorite endeavor. And yet, paradoxically, it was just one of those forbidden books, *La Nouvelle Héloïse,* that

gave form and substance to such exhilarating notions as subli-
mated love, honor, and loyalty and raised Henri's inner horizons
above the petty frustrations and grudges that threatened to twist his
naturally affectionate, outgoing nature into that of a vindictive,
hypocritical cynic: "During these four or five years, my heart was
filled with a feeling of helpless hatred. . . . My reading of *La
Nouvelle Héloïse* and the scruples of Saint-Preux made me a profoundly honest man; I could still, after having completed this reading with tears and in ecstasies of love for virtue, commit rascally
tricks, but I would have felt like a rascal. Thus it was a book read
in great secrecy and despite my relatives that made me an honest
man." [6]

Another discovery made at Claix was an edition of Voltaire's
works. Since the volumes were closely stacked together, Henri
could take out one or two at the time and separate the rest slightly
so that it did not show. Curiously enough, though, while Voltaire
was revered by Dr. Gagnon, he never really appealed to young
Henri, and this antipathy never abated. [7] Stendhal himself found it
difficult to explain this reaction, since there were so many reasons
why he should have been an admiring disciple of Voltaire. Like so
many members of the post-Enlightenment generation, Stendhal
had a certain image of Voltaire which was almost a caricature of
the *philosophe*. He regarded him as a witty writer and storyteller, a
talented historian, and competent playwright, but as a superficial
thinker and a man who knew nothing about the finer, more delicate feelings of which the human heart is capable. But if he professed never to have loved Voltaire, he remained a constant and
attentive reader of his works, especially of his *contes*, which he
greatly admired for their style and which he came to consider as
the best antidote against what he detested most in the style of his
contemporaries: bombastic verbosity and flatulence. [8]

Don Quixote de La Mancha, in an old illustrated edition, was
another high point in his early readings. He also got hold of an illustrated edition of Molière, but he who would later aspire to
become the Molière of his age was not at first overly impressed.
The main reason for this initial coolness was, as he later surmised,

the realism with which Molière depicted bourgeois manners and
morals. Scenes of dissimulation, hypocrisy, and familiar wrangling
were all too familiar to Henri to amuse him: "I had a horror for
the bourgeois and base details which Molière used to express his
thought. These details reminded me too much of my unhappy
life." [9] What the boy sought in books, above all else, was an escape from the real world and not a vivid recreation of surroundings
he thoroughly loathed. From the outset he rebelled against a form
of literary realism that depicted too faithfully the dull, dreary
aspects of everyday life.

But that despite these initial reservations concerning Molière,
the playwright was to occupy a very special place among Stendhal's literary masters and models is made abundantly clear by the
numerous references and comments, spread over an entire lifetime, in the novelist's diaries, notebooks, correspondence, and
other works. That the middle-aged Stendhal, setting down nostalgic recollections of his early years, should have stressed the negative lesson derived from Molière, while at the same time stating
that his first ambition in life had been to become the Molière of
the nineteenth century, should not strike us as a totally contradictory and hardly believable statement. It is worth remembering,
in this connection, that Stendhal never recoiled before the desire
to provoke the reader with a quip or a paradox. Therefore, while
other youthful idols, such as Rousseau, at first received far more
fulsome praise than Molière, the latter was to grow in stature
through the years. To be sure, young Beyle's *espagnolisme* caused
him to equate an unadorned portrayal of French manners and
mores with a lack of true literary genius and creative imagination.
Throughout his adult life, he would continue to evince the same
predilection for a literary and artistic vision that exalts idealism,
generosity, and chivalry. Yet, he grew increasingly aware that the
lesson of a Molière was a salutary one, for it forced him to face
contemporary society, not as he fondly liked to imagine it, but as it
was in reality.

It is symptomatic of Beyle's relentless search for self-
knowledge that Molière, like the other authors who caught his at-

tention or fancy, was envisaged as a tool, a means to gain a better understanding of human nature in general and of French sociological types in particular. Molière both fascinated and repelled Henri because his plays helped the rebellious son of a typical bourgeois to gain perspective in his difficult dealings with men like his father.

Chérubin Beyle, with his rigidity, gaucherie, and total lack of charm, and with his single-minded devotion to social advancement and material enrichment, came to symbolize a kind of mentality which the future author of *The Red and the Black* would always hold in abhorrence. At the same time, however, Molière was the first who showed young Beyle the dramatic possibilities that such seemingly unrewarding types can afford an author of talent. It did not take too long, therefore, before Molière became identified with the boy's growing dream of embarking upon a successful career as an author of comedies who would make people laugh at the expense of the follies and stupidities of contemporary types like Chérubin Beyle: "I had resolved to write comedies like Molière." [10]

The leaders of the Revolution were deeply concerned with the need of establishing, throughout France, free, public and universal education at the expense of the state. Consequently, by a law dated 7 ventôse, year III, of the revolutionary calender (February 25, 1795), the National Convention decreed that in each Department a Central School be established. The purpose of these schools was not merely to replace the old, private, and religious— primarily Jesuit—schools with lay, nondenominational institutions of learning, but also to insure that the future citizens of a new France would be presented with a program of study in keeping with the philosophic tenets of the Enlightenment and with the revolutionary principles of civics and patriotism.

The men who played a considerable role in shaping these new schools were Joseph Lakanal, who was primarily interested in the establishment of scientific, literary, and educational institutions, and Antoine Destutt de Tracy, a philosopher and psychologist who belonged to the school of Ideologists, disciples of Locke,

Condillac, and Helvétius. Destutt de Tracy and the Ideologists were proponents of sensationalism, the theory that all thought and knowledge derive from sensory perception. Quite aside from his association with the Central Schools, Destutt de Tracy was to play a major part in helping Stendhal develop his own philosophic system.[11] Interestingly, priests were not automatically excluded from the teaching cadres of these schools, as long as they had sworn allegiance to the new regime and appeared sufficiently imbued with the new ideals of civic loyalty.

In 1796, a Central School opened in Grenoble. In addition to the traditional curriculum emphasizing literature and the humanities, it boldly introduced the newer subjects and disciplines, particularly the sciences. On the other hand, theology and religion had been eliminated from the program. This experimental orientation, made exciting by competent and sometimes inspiring teachers, opened up for Henri Beyle a whole new world of ideas which enabled him to complete his break from his father and the dogmatic abbé Raillane.

It was not until much later that Beyle personally learned from the philosopher and psychologist, Destutt de Tracy, that he had been largely responsible for the law which permitted the establishment of Central Schools. This greatly reinforced Beyle's growing admiration for the Ideologist who made such an important contribution to his own ideas concerning man's behavior and emotions.[12]

Dr. Gagnon, in his capacity as the respected head of the committee whose duty it was to submit the names of teachers to the Departmental Administration and to organize the school, had a great deal to do with persuading Henri's father to allow him to attend an educational institution which, after all, was a direct product of the Revolution. To be sure, Grandfather Gagnon was roundly scolded by his daughter Séraphie for his willingness to serve on the organizing committee, but he ignored her entreaties and, when the school was formally opened, he was the one who pronounced the inaugural speech. Henri was beside himself with joy and pride. He was thirteen when he entered the Central

School in November 1796 and he pursued his studies there until he had reached his sixteenth birthday, in 1799.

From the outset, the young Beyle showed a special gift for those subjects that call for logic in thinking, and it was at the Central School that he discovered mathematics. It was not an immediate love affair, however. But when it dawned upon him that excellence in this field would enable him to pursue his studies at the Ecole Polytechnique in Paris, that is, to escape from Grenoble, his ardor and willingness to work hard knew no bounds. His interest in mathematics was not merely opportunistic.[13] He developed a real and enduring passion for an intellectual discipline which, as he later put it, tolerates no hypocrisy or imprecision. At fourteen he was convinced that only mathematics furnishes solid, incontrovertible truths.

During his first year, however, Henri did not stand out as an exceptional student. The end of the year examinations were held in the presence of a jury, and Dr. Gagnon, as one of the founding members of the school, was on the examining committee. In the mathematics examination, candidates climbed up to a blackboard by way of a stepladder, so that the demonstration could be seen by all. Consumed with shyness, Henri presented a lackluster performance. Dr. Gagnon gently chided his grandson: "You only knew how to show us your big behind." [14] Henri was stout and shortish, hence the jocular reproof.

In his second year, Henri began making significant progress and threw himself into his work with redoubled efforts. Shedding little by little his timidity, he learned to like and respect his teachers and began taking an interest in his schoolmates. He also learned the value of competitive and sustained intellectual effort and was initiated, sometimes roughly, into the intricacies of getting along with the boisterous, aggressive boys his own age. His private tutoring with the hated abbé Raillane had failed to awaken his lively curiosity and nimble intelligence. He now acquired regular habits of work and study and became acquainted with an orderly, disciplined approach to knowledge, ideas, and culture. The abbé Raillane had stressed rote learning and passive memorization.

For the first time, Henri was encouraged to ask not only the "how" but also the "why" of things. It is worth noting that, of all French writers, Stendhal is the only one who spent some of the most crucial years of his early adolescence in an institution that was a creation of the Revolution. His exposure to this intellectual milieu was to leave an indelible mark on his mind and philosophy of life.

Overprotected and unduly fretted over by his fussy and ever-anxious family, he had developed character traits that might well have had disastrous results had he not become a student, along with many others from varying walks of life, at the democratic and forward-looking Central School. Both his intelligence and character benefited immensely from this experience. After an initial period of groping and adjustment, he eagerly plunged into an environment where he was no longer in the center of the stage but had to jostle for recognition. He was also duly indoctrinated into the political beliefs of the Revolution, to which he had been, from the outset, sympathetically inclined anyway. He no longer felt isolated and an outcast because of his enthusiasm for the revolutionary cause. A chasm now separated Henri, not only from his father, but also from his skeptical, aloof grandfather.

All his life Stendhal remembered the Central School of Grenoble with great affection. He was very disappointed when, in 1803, these schools were abolished and replaced by lycées reverting to the more traditional and conservative approach to learning and eliminating the courses in politics, logic, and ethics he had found so challenging and exciting.

Among the more remarkable teachers who were associated with the Central School at Grenoble in Beyle's time, the abbé Claude-Marie Gattel, professor of grammar and rhetoric, taught him to present his ideas in a clear, logical sequence. The abbé was, like the other teachers at the school, a disciple of Locke and Condillac.[15] Jean-Gaspard Dubois-Fontanelle was in charge of French literature and the history of literary genres. He taught his pupils to appreciate not only the Greek, Latin, and classical French authors, but also Shakespeare, Goldoni, and Goethe.[16]

Dubois-Fontanelle was a native of Grenoble who had long lived in Paris and abroad and who, for several years, had edited an influential literary periodical, the *Gazette des Deux-Ponts*, which specialized in what would today be called comparative literature. A prolific and resourceful editor, publicist, and writer, he had also authored translations from Latin and English, light verse, tales in the Voltairean tradition, and plays. Yet, despite an untiring activity, he failed to achieve the kind of literary success of such comparable authors and critics as La Harpe or Marmontel. He had remained fairly impecunious, and by the time he accepted the position as teacher of literature at the Central School of Grenoble, he was weakened with old age and crippled with gout. He was therefore grateful to have found a measure of security in becoming a teacher with board and lodging in his native city. Moreover, he quickly became something of a local celebrity, especially when one of his plays, a tragedy entitled *Éricie ou la Vestale*, which had been banned and had caused a furor under the Old Regime for its anticlerical message, was performed on the stage of the Grenoble municipal theater.

While Dubois-Fontanelle failed to stir Henri's enthusiasm, probably because he lacked fire and spirit as a teacher, he was undoubtedly responsible for opening the boy's mind to foreign literatures. Like most men of letters of the eighteenth century, Dubois-Fontanelle remained sincerely loyal to such French classics of the seventeenth century as Racine and Molière. He was also a follower of Voltaire and a stalwart defender of neo-classical canons of literary and artistic beauty. But as the ex-editor of a magazine that specialized in foreign literatures, it was natural that he should introduce his students to Shakespeare. Not too surprisingly, however, his praise was mixed with the typical Voltairean reservations concerning the Bard's language and mixture of the tragic and comic. And when he read scenes from *Hamlet* for his young audience, it was in Le Tourneur's edulcorated translation. This first contact aroused Henri's interest in English literature, an interest that was to grow through the years. In general, Dubois-Fontanelle's thorough and systematic approach was beneficial, for it corrected and completed the young scholar's previous rather haphazard readings.

Another teacher who quickly became one of Henri's favorites was Louis-Joseph Jay, whose subject was drawing and the history of art.[17] An eloquent speaker, full of initiative and ideas, Jay was very popular with the students. And as an ardent revolutionary and loyal Jacobin he could not but appeal to young Beyle, if only for that reason. In his lessons, Jay also underscored the impact of geographic, political, and cultural factors on artistic creativity, an approach that must have played a significant part in shaping Beyle's own ideas on a field of human endeavor which was to preoccupy him for the rest of his life.[18]

That Henri grew independent of his family during the three fruitful years he attended the Central School is understandable, especially in view of the fact that the school harbored political principles completely contrary to those cherished by Chérubin Beyle. Young Beyle had always been rebellious by nature, an inclination unwittingly reinforced by his father's heavy-handed authoritarianism. He was now entering that critical age at which boys go through their crisis of adolescence and, in this process, question all the values of their elders. Even his physical appearance changed, although his looks did not improve noticeably. He grew somewhat taller, but remained stoutish and heavy-set. What he lacked in outward mien and presence, however, he amply made up thanks to his high spirits, quick mind, and friendliness. When invited to the house of a classmate, he felt, despite his lingering timidity, the irrepressible need to shine, especially when a pretty young girl was present. His imagination emboldened by his recent secret reading of romantic and spicy tales of love and seduction, he eagerly responded to the sight of appealing young members of the opposite sex.

To his classmates Henri Beyle must at first have seemed a rather odd fellow, with his big head, short legs, and stocky body usually draped in a long, loose-fitting gray coat that reached almost to his feet. But thanks to his intelligence, forceful personality, energetic manner, and willingness to take risks—to receive punishment and mete it out as the occasion required—he gradually established his authority as a natural leader among the students, especially within a group of boys with similar backgrounds and kindred interests and on whose loyalty he could depend.

He was to keep up a lasting, sometimes even lifelong, relationship with several of these special friends. One was Félix Faure, son of a self-made man who had amassed a sizeable fortune as Receiver General of Finances for the province of Dauphiné, who himself was to rise to a position of eminence as magistrate and peer of France.[19] Henri met Félix Faure in his mathematics class and liked his air of brooding melancholy and proud aloofness. Although Beyle was to maintain contact with Faure after his departure from Grenoble, he became increasingly aware of his friend's huge vanity and rather callous egotism. Yet, although Félix Faure was, according to Stendhal, the least intellectually outstanding member of the Central School group, he was the one who had the most successful career and became the wealthiest, an ironic twist of fate that hardly surprised the aging novelist setting down his reminiscences and meditating upon the divergent destinies of his school-day friends. What also contributed to his eventual estrangement from Félix Faure was the latter's growing conservatism in politics.

Another close companion of Henri Beyle at the Central School was Jean-Antoine Plana, whose family hailed from Piedmont, Italy. Plana outshone Beyle in mathematics and was to become a distinguished *savant* upon returning to his native Italy. Yet another enduring friendship was with Louis de Barral, scion of one of the most influential families in the district—his father was President of the Grenoble Parlement under the Old Regime but a warm partisan of the Revolution and, later, of the Empire.[20] Louis de Barral immediately made an enormous impression upon Henri. He was a handsome, impeccably dressed young man with an aristocratic demeanor and a great love of poetry. His way of reciting Voltaire's verses even caused young Beyle to relent, at least in part, in his hostility toward that writer. Barral's mother was a *grande dame* in the most typical Old Regime tradition. When she made an appearance on the terraced Promenade of the Jardin de Ville of Grenoble in a fashionable dress of white satin, her hair powdered and done in an elegant chignon, a lapdog in her arms, she was followed, at a respectful distance, by an admiring throng of idlers. This great lady had all the refined manners of her class, and Dr. Gagnon, a great connoisseur in such matters, never failed to point out, when referring to her, that she was the *comtesse de Grolée* and belonged to one of the most ancient aristocratic families in France. When her husband, Joseph-Marie de Barral, marquis de Montferrat, refused to emigrate with the other aristocrats, he lost his position as President of the Parlement, but was not otherwise troubled by the revolutionary regime. Henri's family, and especially his father, sternly disapproved of the ex-marquis's decision to stay in France and viewed his cooperativeness as a betrayal of his class. Henri, for his part, kept making sad comparisons between the elder Barral's gracious manners, witty conversation, consideration for his children's self-respect, and his love of literature, especially poetry, which he imparted to his son, with his own father's rigid pedantry and grubby preoccupations.

Dissimilar though they were in appearance and even in personality, Henri Beyle and Louis de Barral were inseparable. They must have formed an odd pair, Henri in his ungainly, drab coat which only emphasized his thick-set and peasant-like body, and Louis, tall, slim, and elegant in his well-tailored and bright-colored suits. It was no doubt a case of the attraction of opposites.

Also a close friend was Fortuné Mante, like Henri an incorrigible debater and *raisonneur*.[21] Resolutely anti-clerical and republican, he shared with Beyle the latter's Jacobin sympathies. Mild and easy-going in manner, he was, in fact, quite hard-headed, shrewd, and unsentimental. Henri admired not only his intellectual ability, but also his handsome good looks.

The youngest and smallest in the group was Louis Crozet, a brilliant student and a lawyer's son like Henri.[22] He too lived on the rue des Vieux-Jésuites. Louis Crozet had the dubious distinction of being the least attractive looking student at the Central

School: his face was pallid and badly pitted by smallpox, his posture was poor, and his gait clumsy. But his little blue eyes shone brightly and his irregular features were animated and expressed intelligence and wit. Of all his contemporaries at the Central School, Louis Crozet is credited by Stendhal with the most outstanding intellectual capacities reinforced by a precocious sagacity, a quality of which he deemed himself totally devoid, especially as an adolescent.

Louis Crozet was to remain a lifelong friend and trusted confidant. He pursued his studies at the Ecole Polytechnique in Paris and became an engineer. With a promising career in the French capital before him, however, he returned to his native Grenoble, where his natural ability was stifled by provincial, bourgeois pettiness. Stendhal was convinced that had his friend remained permanently in Paris, he would have had a career truly commensurate with his capacities and, despite his bad physique, would have made his mark in society. Stendhal also greatly valued his friend's generosity and selflessness.

At the Central School, Beyle and Crozet decided not only to study together, but also to write essays in manners and morals which they called *Characters* (in honor, no doubt, of La Bruyère, the famed seventeenth-century moralist). These they submitted to each other for frank criticism and evaluation and vowed not to allow vanity or *amour-propre* to interfere with their judgments. Later in Paris, they pursued this common program of self-education and broadened the scope of their readings, covering such disparate authors as Montaigne, Shakespeare, Machiavelli, Montesquieu, Helvétius, and Adam Smith.

Yet another student at the Central School Henri befriended was Romain Colomb, son of a retired Grenoble merchant and related to the Beyle family through his mother, who was a first cousin of Henriette Gagnon.[23] Romain Colomb was a bit too bourgeois and stolid in his outlook to win Henri over completely. But his loyalty and affection remained constant through the years, and Stendhal appreciated more and more the fact that he could always depend upon his steadfast friendship.

Among Beyle's classmates, François Bigillion, who was to kill himself in 1827 partly as a result of marital difficulties, had a special place in his affections.[24] Like Henri, he was an ardent patriot and revolutionary. He had a certain advantage over his classmates which the young Beyle particularly envied. Since his childhood, he had enjoyed a kind of liberty unknown to Henri, for his father, absorbed in a life of pleasurable pursuits, paid scant attention to him and his younger brother and sister. A country bourgeois, the elder Bigillion lived at Saint-Imier, a picturesque village in the Isère valley, one postal stage east of Grenoble. He had rented a small apartment in Grenoble for his two sons and daughter, leaving them under the supervision of a servant who was herself only seventeen years old and coming only for occasional visits.

Henri became very fond of François and even more of his charming young sister Victorine, who was the same age as he. Victorine was pretty, full of piquancy, if a bit on the thin side. It was during the year 1796–97 that Henri's friendship with François and Victorine Bigillion was at its most intimate. The two boys often launched on long walks along the medieval ramparts of Grenoble, from which one could enjoy beautiful panoramas, and engaged in those endless discussions about life characteristic of youth in the course of which they would exchange mutual confidences and projects for the future. As for vivacious Victorine, she stirred Henri's feelings and sexual fantasies as she sat next to him during his frequent and prolonged visits to the apartment she shared with her two brothers. Overcoming his initial shyness, he began having intimate conversations with her and eventually even told her about his difficulties with his family. She evidently responded to him, despite his physical unattractiveness, and to Félix Faure, who tried in vain to get into her good graces, she cryptically spoke of an unnamed lover: "The man I love is homely, but nobody will ever criticize him for his ugliness, he has so much wit!" [25] This mysterious "man" was none other than Henri, as the hapless Félix Faure was to discover only much later. Notwithstanding these melodramatic words, the relationship between Henri Beyle and Victorine Bigillion was a pre-adolescent infatuation rather than a real amorous attraction. With François, Victorine, and their young brother Rémy, who was only twelve, Henri spent many delightful hours, with no adults to inhibit their games, frolics, and chatter.

One evening at supper with his family, Henri was rash enough to mention the Bigillions, without however revealing anything about his feelings for them. To his distress, he heard his relatives express scorn for Victorine and her brothers, for the Bigillions belonged to the rural bourgeoisie, whereas the Beyles considered themselves virtually as members of the nobility. "Isn't there a daughter? No doubt some country damsel?"[26] Once more, Henri was infuriated by his family's snobbishness and class consciousness.

Thanks to his Aunt Elisabeth's complicity, Henri was his own master several evenings of the week. Emboldened by his initiation into the mysteries of the theater through his uncle Romain, he sneaked into the theater and purchased the cheapest ticket, admitting him to standing room. This is how he met the young actress, Virginie Kubly.[27] She was, from all contemporary accounts, an attractive, shapely, and rather tall young woman, with the delicate-looking slenderness of early youth. Her face, Henri noted, was serious and often melancholy, and she had a slightly aquiline nose. She played leading and ingénue roles in comedies and also sang in light opera.

Born Marie-Gabrielle Ramond in 1778, she had already appeared in Grenoble in 1795 and came back at the end of 1797, by then married to a Swiss actor, and it is under her husband's name that she appeared on the posters. She was nineteen and Henri had reached his fifteenth birthday when he watched her perform and fell madly in love with her.

Quite suddenly, Henri grew indifferent to everything around him. His detachment from family affairs and squabbles became such that he even lost all hatreds and resentments. Only one person occupied his every thought, Mlle Kubly. A mysterious new madness took possession of his being and, since his acquaintance with the phenomenon of love had thus far been of an exclusively bookish nature (his infatuation with Virginie Bigillion could hardly be called that), he found it impossible to identify the tumultuous feelings that pervaded him each time he rapturously watched Mlle Kubly on the stage. She excelled in romantic comedy, but her voice lacked power and was narrow in range.[28] Yet when she sang the leading part in an *opéra comique* by such an eighteenth-century master of the genre as André Grétry, Henri was in seventh heaven. All the light operas in vogue in the late seventeen-nineties acquired for the enamored youth a quality of sublimity through the enchanting presence of Mlle Kubly.

Thus Beyle's passion for music, which was to play such a large part in his life, was born, and it is appropriate that it was kindled by the ineffable raptures of a shy, first love. Stendhal would always associate music with tender, amorous, or nostalgic feelings. It was not until 1800, however, that at La Scala of Milan he would be privileged to hear for the first time great opera, sung by accomplished artists. All his life love and music would be inextricably and delightfully associated in his mind and sensibilities. Listening to Mlle Kubly's thin but pure and clear voice, observing her fine-featured and pensive face, Henri dreamed about happiness and love as depicted in Rousseau's novel, *La Nouvelle Héloïse*.

If someone said in his presence *la* Kubly, he found it hard to contain his horror and rage at such disrespect. His emotional involvement with the young actress and singer heightened his growing passion for the theater and opera, and while she was by no means an outstanding artist, her youthful charm and vulnerability gave him an intimation of what stage presence means. Once she appeared, his world was transfigured, and nothing could be commonplace or vulgar.

But this young woman who so completely engaged his thoughts and feelings could be adored only from afar. Henri would avidly absorb every sound and sight and fill his mind and soul with that magical, gracious presence, brightly illuminated on the distant stage. He never mustered enough courage to go backstage and introduce himself to her. But one morning, while walking in the Jardin de Ville, thinking of her, as usual, he suddenly caught sight of her at the other end of the lane. The joy of seeing so close up the object of his adoration was too much; overwhelmed, he fled in panic. [29]

This peculiar combination of intensity of feeling and paralyzing timidity would be typical of Stendhal's attitude toward all the women he truly loved. Boldness of approach and calculating amorous strategy would be possible only where his feelings were not really involved.

Virginie Kubly, who was a member of a traveling group of actors, so common in seventeenth- and eighteenth-century France, left Grenoble in April of 1798, and Stendhal would never see her again. After her departure, Henri's passion for her consumed itself fairly rapidly. But the memory of those ecstatic hours spent in the theater of Grenoble left him with an abiding love of the stage and the opera. It was, after all, in the complicity and anonymity of a theater audience that he had come upon a vision of youth and beauty that had enchanted his imagination and cast a spell on his senses.

Absorbed by his studies, school activities, and new relationships, Henri Beyle hardly noticed the swift-changing political scene. Robespierre had fallen in 1794, the Jacobin Club which he had surreptitiously visited had been closed, and in October of 1795 the rule of the Directory had begun. The political regime that succeeded Robespierre and the Committee of Public Safety had been brought about by a *coup d'état*, and it was to be killed by a *coup d'état*. The common bond that united the Thermidoreans was their hatred and fear of Robespierre. A counter-revolution had set in and it was marked by the repudiation of Jacobin politics.

As the young Beyle was going through the difficult crisis of puberty, everything about him reflected the gallant and pleasure-seeking ways of the Directory. The solemn austerity of the Jacobins was being replaced by the gaiety, amenity, and frivolity of the elegant youths who emerged during the Thermidorean reaction. In

the Jardin de Ville of Grenoble fashionable young women prom-
enaded, wearing light-textured, free-flowing dresses that boldly
revealed their arms and bosoms, while their male counterparts
strutted about in elaborately embroidered coats with jabots and
cravats.

At the end of his third and last year at the Central School,
Henri Beyle scored a brilliant success in his final examinations.
He was deemed worthy of pursuing his studies at the prestigious
Ecole Polytechnique, in Paris. Henri's fondest dream of getting
away from Grenoble was thus realized.

On October 30, 1799, he bade farewell to his father and his
family and boarded the stagecoach for Paris. He was so carried
away at the prospect of finding himself soon in the French capital
that he hardly noticed his father's sadness which, as always, left
him unmoved. "He was weeping a little. The only impression his
tears made upon me was to find him quite ugly."[30]

V

Paris and Loneliness

THE HEAVY STAGECOACH rumbled northward, crossing an autumnal and rain-swept countryside. His mind filled with delightful thoughts and images of his forthcoming life in the French capital, Henri Beyle barely took notice of his co-travelers or heard what they said among themselves in order to while away the time agreeably.

It was on one of the last stops of the journey that Beyle and his traveling companions learned the momentous news of the 18th Brumaire (November 9, 1799). General Bonaparte had sent his grenadiers into the House of Deputies and the Republic had come to an end. At the time, the political significance of Bonaparte's successful coup d'état completely escaped young Beyle. But he was nonetheless aroused by this startling turn of events and fully expected Bonaparte to become the next king of France, something that did not displease him, since the image he had of the youthful and fearless general matched his concept of what an ideal monarch ought to be.[1]

The large diligence ponderously progressed by stages toward Paris. Beyle's excitement was such that it obliterated any of the sights and incidents of his six-day voyage. With the exception of the news of Bonaparte's coup d'état, the experience of the journey—the first of many Stendhal would undertake—remained a blur in his memory. He was too absorbed by his *idée fixe*. Once settled in the capital, he would meet a beautiful woman, far more

85

seductive than Mlle Kubly or Victorine Bigillion, probably an actress, and she would promptly fall in love with him and become
his mistress. Life would be one enchantment after another.[2]

At last the stagecoach reached the suburbs of Paris. The date,
a memorable one for Henri Beyle, was November 10, 1799. The
first impressions, which were to be confirmed in the following
days, were of utter disappointment: "The surroundings of Paris had
appeared to me horribly ugly; there were no mountains! This
disgust rapidly increased during the following days." [3] Accustomed
to the verdant prospects and lofty peaks of his native Dauphiné,
Henri Beyle was unprepared for the flat landscapes of the Ile de
France province.

In the old and aristocratic Faubourg St. Germain, on the Left
Bank, Henri Beyle was deposited in front of a small hotel, the
Hôtel de Bourgogne, in the rue Saint-Dominique. It was conveniently located, within walking distance of the Ecole Polytechnique, on the rue de l'Université. For the sake of economy, however, he promptly moved to a rooming house in the same
neighborhood.

He eagerly set out to discover Paris. At this point, something
curious happened which Stendhal himself was always at a loss to
explain. Instead of registering, as was fully expected of him and as
he himself had planned to do, at the Ecole Polytechnique, he
aimlessly wandered through the streets of the capital, mingling
with the crowds, buying books, and gawking at the shop windows
and their wares.

Why did young Beyle pass up the opportunity of becoming a
student at the Ecole Polytechnique, which would have assured
him of a career and of a secure future? His new-found taste of
freedom was no doubt so heady as to obliterate everything else. To
come and go as he pleased, to view the world, not from the limited vantage point of the windows of the houses of his father and
grandfather to be freed at last from the constricting bonds of his
family—all this contributed to his desire to perpetuate this delightful state of affairs indefinitely.

The main reason for Henri Beyle's failure to enroll at the

Ecole Polytechnique may very well have been a subconscious one. Despite his spectacular success in mathematics in his last year at the Ecole Centrale, he may have sensed that he was not a naturally gifted mathematician and that his accomplishments in this field thus far were primarily the result of hard work and a dogged determination to leave Grenoble and escape from his family. Now that he had achieved this goal, the impelling force that had motivated him suddenly vanished.

While former Grenoble classmates inferior to him in mathematics easily passed the entrance examination at the Ecole Polytechnique and in due time became full-fledged Polytechnicians, Henri spent his days in idle and aimless ramblings and revery. Upon writing his autobiography, Stendhal wondered why his father had not taken the trouble to force him to present himself at the Ecole Polytechnique and to take the entrance examination which he would have passed without any difficulty: "Probably he trusted the extreme passion for mathematics he had observed in me. My father, besides, was affected only by what was near him." [4]

In the depth of the provinces, Henri had pictured Paris as a place of enthusiasm, excitement, and revolutionary fervor. But the days of street festivities and popular rejoicings, which had marked the early stages of the Revolution, had been followed by far tenser times. The city was now warily bracing itself for the new regime introduced by Bonaparte's *coup d'état*. In the face of what he saw all his high expectations were brutally dashed to the ground. For the first but by no means last time he found that the confrontation between one's dreams and reality is more often than not an utterly disheartening experience.

But if Henri Beyle himself failed to become a student at the Ecole Polytechnique, he compensated for this as a novelist by having some of his fictional heroes acquire this distinction: Octave de Malivert in *Armance*, Lucien Leuwen in the novel bearing that name, Fédor de Miossens in *Lamiel*, the duc de Montenotte in *The Pink and the Green* are all alumni of that distinguished institution.

In his small, depressing, sparsely furnished attic room, with
its tiny window and ineffective iron stove, Henri Beyle gave himself over to melancholy thoughts. In lieu of the brilliant social life
he had anticipated, he had seen only crowded and muddy streets
and bustling, indifferent crowds. On the morrow of the Directoire,
Parisians were eager to forget the recent traumatic events and to
make up for time lost. Elegant dandies and their provocatively attired lady companions, their charms daringly exposed by their low-
cut, transparent dresses dictated by the latest fashions, thronged
the balls and festivities to which young Beyle was never invited.
Spending his days in depressing idleness, neglecting to eat properly, exhausting himself in long, aimless walks through the Paris
streets or shivering in his room, Beyle became utterly disoriented.

The older, more knowledgeable Stendhal, pondering the reasons for his first disastrous contact with big city life, ascribed much
of his initial bitter disillusionment and helplessness to his romantic, impractical nature. Unlike his friends and companions from
the Central School, who were all endowed with common sense
and even a healthy dose of cunning and craftiness, he had always
been an incorrigible dreamer. As a young man of sixteen, he was,
in his own words, "one of the least reasonable souls and one of the
most susceptible to emotion that I have ever encountered!" [5]

While his friends from Grenoble spent their time taking
courses, planning their future, and shrewdly managing their
meager finances by haggling over their rents, groceries, and bun-
dles of firewood, he plunged into interminable reveries and fantasies: "A charming woman will have a carriage accident ten paces
from me, I shall come to her help and we will adore each
other." [6] Constantly in a state of intense emotion—whether it be
an outburst of enthusiasm or a fit of gloom—he never paid attention, save when obviously taken advantage of, to the practical details of everyday life. His sensibilities had grown too keen for his
own well-being and peace of mind. What barely affected others
wounded him to the quick. His enthusiasms were far in excess of
their cause, his sympathies too intense and sincere to be rewarded
by similar sentiments, his fancies incommensurate with reality.

His monthly allowance from his father was adequate. In addition, his grandfather and Great-Aunt Elisabeth had given him some money before his departure from Grenoble. What he yearned for desperately was the companionship of a friend, and above all the love of a woman. But he was too timid to take any kind of initiative, and he had a horror of the prostitutes of whom he caught glimpses in the street. Except for his flashing and expressive eyes and his curly black hair, he had few physical assets. In this respect, Beyle's disappointment during his first stay in Paris was not greatly different from that of countless other provincials and foreigners—from Rousseau to Chateaubriand—who before him had gravitated toward the capital, innocently expecting to find there the immediate realization of their fondest dreams.

In Grenoble, Beyle's enemies had been well-defined ones: they took the tangible form of individuals who embodied attitudes, beliefs, and prejudices that he had come to detest. Contrary to all his plans, however, Paris inspired in him a sense of such intense dislike that he came very close to feeling homesick. With the benefit of hindsight, he was able to diagnose accurately the basic reason for this deep malaise: "In fact I had loved Paris only out of profound disgust for Grenoble." [7]

The change in environment, habits, and diet, coupled with the unexpected disappointment and disorientation, soon got the better of Beyle's vigorous constitution. He fell seriously ill and spent the better part of December, 1799, in bed. Fortunately for him, loyal relatives on his mother's side, the powerful and influential Darus, to whom he had paid only a perfunctory visit upon his arrival in Paris, came to the rescue, bringing a reputable doctor, providing a nurse for proper care and, after he had sufficiently recovered, moving him to a spacious room of their handsome mansion on the rue de Lille.

Noël Daru, a first cousin of Dr. Henri Gagnon, had, after completing his law studies, left Grenoble for Montpellier in order to enter the employ of the count of Saint-Priest, who held the important post of governor of the province of Languedoc. A hardworking, astute administrator, Daru rapidly rose in the government hierarchy, shrewdly managed his finances, and, having retired in 1787, settled in Paris. Successful speculations under the easy-going and corrupt regime of the Directoire increased his wealth significantly, enabling him to purchase, on the southeastern corner of the rue de Lille and the rue de Bellechasse, an attractive mansion which had belonged to the ill-fated *philosophe* Condorcet.

Skilfully steering clear of the Revolutionary partisan politics and essentially a man with a practical turn of mind and a financial flair, Noël Daru kept at a prudent distance from doctrinaire passions and ideologies. He thus avoided persecution and ruin. The end of the Terror found him solidly entrenched in the important circles of French society.

A tall, impressive figure of a man of seventy when he entered Henri Beyle's life, he nevertheless made an unfavorable impression on his young relative and protégé. The elderly Daru was given to lengthy, sententious speeches. Politely listening to M. Daru as the latter droned on about his loyal devotion for Dr. Gagnon, Henri was somehow made keenly aware of his own inadequacy. Instead of putting him at ease, M. Daru only increased the youth's painful self-consciousness with his authoritarian and condescending manner.

It is obvious, from Stendhal's comments in *Henry Brulard*, that he never overcame his first negative reaction to M. Daru *père*. The latter's aptitude for personal survival in times of turmoil he attributes to a basic indifference to everything that did not concern his immediate gain and advantage. His sole, overriding passions were ambition and vanity. The great ideological issues of his day, on the other hand, left him completely cold. Hence his clearheadedness during the revolutionary storm, an immensely valuable asset at a time when political passions and hatreds caused so many heads to roll. But it is precisely this cool egotism, this opportunistic and realistic perception of men and events, this calculating and self-seeking philosophy of life that repulsed the idealistic young Henri Beyle. M. Noël Daru reminded him too much of his own father.

Madame Noël Daru, who hailed from Montpellier and had presented her husband with nine offspring, equally failed to appeal to Henri. She offered a rather striking contrast with the tall, distinguished-looking Daru. A tiny, shriveled old woman, she retained a stiff, small-town manner that would have befitted the spouse of a minor provincial sub-prefect. Like her husband, however, she was eminently prudent and cautious and absolutely incapable of generous, selfless feelings. Any enthusiastic, magnanimous sentiment was alien to the Darus. But by the same token, they were equally incapable of vengeful wrath or hatred.

The Darus transmitted this eminently shrewd, reasonable, and unemotional disposition to their children, particularly to their eldest son, Pierre, destined to have a brilliant career under Napoleon. A demon for work, capable and ambitious, but authoritarian and prey to fits of rage, Pierre Daru, sixteen years Henri Beyle's senior, was the very opposite, in temperament and outlook on life, of his young cousin. No doubt the crushing responsibilities that would constantly weigh upon him contributed in no small measure to his abruptness of manner and irascibility. But like his father, he went out of his way to help his indecisive and impractical cousin from Grenoble. Henri was taken to the theater and invited to parties and literary meetings, for Pierre also had some literary ambitions, having written poems in the neoclassical style. But even in literary matters, which might have drawn the cousins together, there was a profound chasm in tastes and predilections, for Henri could not but disapprove of Pierre's narrow traditionalism.

But whatever antipathies Henri Beyle was to harbor against his powerful protectors, he could never accuse them outright of not doing their utmost—at least according to their own lights—to further his chances of success in the world. The Darus, if anything, had a strong sense of familial duty and loyalty, and it must be said that they consistently showed notable patience and forbearance, through the years, in their dealings with their unpredictable relative from Grenoble.

From the outset Henri Beyle got along best with Martial

Daru, a younger brother of Pierre, who was not only closer to him in age—being nine years older—but also more outgoing, cheerful, and fun-loving than his formidable brother Pierre. Martial, moreover, turned out to be a helpful ally, one who could be relied upon to plead his cousin's case whenever necessary. At twenty-six, Martial was a handsome man and one of the more elegant and popular young dandies in post-Revolutionary Paris. He was, moreover, much sought after by the fashionable ladies. To be sure, his intellectual endowments and character were not on a par with those of his more gifted, ambitious, and energetic brother Pierre, and he was possessed of an inordinate amount of vanity. But he was also capable of real kindness and of friendship. No wonder Henri was far more at ease in his company than in that of the authoritarian Pierre. And it was Martial's handsome looks, elegance of dress, and ease of manner, and above all his success with women, that most impressed Beyle and aroused his admiration and secret envy. Martial Daru quite naturally assumed the role that gallant uncle Romain Gagnon had played in Grenoble. To cut as dashing a figure in the salons and to count as many mistresses as Martial became Henri's favorite fantasy.

In actuality, however, Beyle still had a great deal to learn to achieve Martial's kind of social and amorous savoir-faire. At the Daru dinner table or in a salon he hardly ever opened his mouth. As a result, his relatives and their friends were nonplussed, deeming him a strange kind of a fellow. Yet it is to the credit of the Darus that they did not immediately conclude that he was plain stupid. He rather struck them as overly proud and perhaps slightly mad. They decided that his case was possibly not entirely hopeless, provided they took him firmly in hand.

As for young Beyle, he was painfully conscious of the fact that his long and awkward silences when in a salon were due not to a lack of ideas or to a keen desire to please, but rather to an embarrassment of riches. His head was so filled with notions acquired in books, his imagination so overheated, his sensibility so acute that his faculties became paralyzed when he found himself confronted with the necessity to chitchat about inconsequential, trivial matters. Not unlike his beloved mentor, Jean-Jacques Rousseau, he found himself taking refuge in silence and sullenness. But unlike Rousseau, he did not turn his back on society and retreat into his own private world of ideas and fancies, but embarked upon a systematic program of self-training in order to "correct" those traits in his character and temperament which hampered him in his efforts to please or at least to communicate with others.

Living with the Darus and accompanying them on their social outings, Henri slowly lost some of his provincial naïveté and shy awkwardness. But there was a price in boredom to be payed for this protection and introduction into Parisian social circles. The atmosphere in the Daru household was stiff and formal and the friends and salons favored by them tended to be equally constrained and tradition-bound. Martial Daru was the only member of the family who could provide a note of levity or escape, in the company of a delighted Henri, from one of those endless and tedious soirées which were de rigueur with the Darus.

Henri Beyle's protectors, especially stern Daru père and diligent Pierre, strongly disapproved of the young man's idleness and lack of purpose. That he had failed to present himself at the Ecole Polytechnique and appeared unable to make up his mind about a profession completely baffled and disturbed these eminently practical and ambitious men. Once more, they took the initiative. Henri was given a position as clerk in the Ministry of War where Pierre was Secretary General.

Bonaparte was secretly reorganizing his army for an Italian campaign, and the overworked Pierre Daru often turned up very late for dinner and rushed back immediately to the office afterwards. As for Henri Beyle, he was now one of an army of seven or eight hundred clerks who toiled under the irascible Daru. Henri was given a desk and on his first day, when asked to copy a letter, managed to misspell *cela* by giving it an extra *l*, a humiliating experience for one who had boasted of winning so many prizes at the Ecole Centrale! Julien Sorel, the hero of *The Red and the Black*, would make the same embarrassing mistake.[8]

In order to please his boss and to make up for his initial blunder, Beyle zealously imitated his cousin's writing style, stuffing his letters and memoranda with administrative locutions and phraseology. He was also hopeful of being promoted, like Martial Daru, to the position of Deputy Commissary of War and of earning the right to wear the dashing red uniform that went with that rank.

During that winter of 1800, Beyle led a diligent but increasingly dull existence, spending his days at a desk, trying hard to turn out letters according to the instructions and guidelines of the War Ministry. He was soon again overcome with that depressing mood of melancholia which was all too familiar to him. His eyes continued to hunger for the mountainous horizons and verdant perspectives of Grenoble and greedily fastened on the few meager and closely clipped lime trees that adorned the courtyard; "They were the first friends I had in Paris. Their fate evoked my pity; to be clipped like that!" [9]

More and more, Beyle felt the necessity to perfect the art of concealing his real self when dealing with others, of creating a social persona which would enable him to maintain his emotional and intellectual distance and sharpen his critical faculties. And here he found the tragic case of Rousseau extremely instructive. Unlike Jean-Jacques, who had trusted his sensibility too implicitly and had not learned the value of emotional control, especially in his relations with others, he would be careful not to let his guard down. His best shield against the malice, indifference, or ill will of those with whom he would come into contact would be a mask of insouciance and flippancy.

It was to his sister Pauline, by now almost fifteen years of age, that he confided his innermost thoughts in long, affectionate letters. He felt, moreover, that it was incumbent upon him to guide his sister in the treacherous ways of the world. He also wanted her to share his latest intellectual discoveries and moral insights. He himself had embarked upon an ambitious program of self-education. His favorite authors, at this time, were Ariosto, Shakespeare, Molière, and Rousseau.

While Henri Beyle was marking time, scribbling at his desk, or daydreaming and watching his beloved trees in the courtyard, highly secret plans for an invasion of Italy were afoot in the War Ministry. Bonaparte, as First Consul, had determined to head an army that would cross the Great Saint Bernard Pass, reoccupy northern Italy and attack the Austrians. Pierre Daru, on whom Bonaparte counted heavily because of his capacity for hard work, had decided that it might be a good idea to send his young cousin along with the invading forces.

Beyle was totally unaware of these feverish and secret preparations. In the beginning of May, 1800, he was suddenly invited to rejoin his cousins, by then already in Italy. His reaction was one of overwhelming enthusiasm. To be able to leave behind Paris and its disappointments and to make his way toward sunny Italy, the land of his dreams, was a prospect that he had not conjured up in his most fanciful plans. On May 7th, Henri Beyle left Paris and set out on the first lap of his journey, via Dijon, to Geneva.

The weather was mild, spring was in full bloom in the countryside, and it was without the slightest regret that Beyle, journeying by carriage, saw the Parisian skyline fade in the horizon. His mood was that of an eager tourist more than that of a soldier, and as he progressed toward the south he looked upon the world around him with growing exhilaration. For the first time, he was having a taste of real freedom, and he was convinced that passion and adventure were at last at hand.

VI
The Discovery of Italy

ENCUMBERED WITH A bulky portmanteau containing his clothes, personal effects, and favorite books, including Rousseau's *La Nouvelle Héloïse*, Henri Beyle reached Geneva on May 18, 1800, in a state of growing euphoria. His exaltation knew no bounds when, fervent disciple of Rousseau that he was, he hastened to visit those shrines associated with the writer's life and works.

His first mission was to make a pilgrimage to the old house, on 40 Grand-Rue (which still stands today), where Jean-Jacques was born in 1712. Everything in and around Geneva reminded him of Rousseau and of *La Nouvelle Héloïse*, the novel that had made the most indelible impression upon his sensibility and imagination. The vistas afforded from the banks of Lake Geneva, so closely associated with the touching Julie and the ever faithful Saint-Preux, filled him with profound emotion. And he felt gratified at the thought that he, too, possessed a sensitive and tender soul and a heart capable of lofty and delicate sentiments.

Geneva was cluttered with military convoys and everywhere disorder and chaos reigned. Beyle remained in the city several days. Pierre Daru had left a slightly ailing horse in Geneva with instructions that Beyle wait for its recovery and bring it with him. When the horse, a young bay, was ready for the trip to Milan, Beyle, a totally inexperienced rider, rashly mounted the beast, slinging behind him that unwieldy portmanteau he had brought along from Paris. The resulting scene, described in humorous detail in *Henry Brulard*, was worthy of a picaresque novel.[1] Beyle must indeed have cut a comical figure on that horse: he was still dressed in civilian clothes, but wore spurs and sported a long sword which hampered his movements. Sensing its rider's clumsiness and irritated with the added weight of the portmanteau, the horse immediately broke into a wild gallop and, leaving the road, made its way toward Lake Geneva. Both horse and cavalier might have ended in the lake if they had not been skilfully intercepted by the servant of a Captain Burelviller who, upon meeting Beyle, took a liking for him and henceforth traveled by his side, teaching him how to ride a horse properly and guiding him throughout the long, arduous, and treacherous journey across the Alps and into Italy.

Before long, Beyle had learned to bridle his horse as well as balance his luggage properly. But if his mount had calmed down, his own mood continued to be one of high excitement. Captain Burelviller sometimes had a hard time quieting him down when a new sight aroused his enthusiasm. At Rolle, a picturesque town situated at mid-point between Geneva and Lausanne and also bordering on Lake Geneva, the bells of a church merrily rang out: "I saw the beautiful lake stretched out before my eyes, the sound of the bell was a ravishing music which accompanied my ideas and gave them a sublime coloring. There, it seems to me, I experienced something most akin to *perfect happiness.*" [2]

While Henri Beyle was still in Geneva, the long, winding columns of Bonaparte's army were progressing toward the Great Saint Bernard Pass which, having already been crossed by the French in 1798 and 1799, was by now familiar to them. Bonaparte's purpose was to take the Austrians by surprise and to inflict upon them a swift and decisive defeat.[3]

The path on which Beyle and his companions rode became narrow, winding, and steep, and a cold, penetrating mist enveloped the column of soldiers and cannons slowly moving upward. Snow and frost surrounded Beyle, and now and then his mount, startled by the carcass of a dead horse or falling stones, would sud-

denly rear, almost causing him to fall to his death. But Beyle had
always loved mountains and if he was not heedless of the hazards
of this perilous journey, his mood was too euphoric to allow him
to take these dangers too seriously.

As one who considered himself a child of the French Revolution, he had cherished the dream of becoming some day one of
those soldiers of the Republic who spread liberty and equality to
the subjugated peoples of Europe. Now reality at last rejoined fantasy. That these "glorious soldiers" were not above pilfering from
their comrades, that many of them looked and acted like lawless
ruffians, and that instead of the feelings of heroic comradeship he
had expected of them, many displayed only ill-tempered selfish-
ness, had a somewhat sobering effect upon him. But this glimpse
of human nature under stress was quickly cast aside in favor of
more cheerful thoughts. Later, however, when the initial excitement of witnessing history in the making wore off, Stendhal increasingly used his military experience as a rich source of reflection upon the vagaries, unpredictability, and darker sides of the
human psyche. A *moraliste* (in the classical French sense of the
word, meaning an observer of manners and mores) at heart, he
was to amass a vast treasure of observations on the vices, foibles,
and follies of mankind during his years of close association with
the military and during his extensive travels throughout Europe.

For the time being, however, he was under the spell of the
majestic and forbidding scenery that surrounded him: "If I day-
dreamed, it was about the sentences with which J.-J. Rousseau
would describe these frowning and snow-covered mountains rising
to the skies, with their peaks forever obscured by large gray clouds
rushing past." [4] This observation, written thirty-five years after the
event, reveals in its subtle and self-deprecatory irony a typical
aspect of the Stendhalian esthetic. From the vantage point of his
experience as a mature writer and novelist, Stendhal evoked with
nostalgia as well as gentle sarcasm the naïve young man of 1800
who so confidently looked forward to emulating Rousseau's descriptive eloquence and mastery. But the young Beyle could hardly

suspect, as he gave himself over to the delightful dream of rivaling with Rousseau in depicting this sublime mountainous landscape, that eventually he would reject precisely this type of stylistic virtuosity, so favored by Jean-Jacques and his Romantic followers.

If the climb to the Saint Bernard Pass was arduous, the journey down presented even greater perils. Before beginning the descent, Beyle, like the rest of the army, took a brief rest as well as some refreshments at the famed Hospice of Saint Bernard. As the long descent progressed, he became soaked to the bones and his horse grew more unsteady, threatening to stumble at any moment into the gaping precipice at the bottom of which a frozen lake was faintly visible.

At last, the air grew milder and the scenery less austere. Foothills on the Italian side were reached and hamlets came into view. Beyle was beside himself with joy at the thought that he was now on Italian soil and had survived the epic journey. "So the Saint Bernard, it's only that?" he said teasingly to his companion, Captain Burelviller, who by now was becoming somewhat exasperated with his foolhardy protégé.[5]

When he reached Fort Bard, overlooking the valley of Aosta, Beyle received his baptism of fire. The Fort had been bypassed by the main French forces and was still holding out. As the sound of cannons reverberated ominously, Beyle, to prove his mettle, deliberately went close to the edge of the platform to be more exposed and lingered there several minutes. In his *Henry Brulard*, Stendhal remarks with a touch of humor that this first contact with enemy fire marked the loss of a kind of virginity as burdensome as the other sort.[6] For he had as yet to experience physical love at the time of the passing of the Saint Bernard.

Before descending into the luxuriant plains of Lombardy, Beyle spent his last night in the mountains with a kindly Italian village priest, who offered him both hospitality and his first lesson in Italian. Approaching the Italian border town of Ivrea, Beyle continued to be enchanted by the countryside, even though it was marred by the usual war wreckage, including a number of dead

horses. At last, on June 1, 1800, in the afternoon, while behind
him Fort Bard finally surrendered to the French army, Beyle made
his entry into Ivrea.

Picturesquely located at the foot of mountains and overlooking a green valley, Ivrea had a population of about ten thousand
and boasted a small opera house. Everything about the town delighted Beyle: the sun-drenched streets, ocher-colored houses, and
especially the women. At once the dangers and physical discomforts experienced while crossing the Great Saint Bernard and facing enemy fire at Fort Bard disappeared as if by magic. Life was
rich with promise of happiness, and all the recent disappointments, especially those suffered in Paris, also vanished in the
bright, warm Italian air. Upon reflecting about that momentous
journey across the Saint Bernard Pass, Beyle came to the conclusion that Fate, at last, was willing to look with favor upon him.
This was to be a turning point in his life. He had had little luck
from the age of seven to that of seventeen. But now things were
definitely beginning to look up.[7]

Beyle's first day in an Italian town was appropriately high-
lighted by a memorable evening at the Ivrea opera house. He
watched a performance of Cimarosa's *Il Matrimonio Segreto* and
was overcome by such a powerful feeling of "sublime happiness"
that almost all details of that ecstatic evening were obliterated in
his memory by the very intensity of his emotions. With characteristic reserve and conciseness, as well as an implied criticism of
such writers as Rousseau and Chateaubriand—who liked to linger
at length over the circumstances of their most intimate experiences—Stendhal simply writes about that unforgettable evening: "I
would lie and fictionalize if I undertook to describe it in detail."[8]
The sweet melodiousness of Cimarosa filled him with a rapture
even greater than that he had known while standing on the edge of
Lake Geneva and dreaming of Rousseau's *La Nouvelle Héloïse* and
its touching heroine. Everything about that evening was perfect. It
was as if a new page had been turned in the book of his life. He
felt that everything that had preceded it, the pettiness and unhap-

piness in Grenoble, the loneliness and disenchantment in Paris, were effaced forever.

So here he was, barely seventeen, and privileged to enter the land of beauty, music, and art. Italy was inextricably bound up in his mind with the most compelling images that had peopled his imagination. It was, above all, the land of sublime women: Verona and the immortal Juliette, Venice and the tragic Desdemona as well as Rousseau's enigmatic and disturbing courtesan Zulietta, Turin and another feminine figure immortalized by the *Confessions*: the modest yet seductive Mme Basile, whom the young Jean-Jacques had silently adored. Shakespeare and Rousseau, Ariosto and Tasso were constantly on Beyle's mind as he went through colorful Italian villages. Passion and prowess had equal shares in his high expectations.

On June 2, Bonaparte had made his triumphal entry into Milan. On the tenth of that month, it was Beyle's turn to set foot in the city. It was one of those dazzling Italian spring mornings, and Milan was in a festive mood. Following his brilliant victory at Marengo on June 14, Bonaparte returned to Milan. In all probability, Beyle, accompanying his chief Pierre Daru, beheld the thirty-one year old general for the first time at the Scala theater.[9] The audience saluted the conqueror of northern Italy with a standing ovation.

Upon his arrival in Milan, Beyle was lodged in the imposing Adda Palace, located at the entrance of the Corso di Porta Nuova (today via Manzoni) near the famed Scala.[10] Although its façade was as yet unfinished, the Adda served as headquarters of the French. It was to be Beyle's temporary home and place of work. He slept in an ornate bedroom and worked in a stately salon with high windows and elegant balconies overlooking the bustling and fashionable Corso. It also boasted a monumental staircase and an immense gallery on the first floor. Beyle was later given lodgings in the equally splendid Casa Bovara on the Corso di Porta Orientale (today Corso Venezia), between the Duomo Cathedral and the Public Garden. The Casa Bovara, which also served as the

French Embassy, was assigned by Pierre Daru to Claude Petiet, Ambassador and Minister Extraordinary of the French Republic in Italy. Senior French officers and staff members, as well as the city's high society, gathered in the evenings at the Casa Bovara for gala dinners and balls. Beyle was thus introduced to the most exclusive Milanese circles.

Milan, in those heady days, reinforced his belief that it was the one place on the face of this earth where his yearning for earthly fulfilment and perfection did not have to be relegated to the realm of the unattainable. His lifelong love for the city was such that it eventually found expression in the wish that his tomb be inscribed with the epitaph, in Italian: "Arrigo Beyle, Milanese." [11] Thus Italy became the land of his choice and he symbolically renounced his French origins and nationality. Unlike Paris, Milan, with its architecture, people, customs, and music, was a perpetual source of keen delight.

To be young and welcomed as a hero by the effusive Italians, to participate in the public celebrations, festivals, and balls that greeted the French soldiers, to behold the architectural and artistic treasures of Milan, to frequent every evening the legendary Scala, to make excursions to the spectacular surroundings of the city, to watch the Milanese women, whose morals were notoriously easy-going, this was the existence young Beyle threw himself into with great gusto.

A constant round of social festivities marked those historic days of June 1800. Milan, which had just suffered thirteen months of repressive Austrian rule following the retreat of the French after their first invasion in 1796, was eager to show its hospitality to Bonaparte and his army and treated them as liberators rather than conquerors.[12] With typical Italian élan and ardor, the Milanese filled the streets, piazzas, and palaces. But it was at the Scala, not only the musical center of the city but also the heart of its social life, that Beyle felt the happiest. Every night he was faithfully at his post, admiring the most fashionable and beautiful women of Milan surrounded by their cavaliers, and listening with ever-renewed rapture to Italian music.

His days were equally filled with delightful activities, for he was by no means bound to his desk. He embarked upon the pleasurable task of visiting systematically the famed artistic landmarks of the city. In the streets he examined curiously the passers-by and found in their manner and deportment, from the humblest types to the most distinguished aristocrats, an animation and zest for life he had seen nowhere before. Whereas the monuments, palaces, and churches of Paris had failed to impress him, and the city in general had struck him as ugly, constricted, and claustrophobic, Milan enchanted him with its broad expanses and sweeping vistas. He tirelessly roamed about the city, visiting, among the notable places of interest, the huge and then uncompleted Duomo Cathedral, the massive Sforza Castle, focal point of conspiracies, assassinations, and popular uprisings since the Renaissance, and for this reason of great interest to Beyle, and the cloister of Santa Maria delle Grazie and its adjacent convent with the refectory which is the repository of the legendary "Last Supper" by Leonardo da Vinci, a work that was to hold a special fascination for Stendhal, art critic. [13]

And in several sidetrips, Beyle completed his discovery of the beauty and poetry of the luxuriant countryside and towns of Lombardy, and especially of its mountains and lakes. Henceforth these last two features were to figure prominently in the privileged sites of his own novelistic landscapes. [14] On these journeys, sometimes conveniently combined with military missions for Pierre Daru, he was able to visit Lake Maggiore and the "divine" Borromean Islands. To his sister Pauline he wrote that these greatly surpassed all scenes of natural beauty he had seen thus far, including Lake Geneva. Several rather long letters to Pauline, dating from that period, and in which he attempted to share with her his feelings and impressions, give us revealing and concrete information his far later *Henry Brulard* fails to provide. [15]

Stendhal's first five or six months in Milan were, in his words, the happiest period in his life, so much so that thirty-six years later, when writing his autobiography, he found it impossible to depict this exhilarating interval in rational, coherent terms:

"How can one give a reasonable account of those times? . . . How can one describe frantic happiness? . . . Upon my word, I can't go on." [16]

His shyness, especially with women, continued to plague him. Enviously he observed his cousin Martial Daru and the latter's boon companions acquiring as mistresses the most beautiful and desirable women in Milan. He diligently studied Italian and made rapid progress in mastering the language. But his growing linguistic facility was no great help in his awkward attempts to emulate the dashing Martial. He was as tongue-tied as ever when in the presence of an attractive member of the opposite sex. He reluctantly had to remain on the sidelines, while officers, sometimes plainer looking than he, enjoyed the favors of the Milanese women.

One of those lucky Frenchmen whom Beyle particularly envied was Louis Joinville, a friend of Martial. He was the proud lover of a dazzling beauty, Angela Pietragrua. [17] The daughter of a Milanese cloth merchant whose business thrived thanks to the patronage of the French officers, she was married to a minor functionary in the Office of Weights and Measures. With her imposing stature, magnificent black hair, flashing eyes, and generous proportions, she seemed to have stepped out of a painting by one of the masters of the Italian Renaissance. She was twenty-three years of age and, in typical Milanese fashion, made no secret of her numerous amorous liaisons, which her husband tolerated good-naturedly.

When Beyle made her acquaintance through Joinville, she was perpetually surrounded by a bevy of young admirers and hardly took notice of the shy young Frenchman who, with the other officers, thronged her father's shop located near the Duomo. Before long, Beyle had fallen desperately in love with the voluptuous Angela.

In his autobiographical essays, Stendhal, analyzing retrospectively the events of this crucial period in his life and especially his first unrequited love, expressed the thought that Fate had, once again, dealt unkindly with him. At a time when he had been in greatest need of the tenderness of a loving woman, he had been cruelly deprived of it.[18] Since that first enchanted stay in Milan, he would, to be sure, love several other women, but with possibly one exception never again would his passion glow with such intensity and fervor. In the face and body of Angela Pietragrua everything he admired and loved about Italy became crystallized.

Despairing of finding supreme happiness in the arms of Angela, Beyle resigned himself to seek sexual fulfilment elsewhere. As he humorously notes in his *Henry Brulard*, he had brought his virginity with him from Paris: "It was not until I reached Milan that I was able to unburden myself of this treasure. What is funny is that I don't remember distinctly with whom." [19] As always when facing an extraordinary experience in his past, Stendhal retained no distinct memory of it, only a blur.

One can safely surmise, however, that his first love partner was a lady of easy virtue, and what he fails to indicate explicitly in his autobiography is that, on this occasion or subsequent ones, he contracted a venereal disease the consequences of which were to plague him for the rest of his life.[20] The illness was then described as the French or the Italian disease, depending on who did the describing, and was treated, according to the medical prescriptions of the time, with bleedings, mercury, quinine, and opium.[21] While his friends continued their round of festive activities, Beyle, pale and feverish, had to spend many a day in bed, as his *Journal* for that period amply testifies.[22]

To be sure, Beyle was by no means alone in his predicament, and both he and his friends who came to visit and cheer him up when he was confined to his room did not seem particularly alarmed by this mishap, a rather characteristic reaction of the age. Syphilis was looked upon as an almost inevitable event in the amorous life of a young man: it was practically the badge of his virility. Thus Beyle was not unduly concerned over his ailment, which only slightly marred his generally happy mood at that time. If we are, quite understandably, ill-informed on the subsequent course of the illness, we do know that throughout his life Stendhal would intermittently suffer from symptoms that point to the onset of the later stages of the disease: attacks of headache, bouts with fever and congestion, digestive difficulties. It may even be surmised that syphilis, inadequately treated, eventually contributed to his premature death at fifty-nine of apoplexy.

Punctilious, conscientious Pierre Daru was a man with strong family loyalties. By pulling the appropriate strings, he hoped to secure for his young cousin and protégé a regular army commission, the necessary prerequisite for an eventual post in the administration of the War Department.

On September 23, 1800, Beyle officially received a provisional commission as a sub-lieutenant in the cavalry. The following month he was assigned to the 6th Dragoons, and, on November 22, he rejoined his regiment at Romanengo and rode with it to Bagnolo, a small cisalpine village near Brescia. Outfitted in his brand new uniform, a sword at his side, on his head a golden helmet with a long black plume, and an elegant green cloak flowing from his broad shoulders, he felt immensely proud and knew that, at long last, he was a real soldier, and what was especially gratifying, a soldier in Bonaparte's *Grande Armée*. At seventeen-and-a-half, Beyle impatiently looked forward to a brilliant career in the army and eagerly anticipated an event-packed life in which heroic deeds would alternate with a succession of amorous adventures and conquests.

Unfortunately, reality quickly brought Beyle down from the heights of his euphoric mood. At Bagnolo, where he was stationed until the end of the year 1800, he became bored and restless and increasingly missed Milan, the Scala, and especially the desirable Angela Pietragrua. He tried to pass the time profitably and to find some meaningful diversion by studying the area, its history and its inhabitants and their customs. Over the years, as he oftentimes found himself faced with periods of enforced leisure, he would perfect the art of whiling away the time and tedium through writing and study; and to be the amateur historian, social observer, and psychologist of a particular European region would be one of his favorite occupations.

It was not long before garrison life, its monotony and discomforts, began to weigh on Beyle. His state of health, since his recent bout with syphilis, continued to trouble him and to cause recurrent attacks of fever. The duties and missions which took him to small Italian towns and villages held little attraction for him, despite his earnest efforts to delve into their history and culture. His letters to his sister Pauline of that period faithfully mirror his growing dissatisfaction. Whereas he had liked and admired everything about Milan and the Milanese, he felt only contempt or indifference for the villagers and peasants of Lombardy. To his sister he wrote that he had never seen more brutish and stupid people and that they were far worse than the rustics of the Dauphiné, for in addition to being ignorant, they were also fanatical, superstitious, cowardly, dishonest, and treacherous.[23] Unlike the city dwellers, they were also actively hostile to the French troops.

His mental outlook swung from the enthusiasm and euphoria that had marked his Milanese period to a state of boredom that rapidly bordered on depression. It is, of course, quite understandable that the high excitement in which he had constantly been for approximately six months could hardly last much longer. It was followed, not too surprisingly, by a psychological downswing. Even his love of Italy and the Italians suffered a temporary eclipse, and to his sister he wrote lengthy letters—always a sign of loneliness and frustration—in which plaintive notes, reminiscent of the Paris period, were sounded.

Beyle soon came to the conclusion that military life had a great many servitudes and very little grandeur. He could not take part in any of the momentous events that were taking place, notably the battle of Castel-Franco and the campaign of Mincio at the end of 1800.[24] In the small towns and villages of Lombardy where his duties relegated him, he felt forgotten and abandoned. When cold weather, heavy rains, or the state of his health prevented him from roaming around the countryside on horseback he was overcome with melancholy and self-pity. In his letters to Pauline he kept begging her to remind their father to send him volumes from the family library. Unable to give expression to the courage, initiative, and energy of which he felt capable, since he was forced to

remain on the sidelines of military action, more and more exasperated by the dullness of his present existence and by the coarseness
and ignorance of his fellow officers, he determined to do everything in order to get away from his regiment.

Beyle's connection with Pierre Daru once more came in
handy. Using his cousin's influence at the headquarters in Milan,
Beyle got himself appointed as a general staff officer and aide-de-
camp to General Claude Michaud, commander of the third division in Bonaparte's cisalpine forces, an assignment he delightedly
assumed on February 1, 1801.[25] This was, however, a rather irregular procedure, all the more so since the recently commissioned
sub-lieutenant did not have the necessary seniority or rank for such
a post. Beyle's transfer and new assignment, therefore, could not
receive the official stamp of approval, and it was no doubt in order
to do the powerful Pierre Daru a favor that the young man was
allowed to assume the duties of an aide-de-camp without actually
obtaining the title.

Furthermore, Beyle had brazenly solicited and obtained this
transfer without bothering to consult Daru who, upon being informed of this, flew into one of his famous rages, for he was acutely
aware of the fact that this rash act on his troublesome young
cousin's part could turn out to be a real embarrassment for him,
rendering him liable to accusations of nepotism. As for Beyle, he
was so pleased to escape from army camp life that Daru's displeasure did not unduly perturb him. On the contrary, he felt he
owed his improved situation to his own efforts and initiative more
than to the protection of Daru. He therefore stubbornly resisted
the latter's efforts to have him give up his new position and rejoin
his regiment. Beyle claimed ill health and even appealed to his
grandfather to plead his case with his cousin. In the meantime,
Daru had written to Dr. Gagnon, inveighing against the recalcitrant young man who had been entrusted to him.[26]

General Michaud, a rather unsophisticated but friendly and
spirited man of about fifty, with a distinguished record in the revolutionary army and with strong Jacobin sympathies, had taken a
great liking for his new aide-de-camp. Beyle was invited by his

new chief on several missions, trips, and hunting parties. And when his duties did not take him to various attractive towns, such as Brescia, Mantua, Cremona, Bergamo, and Verona, he could lead an agreeable and carefree existence in Milan and devote himself to his favorite pursuits. It was during this period, toward the end of April 1801, that at La Scala, in the loge reserved for staff officers, he met in person Choderlos de Laclos, by then an aging artillery general. Thirty years earlier, the author of *Les Liaisons dangereuses* had been stationed in Grenoble and Beyle well remembered all the scandalous rumours he had heard as a child concerning this notorious book and the men and women depicted in it. Beyle was all the more moved by this encounter since, in his recent efforts to overcome his shyness and awkwardness with women and to educate himself in matters of love and seduction, he had lately reread the novel with renewed interest and admiration. Whether the elderly Laclos was equally pleased to meet a young officer hailing from a town of which he no doubt had vivid memories, we don't know, although Stendhal, in his *Souvenirs d'égotisme*, assures us that the writer waxed sentimental and emotional during his conversation with his admirer.[27]

On September 18, 1801, Beyle's unofficial service on General Michaud's staff came to an abrupt end when he was sternly ordered, this time by his commanding officer of the 6th Dragoons, to rejoin his regiment forthwith. No doubt Pierre Daru had something to do with this turn of events. Beyle could hardly ignore this direct command. With a heavy heart he took leave of the fatherly General Michaud, paid his respects and bade a sad farewell to his lively Milanese friends and to the elusive Angela Pietragrua and, mounting his horse, started on his trip to the small town of Bra, in Piedmont, where his regiment was now stationed.[28] Upon reaching his destination on October 26, he fell seriously ill. His despair at having failed in his attempt to achieve a measure of independence in the army in all likelihood had something to do with this physical breakdown.

To be forced again to rub elbows with uncouth soldiers and barely literate officers, to have as his sole horizon the countryside and villages of Piedmont, to have to resume the dreary routine of army life without the excitement of military action, this was more than he could endure. While bouts of fever increased his physical discomfort, somber ennui, that spiritual ailment common to sensitive and imaginative beings who expect too much of life, gnawed at his soul. In a mood of acute loneliness, boredom and melancholy, he requested, and was granted, a leave for reasons of health and allowed to convalesce in his home town. At the end of December 1801 he left Italy and started on his journey to Grenoble. Ten years would elapse before he was to set foot once again on Italian soil.

VII

First Literary Efforts

DESPITE HIS frequently-expressed dislike for his native city, Beyle, with characteristic indifference to authority, prolonged his leave and stayed in Grenoble from January until April 1802.[1] The town and its gossips no longer held any terrors for him, for he was warmly welcomed as a hero and invited out a good deal. His relationship with his father, however, continued to be an uneasy one. More than ever, Chérubin Beyle was involved in land speculations and farming experiments which tied up all his assets. On the other hand, Dr. Gagnon's mind was as sharp as always despite his advanced years. And his sister Pauline, with whom he had corresponded so voluminously since his departure from Grenoble, by now an attractive, vivacious young girl of sixteen, was a delightful companion.

Beyle's frame of mind was presently introspective. He had determined that, with his fanciful imagination and tendency to view the world not as it really is but through the extravagantly idealized notions derived from such novels as *La Nouvelle Héloïse,* he needed a strong antidote in the form of a rigorous, systematic philosophy of life. In order to face the trials and tribulations that would no doubt come his way, he would have to ponder, more diligently and soberly than ever before, the mysteries, contradictions, and weaknesses of the human heart. His *Journal,* begun the previous year, 1801, would permit him to jot down, without benefit of any literary embellishment, and on a day-to-day basis,

111

his most intimate thoughts, emotions, and sensations while they were still present in all their vividness. No event would be considered too insignificant or trivial for notation, and absolute truthfulness would be the order of the day. Only in this manner could such a diary provide him with the kind of psychological data, based upon events and his on-the-spot reactions to them, which would make the experiment worthwhile.

And Beyle scrupulously adhered to his self-imposed rule. Hence the immense human, psychological, and documentary value of his diaries, despite their fragmentary form. The style in which he consigned his thoughts and feelings now appears remarkably modern, for, unlike that of his contemporaries, it is direct, natural, concise, simple, and devoid of those elaborate descriptions and rhetorical adornments so common to the Romantics. It is also at times not only abrasive but also singularly explicit, especially in sexual matters. It was his diary, moreover, that helped Beyle evolve his own style as a novelist, for just as he came to cherish truthfulness and spontaneity above all else in his moral philosophy, he would prize directness, vivacity, and naturalness in the literary expression of his ideas and observations. To concern himself with rhetorical niceties and stylistic effects, in his eyes amounted to being guilty of mendacity. All his life he was to remain faithful to this ethical and esthetic creed, even at the expense of an immediate success with the contemporary public.

Beyle's need to systematize the mass of information accumulated in the course of his readings and in his own experience found another outlet in his correspondence. From his studies Beyle hoped to evolve a coherent doctrine, the *Filosofia Nova*.[2] Beyle's philosophy essentially derived from the sensationalists, determinists, and behaviorists of the eighteenth century, notably Locke, Condillac, and Helvétius, and their disciples, the Ideologists Cabanis and Destutt de Tracy. Beyle readily endorsed their mechanistic psychology and the principle of conditioning through training, education, and habit. All our notions derive from our sensory perceptions and the most elaborate mental concepts are based upon the data provided by our physical senses. Imagination cannot create anything *ex nihilo*, but depends upon the raw materials furnished by our power of observation and our memory. Man is not essentially a rational being, but rather one dominated by his passions, impulses, and appetites. His fundamental purpose, on this earth, is the pursuit of happiness, the fulfilment of his passions.

But in order to achieve this legitimate goal, it is necessary to acquire a thorough understanding of human nature and the way in which it responds to the various forms passions assume when they are modified by social customs and restrictions. Hence Beyle's abiding interest in those fields of human activity, intellectual and artistic disciplines, and literary forms of expression that expose man's deepest desires, needs, and passions: philosophy, psychology, art, history, and in the domain of belles-lettres, autobiography and memoirs, tragedy and comedy, and the novel. He also perused a number of philosophical treatises, but on the whole preferred the more informal, personal essay form in the French *moraliste* tradition going back to Montaigne.[3]

Like the eighteenth-century sensualists, Beyle denied the existence of free will and firmly believed that all our actions are determined by our physical make-up and our past experience. Yet he differed from the behaviorist school in that he was also convinced that the individual could, in a large measure, shape his own destiny by knowing what options are open to him and by choosing his course of action with as full an understanding as possible of what is best for him in each particular situation.

Such a method naturally calls for a very high degree of self-awareness, and it is to the end of realizing true happiness within the limitations imposed by nature and society that Beyle determined to bend all his efforts. Henceforth he would submit all significant facts furnished by his own experience as well as those observed in others and culled in books to the crucible of a systematic analysis. With the passing years, this intellectual process became a habit, almost an automatic reaction to people and events. An unexpected consequence of this was that Stendhal, who would always so greatly admire the qualities of energy, spontaneity, and

single-mindedness of purpose, found himself, in critical moments
that called for quick decisions, quite frequently unable to follow a
direct, simple course of action. He who so vigorously applauded
great men of action, capable of acting boldly and ruthlessly, became an observer at least as much as a doer. The momentous
events of the Napoleonic era with which his own destiny had
become so inextricably bound up failed, in the final analysis, to
involve his entire being. His rapid disenchantment with army life
and his decision to resign his commission clearly testify to early
loss of interest in the hero myth which had played such a vital part
in his youthful dreams and fantasies. Yet he continued to be spell-
bound by a Bonaparte and by the combination of psychological
and sociological factors that had gone into shaping this extraordinary being.

As for Beyle himself, he had to recognize with growing
awareness that he was not cut out for a life of pure action. Diffidence, doubt, and inner conflict all too frequently invaded his
inner landscape, forestalling clear-cut commitments and alle-
giances. But it is precisely this acute self-awareness as well as his
sharp powers of observation which enabled him to preserve his independence as a man and his freedom as a writer and artist at a
time when brilliant if less self-sufficient and more irrepressibly ambitious men were sucked in and eventually shattered by the relentless political forces of that tumultuous era.

In the final analysis, Stendhal's intellect and sensibilities are
richer—as well as more elusive—than the set of philosophic principles he evolved on the basis of his study of the sensualists and
ideologists. Similarly, his lifelong involvement with the Napoleonic myth and persona constitutes only one facet—albeit a crucial
one—of his quest for self-fulfilment. Napoleon came to signify for
him a form of greatness and genius comparable to what he had
always admired in the heroes of Plutarch and other authors and,
more recently, in the leaders of the French Revolution. What
made Napoleon particularly compelling for Stendhal was the fact
that he did not belong to the past, or to a fabulous, mythical world
of fictional beings. Napoleon was not only a living contemporary,

he was also observable and reachable, and Beyle avidly collected all the facts and anecdotes that could help him form a complete picture in his mind of this paradigm case of a man of transcendent will and genius.[4]

Since his departure from Italy, Beyle had not devoted his energies solely to study, and he prolonged his stay in Grenoble not merely to be with his family and friends. A new romantic interest kept him in his native town. The object of his affections was Victorine Mounier, daughter of a former protégé of Dr. Gagnon, Joseph Mounier.[5] The latter, one of several offspring of a modest merchant draper, had resisted his father's efforts to have him stop his studies at an early age in order to work in the family shop. The kindly Dr. Gagnon took an interest in the bright young boy and persuaded the elder Mounier to allow his son to prepare for a professional career. In due time, Joseph Mounier earned his law degree and rose to the post of judge in the Grenoble courts of law. By 1788, he was playing an active role in Dauphiné politics and, in 1789, as a Deputy to the Estates General at Versailles, he participated in the famous Tennis Court Oath. As he watched the Revolution accelerate its leftward movement, however, Mounier who, like his colleague and fellow Grenoblois, Deputy Antoine Barnave, was no Jacobin but rather favored a constitutional monarchy, prudently decided to renounce revolutionary politics and to emigrate. In this respect, he was luckier, or shrewder, than Barnave, who was guillotined during the Terror. For several years he kept his distance from France, but with the ascendancy of Bonaparte he evidently felt that it was safe to return to Grenoble. Widowed during his exile, he had a son, Edouard, and two daughters. Victorine was the eldest and nineteen years of age, just like Beyle, when the latter called at her home upon his return from Italy, in January 1802.

Following Beyle's disappointment with the alluring but indifferent Angela Pietragrua, there was a void in his heart which he was eager to fill. Victorine Mounier was an attractive but proud and reserved brunette, and she greatly impressed him with her artistic accomplishments. Watching her play Haydn in preparation for a musical soirée, he became convinced on the spot that he was in the presence of an exceptional human being, one fully deserving of his love and devotion.[6] Whereas Angela had aroused his senses through her physical charms, Victorine's appeal was of a more spiritual nature. She deeply moved his soul and heart. She was as restrained and withdrawn as Angela had been lively and outgoing. But it was precisely this reserve, tinged with melancholy, that captivated him. His recent misadventure with too facile ladies may also have contributed to this need for a more ethereal relationship. No doubt he was still feeling the unpleasant aftereffects of his bout with syphilis and therefore yearned for the kind of platonic love that had fired his imagination as a lonely youth in Grenoble and Paris.

Victorine's outward appearance, while pleasing, was not of the spectacular kind. Yet for several years to come any woman encountered in Paris or elsewhere who even remotely resembled her would deeply stir his emotions.[7] With her pale and serious face, large, pensive eyes, and lithe, graceful figure, and with her dignified, melancholy demeanor Victorine denoted, Beyle assured himself, a superior soul that could communicate with him on a higher plane.

As always when in the presence of a woman who made a strong impression on him, Beyle found it impossible to overcome his timidity. Instead of revealing his feelings to Victorine, he assiduously cultivated the friendship of her brother, Edouard. He thus hoped to reach her through him, although he was none too fond of the fellow, who evidenced a vain and shrewdly calculating character, the very opposite of Beyle's own temperament.

In the early part of March 1802, Victorine and her family suddenly left Grenoble. Joseph Mounier had been appointed Prefect of the district of Ille-et-Vilaine, in the northwestern part of France. After a brief stay in Paris, the Mouniers settled in Rennes, where Joseph Mounier's new duties called him. Victorine's departure from Grenoble prompted Beyle to follow her, to abandon definitively his military career, and to settle in Paris, because it was closer to Rennes than Grenoble, or at least so Stendhal assures us in his *Henry Brulard* and *Souvenirs d'Egotisme*. [8]

What is certain is that, his father having reluctantly given him some money, he precipitously left Grenoble on April 5, 1802, and after a short stay with his uncle Romain Gagnon in the latter's country house at Les Echelles, he arrived in Paris on the fifteenth of the same month, only to learn of Mounier's appointment and impending move to Rennes. [9]

It is doubtful that Beyle's love for Victorine was the sole cause of his departure from Grenoble and his decision to settle in Paris instead of rejoining his regiment. His recent experience in the army had convinced him that a military career was not for him and, in his readings, he was returning to his beloved literary masters: Montaigne, Molière, Corneille, Racine, Shakespeare, Montesquieu, Rousseau. He was also once more contemplating a career as a playwright. His mind was made up. On July 5, he sent a short, rather curt letter to the War Ministry officially signifying his resignation of his commission as sub-lieutenant of the 6th Dragoons, an act which infuriated Pierre Daru, whom he had once again failed to consult or notify. [10]

In the contest of wills between the high-powered, authoritarian Daru and the rebellious, unpredictable Beyle, the latter had won out and demonstrated that he would accept his influential cousin's protection on his own terms or not at all. It was also, perhaps unconsciously, his revenge for what he regarded as Daru's highhandedness in forcing him to give up his pleasant assignment with General Michaud and resume garrison duty, which he abhorred.

On the same day he sent in his resignation, Beyle wrote a long, friendly letter to Edouard Mounier in Rennes, which in fact was meant for Victorine, and in which he expressed his relief and satisfaction at having regained his freedom as a civilian. [11] He had come to the clear realization that his individuality and whatever talent he might have would be irrevocably stifled if he allowed the army and his powerful cousin to dictate his conduct and control his life. Bonaparte's Grande Armée had by now lost much of its glamor for him. His craving for glory, however, had not abated. It had merely assumed a different form.

Stendhal's abortive military career is by no means the only such case among French writers. Vauvenargues, the eighteenth-century moralist and author of maxims, and Alfred de Vigny, the nineteenth-century poet, followed a similar course in their respective reactions to the frustrations, wastefulness, and absurdities of army life. But Stendhal, in particular, would always be openly impatient of institutionalized authority, no matter what ultimate advantages or benefits he might derive from a greater willingness to accommodate and please his hierarchical superiors.

Interestingly, Chérubin Beyle had encouraged his son to resign his commission, for as a loyal monarchist and devout Catholic, and as a stout opponent of the French Revolution, he regarded Bonaparte and his army with immense suspicion. To see his only son don the uniform had greatly displeased him, although he did not wish to express his discontent openly since the powerful Darus had been responsible for this turn of events.

After his arrival in Paris Beyle first stayed in a house on the rue Neuve-Saint-Augustin (today rue Daunou), where his old friend from Grenoble, Félix Faure, also resided. He soon thereafter moved into a sixth-floor room of the Hôtel de Rouen, in the rue d'Angivillier (no longer in existence), from which he had a splendid view of the colonnade of the Louvre. To watch every morning and evening the rising and setting of the sun behind this historic colonnade stimulated his imagination, and he fancied seeing the august shadows of Louis XIV and of Corneille and Pascal lurking about.[12]

Beyle now contemplated the prospect of living in Paris in quite a different light from that which had marked his first disappointing stay in the French capital. His adventures and misadventures in the army and his travels in Italy had given him greater self-confidence and a more independent, cosmopolitan outlook on life.

With the exception of Félix Faure, who had also renounced

the Ecole Polytechnique and was working for a bank, and two other former classmates from the Ecole Centrale, Fortuné Mante and Louis Crozet, who had both duly pursued their studies and were now in their last year at the Ecole Polytechnique, he saw few people and led a fairly well-regulated, scholarly existence. In the morning he read, took copious notes, wrote lengthy letters to his sister or to Edouard Mounier,[13] studied Italian as well as English, and worked on projects for plays. In the afternoon, he exercised by taking walks in the Tuileries Gardens, attended the public lectures at the Collège de France by the famous critic Jean-François de La Harpe, or pursued his readings at the Bibliothèque Nationale or the Bibliothèque du Panthéon (today Sainte-Geneviève). In the evening, he paid visits to his friends or acquaintances or attended the theater.

More than ever, the theater was his great passion, and it is as a playwright that he fervently hoped to make his mark and achieve an imperishable renown. Since the seventeenth century, the way for an aspiring writer to conquer the literary world was by mastering one of the classical genres, for these required imagination and loftiness in conception and virtuosity in execution and technique. Had not Voltaire obtained his first great success with a tragedy, *Oedipe?* Beyle decided to tackle the most demanding genre, tragedy in verse. His play, *Ulysse,* would pick up matters where Homer had left them after the hero's return to Ithaca.[14] But what plot could be concocted that would match in dramatic interest Ulysses's legendary adventures? Beyle racked his brains but could come up with no satisfactory solution and gave up the whole idea.

But ambition goaded him and he lacked neither a sense of purpose nor the willingness to persevere in his efforts. Patiently he dissected the plays of Corneille, Racine, Voltaire, and especially Shakespeare, who now superseded by far the French classical and neo-classical tragedians in his estimation. In his desire to appreciate fully Shakespeare's genius, he took English lessons with an Irish Franciscan friar and worked on a translation of *Hamlet.* Filled with admiration for this masterpiece, he cheerfully resolved to write his own *Hamlet!* He would reduce the number of characters to five, regularize the play according to the precepts of classical dramaturgy and, at the same time, give greater emphasis to the role of Ophelia and to the love element. Naïvely he believed that a masterpiece could be assembled with borrowed ingredients, recipes, and formulas rearranged to suit the trends and predilections of the contemporary public. In this respect, he was more faithful than he himself realized to the theory and practice of Voltaire the playwright. Not too surprisingly, however, he soon gave up his rash project of competing with the Bard. But this first-hand contact with Shakespeare's plays was to be fruitful in a different way.[15]

Turning from tragedy to comedy, Beyle launched into a systematic study of the theory and technique of comedy. He meditated on the psychological workings that produce laughter, read treatises on the subject, studied satire and irony as well as the art of caricature and, with a renewed interest in Molière, examined every facet of his art to see what useful lessons he could derive from the greatest practitioner of the genre.[16] Before long he came to the conclusion that comedy demands a profound knowledge of the human heart, a supreme skill in depicting character and combining situations, and a complete mastery of the expressive possibilities of style and language. Furthermore, great comedy has to be serious in purpose and is at its best when it comes close to tragedy. Hence Beyle's special admiration for Molière's *Le Misanthrope* and *Tartuffe*. Over the years, even after having renounced becoming another Molière, Stendhal continued to take a lively interest in everything that pertains to comedy and satire. There is no doubt that, as one of the most penetrating Stendhal scholars has so convincingly demonstrated, everything he learned in this field eventually found an application, albeit indirectly, in his novels.[17]

When it came to putting all this theoretical knowledge to practice in the actual writing of a comedy, Beyle was in trouble. One of the principal reasons for his difficulties was that he stubbornly stuck to the notion, inherited from his elders, that any work of literature destined for posterity should be written in verse form. Frequently, the exertions of several hours produced only two or three lines of verse, and their obvious awkwardness was disheartening. Nevertheless, Beyle doggedly persevered and *Letellier*, the most interesting and elaborate of these efforts at a serious comedy with a message, reveals something about the aspiring playwright's frame of mind. It presents two men, a reactionary monarchist and partisan of the Old Regime pitted against a forward-looking Republican. Beyle's Jacobin sympathies and loyalty to the Encyclopedists are obvious in his treatment of the two central characters. The idea for the play was an arresting one and testified to its author's ardent desire to adapt the theater to the new spirit of his age. In several ways it also continued the eighteenth-century approach to comedy as a serious, instructive genre, concerned with current events and ideological conflicts. Unfortunately, *Letellier* is wooden in characterization, and its form, burdened by the classic alexandrines, bereft of sparkle and humor.

Beyle did not give up his *Letellier* as easily as his other youthful projects. The unfinished manuscript of the play accompanied him throughout his peregrinations, and as late as 1812, during the Russian campaign, he managed to make a few observations and corrections on the projected play.[18]

Beyle's liberal and republican convictions were beginning to alienate him from Bonaparte's regime. As he meditated on the psychological phenomenon of laughter and its mechanism, he could not but be keenly aware of the fact that his political sympathies, so apparent in his *Letellier*, were running counter to contemporary events. On May 18, 1804, Bonaparte became Napoleon I and had himself proclaimed emperor by a subservient senate. On December 2 of the same year, in the Cathedral of Notre-Dame, he took the crown from the hands of Pope Pius VII and placed in on his own head. Beyle's idealization of Bonaparte as the supreme embodiment of human energy and will was to crystallize many years later, when the fall of the Empire and subsequent political developments would make a whole generation of writers and poets look back with nostalgia upon the Napoleonic era.

The fact that Bonaparte, whom Beyle had thus far regarded as the spiritual heir of the French Revolution and the living incarnation of its military achievements and genius, was turning himself into an imperial ruler left him in an apprehensive, perplexed frame of mind. This unease reflected on his esthetic preoccupations, for he held that true comedy had to express the ideals and aspirations of a free people and satirize unquestioned prejudices, traditions, and customs. As one who regarded himself as a potential nineteenth-century Molière, Beyle felt that it was his destiny to mock, ridicule, and attack more directly and boldly than the great seventeenth-century playwright socially nefarious types and characters.

In this respect, as in so many others, Beyle combined and synthesized the major trends of seventeenth- and eighteenth-century literary traditions. Comedy had to be, according to seventeenth-century tenets, truly amusing; but it also had to be, according to eighteenth-century ethical dictates, instructive and socially relevant. It is one of the most constant and characteristic features of Stendhal's life and career that he invariably found himself out of step with the political and esthetic trends of his time. While Napoleon was reinstating religious institutions and creating an imperial court and nobility, Beyle steadfastly clung to his ambition of writing plays suitable for a people at last freed from political oppression and religious prejudice.

Mulling over his thoughts in his room, Beyle sometimes felt overtaken by self-doubt and a general sense of futility. It was moments such as these that brought about an irresistible need to break out of his spiritual isolation. His thoughts turned, once again, to the ever unattainable Victorine. For a while, at least, she continued to occupy a special place in his affections. But his roundabout scheme of mollifying her by engaging in a heart-to-heart correspondence with her brother produced no results. Her absence combined with her persistent silence began to have their effect. For a short while, he considered resorting to dramatic measures. He would make a surprise trip to Rennes and quite simply ask M. Mounier *père* for his daughter's hand in marriage. But the folly and impracticality of such a step were obvious. Moreover, in his own mind he could not bring himself to make a lifelong commitment to a young woman whom, after all, he had only glimpsed during his Grenoble interlude. His exalted image of her spiritual perfections was perhaps a figment of his overheated imagination. His passion for Victorine Mounier, in the last analysis, had been a very cerebral, one-sided affair.

With the recognition of the highly unsatisfactory nature of this relationship came a desire to make a more tangible, less complicated conquest. Beyle began noticing the more experienced, mature women in the Paris salons where he made his social calls. One such woman was the genial, good-natured, and pretty Madeleine Rebuffel, married to a relative of the Darus and the Gagnons, and therefore within the narrow circle of people with whom he was on informal, even intimate terms. Matters were further facilitated by the fact that she was separated from her husband and occupied her own apartment in the spacious house of the Darus, on the rue de Lille. She was the mother of a vivacious, precociously coquettish daughter, Adèle, who had reached her fourteenth birthday in 1802.[19]

While enjoying the favors of Mme Rebuffel, Beyle could not help but notice the enticing charms and ways of Mlle Rebuffel. What ensued, and is so clearly reflected in the *Journal*, was a game of seduction and deception worthy of Don Juan or Valmont, Laclos's famous rake in the *Liaisons dangereuses*. Adèle allowed her "cousin" to kiss her hand and treat her with a familiarity bordering on amorous intimacy, while her mother, although jealous and suspicious, concealed her feelings behind a façade of light-hearted casualness and maternal benevolence. As for Beyle, he played his part with gusto, noting in his *Journal* the particulars of his dual strategy and fully relishing the piquancy of the situation.[20]

As for the Rebuffel ladies, they showed Beyle that love need not be an overwhelming passion that causes its victim untold suffering and anguish. When it engages the senses rather than the heart, it could be a delightful game, a pastime, and a source of immense satisfaction for one's amour-propre. Furthermore, he found in the mother, and especially in the daughter, excellent pupils of dramatic recitation. Classical tragedy was enjoying a greater vogue than ever in the salons of Paris and a favorite social diversion was to declaim scenes from the classical repertoire. Beyle noted with keen pleasure that his strong voice and emotional delivery produced a great effect upon Adèle. The young girl's fetching flirtatiousness and the tantalizing privileges she permitted Beyle to snatch from her made him believe for a while that she might extend these intimacies to their logical conclusions. As he soon found out, however, he was by no means the sole beneficiary of Adèle's roguish glances, secret kisses, and words of endearment. He realized, to his dismay, that Adèle was one of those cold and designing young women whose main endeavor in life is to toy with men's feelings, a Mme de Merteuil in the making (that superiorly Machiavellian character—the female equivalent of Don Juan—in the *Liaisons dangereuses*).

Yet, despite these reservations, Adèle's spell over Beyle's senses was so powerful that her mere physical presence caused all his doubts to vanish and invariably reawakened his desire to become her lover. Until 1808, when she contracted an advantageous marriage with Alexandre Petiet, one of Napoleon's protégés and high-ranking administrators, she continued to flirt with Beyle without granting him the ultimate favors, although she had bestowed these upon others, notably upon the dashing and ever lucky Martial Daru.

When not preoccupied with Mme and Mlle Rebuffel or engrossed in books and literary projects, Beyle assiduously haunted the Théâtre-Français, carefully studying and evaluating the performances of the noted actors and actresses of the day: Talma, unsurpassed in leading roles of Corneille and Racine and the favorite tragedian of Napoleon, Mlle Mars, then a rising star and brilliant interpreter of Molière and Marivaux who was later to specialize in the great Romantic roles, Mlle George, who shone in the French classical repertoire, Mlle Duchesnois, who transcended her physical unattractiveness with her enormous talent and whom Beyle heatedly defended against her detractors. In the controversy that opposed the young, beautiful, and highly vaunted Mlle George

(Napoleon himself was one of her admirers) and the older, less publicized Mlle Duchesnois, Beyle took up the cudgels for the latter, partly because he sincerely considered her the better of the two actresses but also out of a sense of fair play.[21]

Always immoderate and excessive in his impulses and enthusiasms, yet intent on being guided by his intellect rather than his feelings, Beyle during his second stay in Paris, presented a curious combination of fervent intenseness and cool rationalization. He was quite pleased with his belief, inherited from the *philosophes* and Ideologists, that the most complex emotional phenomena and intellectual processes can be controlled by simple, logical formulae. Similarly, the difficult art of writing comedies, which greatly preoccupied him at this time, could be mastered, he thought, through the study of great works in that genre, especially Molière, through the observation of behavioral patterns in real life, and through the application of this theoretical and practical knowledge in light of basic, general principles.

On the whole, his second stay in Paris was turning out to be a far more profitable and pleasant experience than his first contact with the French capital. The city held no more terrors for him. Eagerly he played his part, both as would-be dramatist, dandy, and Don Juan. Inevitably, he was infected by the general thirst for diversion and pleasure which always follows periods of unrest and upheaval. Despite his very limited financial resources, he was determined to dress in the latest fashion and he frequently appealed to his father for advances on his monthly allowance of 200 francs.[22]

In June of 1803, Beyle returned to Grenoble, where he remained until March 30 of the following year.[23] Perhaps the hope of persuading his father to contribute more generously to his support had something to do with this decision to stay for a while with his family. It was also more economical to live in Grenoble. But what he discovered about the state of his father's finances was disheartening. Chérubin Beyle's incorrigible love of speculation had left him, more than ever, short of liquid assets.

Much of the summer of 1803 was spent in the country house

of Claix, which had always held pleasant associations for Beyle. With his beloved mountains in the background and nature all around him, he pursued his reading and study in an atmosphere of relative serenity and tranquillity. Predictably, however, life in the provinces began to weigh on Beyle and, with the passing months, he increasingly yearned to return to Paris. In the beginning of April 1804 he was back in the capital. Instead of journeying from Grenoble to Paris by the most direct route, he had traveled by way of Geneva, which he wished to see again, probably because he hoped to recapture some of the exhilarating thoughts and emotions that had marked his first visit in that city four years earlier.[24] Spending several days in Rousseau's native town evoked nostalgic memories and everywhere he went he sensed, once more, the haunting presence of Jean-Jacques's spirit. In that mood he wrote a lengthy letter which, by its style, tone, and themes, could have been penned by Rousseau himself.[25]

VIII
Marseilles Interlude

SHORTLY AFTER HIS return to Paris, Beyle decided to take lessons in acting and elocution. The teacher he selected was Jean-Henri Dugazon, a retired actor, whose Jacobin politics on the one hand and his Old Regime gallantry with his lady pupils on the other made him a popular tutor among stage-struck youths like Beyle. It was through Dugazon that Beyle met and fell in love with a struggling young actress, Mélanie Guilbert, who had adopted the stage pseudonym of Louason.[1]

Mélanie Guilbert hailed from Caen, in Normandy, where she was born in 1780 of a typical bourgeois couple with very limited financial resources but impeccable respectability. At the age of twenty, an unhappy love affair had left her in the highly unenviable position of being an unmarried mother. Such a scandal in the staid provincial milieu of her family and entourage made it impossible for her to remain in Caen. More out of necessity than choice, she resolved to go to Paris and try her luck as an actress. To be a self-supporting, independent woman in the early nineteenth century was indeed no easy task, and the only respectable professions open to the second sex were such demeaning posts as maid or governess. No doubt, the glamor and excitement of the theater had a far greater appeal for an attractive young woman like Mélanie Guilbert. And since her reputation was ruined anyway, she had little to fear from the loose morals generally associated with theater people.

Mélanie was elegantly tall and slim, with a classically regular profile and large blue eyes. Beyle's first mention of her is dated December 31, 1804, and it merely refers to the fact that she recited passages from Racine's *Andromaque*.[2] Little by little, however, he came to look upon her as a friend, one capable of understanding the delicacy and complexity of his soul. The thought soon occurred to him that he might do worse than become emotionally attached to Mélanie. For one thing, it might cure him of his lingering and unrequited love for Victorine. For another, he hoped that he would find in Mélanie qualities of tenderness and gaiety that would make of love a happy experience. An easy intimacy was soon established which allowed long talks, promenades, and exchanges of confidences. Mélanie began to speak more freely about her background, her family, her illegitimate child, and her projects.

For the first time, Beyle fell in love with a woman who was willing to give herself to him wholeheartedly and completely. His own complicated nature and excessive timidity, however, delayed the inevitable outcome of their love affair. His peculiar mixture of sincerity and calculation, of spontaneity and duplicity oftentimes strained their otherwise happy relationship. Together they took leisurely walks in and around Paris and enjoyed many a tender tête-à-tête. Beyle was aware that his love for Mélanie lacked the intensity of what he had felt for Angela Pietragrua or Victorine Mounier, but he increasingly valued his relationship with a woman who charmed him, yet left him sufficiently clear-headed to remain in control of his thoughts and emotions.[3]

When in April of 1805, she informed him that she had been offered and had decided to accept an engagement at the Grand Théâtre in Marseilles, with a contract whose attractive terms she could not afford to ignore, he told her that he would go with her.[4] For once, however, Beyle's amorous interests and professional plans were not at odds. Living on his father's barely adequate allowance, paid rather irregularly at that, was not exactly the answer to his dreams of success and affluence. He therefore had to find another sure-fire method of achieving financial independence. It so happened that Fortuné Mante, a friend and classmate from Grenoble who had completed his commerical studies, was about to embark upon his career by associating himself with a firm in Marseilles that combined banking and the import of colonial products. The idea of becoming a banker and businessman struck Beyle as the solution to all his problems. Mante was a scion of a respected Grenoble family, and Beyle felt confident that this association would be a fruitful one.

From May 8 to May 14, Beyle and Mélanie traveled together in a crowded stagecoach from Paris to Lyons, where they parted, she to pursue her voyage to Marseilles, he to repair to Grenoble, in order to enlist financial support for his new venture. In Grenoble, disappointment awaited him. His father once more failed to be properly impressed by his calculations and plans. When he left to rejoin Mélanie in Marseilles, he was as empty-handed as before and a good deal less sanguine about his prospects in the world of business and finance.

But if being apprentice bookkeeper did not quite live up to Beyle's expectations, his devotion to Mélanie at last found its reward on July 29, as an entry in awkward English in his diary discreetly attests.[5] Until the end of December of that year the two lovers occupied adjoining rooms in the same boarding house. After work, Beyle either accompanied Mélanie to the theater, or if she did not perform that evening, helped her memorize her roles. He had also resumed working seriously on his own projects of plays, and his association with an actress revived all his ambitions as a playwright.

To his sister Pauline Beyle wrote about his new-found bliss with Mélanie, urging her to convince their father to send him badly needed funds and also asking her, if anything untoward happened to him to take care of his mistress and her little girl, whom he called either "my" or "our" daughter. Carried away by happy thoughts, he painted in his letters to his sister a glittering picture of the life they would all one day be able to lead together when he and Mante, having made their fortune, would be free to settle down with a select circle of common friends. He also assured

Pauline that she and Mélanie were meant to cherish and understand one another. Furthermore, Mante was a fellow with excellent qualities. By marrying him, Pauline would cement their relationship forever. They would all live in an elegant townhouse in Paris and entertain the intellectual and artistic luminaries of the day.[6] It was just a matter of forming a banking partnership with Mante and obtaining from their respective fathers the necessary funds for such an enterprise.

Harsh reality soon intruded upon these fond hopes and fanciful visions. Marseilles, during these hot summer months of 1805, made an unpleasant impression on Beyle. He found the surrounding countryside dry and arid and barely relieved by an occasional olive tree or by some verdure. With Mélanie he sometimes managed to escape from the stifling heat of the city proper by picnicking on the bank of a nearby stream.[7] But these outings were perforce all too rare and did not offer sufficient compensation for living in a town Beyle increasingly found barely less provincial and loathsome than his native Grenoble. He was also repelled by the Marseillais, whose single-minded pursuit of profit, boisterous earthiness, and love of pleasure struck him as vulgar and materialistic.

During the day, Beyle either sat on a high stool, working on rows of figures in a ledger, or occasionally supervised the unloading of goods from the ships or the customs operations. The firm which had hired him through Mante's recommendation, Charles Meunier and Co., which specialized in the import-export business, was not doing well at all. France was at war with England, which used her maritime superiority to enforce vigorously a blockade of her continental foe. Firms like Meunier and Co. had been in a precarious position since tension between the two countries had increased. Not long after Beyle's arrival in Marseilles, the battle of Trafalgar took place on October 21, 1805, and Nelson's victory over the allied French and Spanish fleets confirmed England's dominance of the seas and reinforced the blockade of the French ports.[8] The bustling commercial life of Marseilles came to a practical standstill.

Mante, moreover, was turning out to be a big disappointment as a person and friend. Three years older than Beyle, he was both phlegmatic by temperament and pedantic by disposition. His passive, insensitive, indolent nature, coupled with rigidity and inflexibility in his judgments, soon brought out his basic incompatibilities with his volatile, temperamental friend.

The sad economic situation of Marseilles had also affected its cultural life, and the Grand Théâtre box office was in a sorry state of affairs. In February it had to close down. In the meantime, the relationship between the two lovers had had its ups and downs. To be sure, there had been those lovely Sundays spent, in the fashion of the Marseillais, in the country. The couple had taken long walks alongside refreshing streams, relishing the quietude of grassy glades and pastoral serenity. In silent delight, Beyle had watched Mélanie bathe naked in the clear waters of the Huveaune river, a sight that reminded him of a painting which had adorned the studio of his Grenoble art teacher, M. Le Roy, and which had held special fascination for him as a boy, for it represented three naked female figures bathing in a stream with a romantically mountainous landscape in the background.[9]

As the colder weather set in with the fall, however, these outings had become fewer and fewer. Beyle came to the realization that happiness could not be a permanent state. Forced to spend their leisure time indoors, the lovers were soon prey to a mood of frustration. There were petty quarrels and mutual recriminations. Beyle made a great show of jealousy, accusing Mélanie of cultivating professionally useful relations with influential men in Marseilles. In reality, however, these accusations and denunciations were a subconscious way of covering up for his own growing disappointment with Mélanie. He had placed her on too high a pedestal, describing her as "sublime" and comparing her to Madame Roland, the heroine of the French Revolution.[10] She had never evidenced intellectual brilliance. She now struck Beyle as dullminded.[11] Only years after their liaison had ended, when a greater experience with women and people in general would give him a broader perspective on such matters, was Stendhal to appreciate more fully Mélanie's exceptional qualities of sincerity, tenderness, and devotion. It was only then that he would realize that there is an intelligence of the heart which is more difficult to measure than brain power, and that Mélanie had possessed this rare quality. Hence the infinite tenderness with which she is mentioned in Stendhal's later works, especially his autobiographical essays.[12]

As for Mélanie, she too soon became disenchanted with her stay in Marseilles. She had dreamed of great theatrical successes. Instead, she had been coolly received by the audience of the Grand Théâtre, probably because her acting style was too restrained and controlled to please the Marseillais public, which favored declamation in the grand, emotional style.

With the closing of the Grand Théâtre and the collapse of her lover's grandiose banking projects, she decided to return to Paris and to try to resume her theatrical career in the capital. She departed from Marseilles on March 1, 1806, leaving behind Beyle who, for his part, was not yet quite ready to admit defeat. He had told Mélanie that he would stay on in Marseilles for a little while and await further developments. In reality, he welcomed this separation, for by now he was eager to be free again. His initial reaction to her departure was one of relief. On May 15, 1806, he notes in his diary: "I'm beginning to find Mélanie stupid. I remember a thousand traits showing little intelligence; after her departure, immediately joy at my freedom; forty or fifty days later, pangs of regret. At present, an accurate appreciation, I believe: a great deal of friendship, even love if she gave up tyrannizing me and always complaining." [13]

After Mélanie's departure, Beyle lingered on in Marseilles, increasingly aware that the banking business, like his previous schemes and plans, was turning out to be another castle in the air. As for poor Mélanie, already so cruelly battered by life, she sadly resigned herself to making a new start on the Paris stage. What she found more difficult to accept was her lover's growing estrangement from her and what she reluctantly had to regard as his obvious desire to break with her permanently. The lovers continued to correspond for a while after their separation. Beyle's letters grew colder and more impersonal while those of Mélanie reflected her anxious, melancholy state.

It is apparent, from the tone of her plaintive, touching letters that, in this relationship, Mélanie had been the more sincerely loving of the two partners. That Beyle's own plans no longer included her, that he did not envisage tying his destiny to hers plunged her into a state of depression which made it difficult to take the necessary steps in order to reinstate herself on the Paris stage. She had to recognize that, once more, she had been too trusting and had given herself too generously. She had fully counted on a stable, permanent relationship and had lulled herself into a state of false security. Knowing how precarious his financial situation was, she even offered to share whatever earnings she would have with him until his own prospects would significantly improve.[14] In vain. To her pressing, precise questions he gave only evasive answers. But it was clear to her that he no longer loved her, that he yearned for his freedom, and that nothing would bring him back to her.

Under different circumstances, Beyle would have been touched by so much loyalty, tact, and loving understanding. But he was in an impatient, restless mood. Surfeited with love, he philosophized that the pursuit of a goal is always more exciting than its realization; that man is so perversely made that he is incapable of achieving a state of permanent felicity. He consoled himself by studying anew the masters of logic and ideology, especially Destutt de Tracy, who would help him to know himself better. For he could not but feel uneasy over his rather shabby treatment of Mélanie. But he was too preoccupied with other thoughts to examine his motives and actions. This would come at a later, more introspective time.[15]

For three months after Mélanie's departure, from the beginning of March until the end of May 1806, he stayed on in Marseilles, idle, bored, and restive. Having realized that he was not cut out for a life of commerce and placid domesticity, he once more gave serious thought to his future. It was high time to redirect his plans and energies. Ambition and a desire, subdued during the months in Marseilles, to plunge himself into action and adventure had again taken possession of him.

Napoleon's star, after such stunning victories as Austerlitz, was shining more brightly than ever. Pierre Daru, Beyle's erstwhile benefactor was now a trusted confidant of the Emperor, a recently elected member of the prestigious Institut de France, an Intendant General of the Grande Armée, and one of the most important men in France. News from Grenoble contributed to rekindling Beyle's interest in what his influential relative could accomplish for him. In his letters to his sister, he urged her to encourage their grandfather to patch things up with Pierre Daru and to bring the latter around to the idea of resuming his patronage of his young cousin. He also wrote to Martial Daru, with whom he had always enjoyed a good relationship, for he knew that he could count on him to intercede on his behalf.[16]

Gone were the days when Beyle looked upon the Emperor and his new Court with a jaundiced eye. His last misadventure had at least had the beneficial result of bringing him down to earth. He was now ready to overlook the misgivings and reservations that, as an idealistic young intellectual with revolutionary sympathies and an eighteenth-century ideology, he felt toward the Emperor and his regime. Such scruples and doubts were a luxury he could no longer afford to harbor if he seriously wished to make his mark in the world. To succeed—and he now desperately wanted to achieve success—he had to overcome those traits of his character and temperament that had thus far held him back: his impractical idealism, his inordinate pride, his impatience with boredom and mediocrity. He was determined to learn to compromise, to forsake his Rousseauistic love of sincerity, to overcome his shyness and awkwardness with people, and to think only in terms of what could further his own social advancement. His immediate goal was to get back into Pierre Daru's good graces.

As for Pierre Daru, he understandably did not immediately agree to let bygones be bygones and to take once more under his wing a young man who had already caused him annoyance and vexation. He had, besides, far too many responsibilities and duties to devote much time to the case of his floundering young cousin. Finally, however, after Dr. Gagnon himself, a highly respected member of the clan whose opinion continued to have great weight with the Darus, repeatedly intervened on behalf of his grandson, family loyalty prevailed.[17] Pierre Daru relented and, without making a definite promise or commitment, indicated that he would endeavor to find for Henri an appropriate position.

Meantime, Beyle decided that, since nothing held him back in Marseilles, he might as well go back to Grenoble while awaiting further news from the Darus. With Mante, his erstwhile banking partner, and a few other Marseilles friends and acquaintances, he dined and strolled through the city and watched a fine sunset from a nearby height. For a while, he pensively gazed at the blockaded port and the blue Mediterranean he was about to leave.[18] On May 24, he was on his way to Grenoble, his mind happily occupied with pleasing thoughts and images conjured up by the prospect of the important career—and its rewards—that awaited him in Paris.

IX

Adventures in Germany and Austria

WITH BEYLE'S DEPARTURE from Marseilles, a new phase in his life and career opened up before him. Wholeheartedly he threw himself into the general current that was sweeping over Napoleonic Europe. Powerful forces, originally unleashed by the French Revolution and affecting whole nations, were at work. Opportunities had multiplied for the energetic and the daring. Talent and ability could be rewarded in the new bureaucracy created by the Napoleonic regime. It helped immeasurably, however, if one had the right connections, and Beyle knew that his moment had come, that he had to make the most of it or be bypassed and forgotten. Deliberately, he embarked upon the task to reshape his temperament, which was too contemplative and introspective to suit the needs of an age of action and upheaval.

After approximately one month with his family in Grenoble, during which he experienced the novel pleasure of agreeing with his father on what would be best for him with respect to his plans for the future, he left for Paris on July 1, 1806. There he renewed his easy relationship with Martial Daru. The summer was spent by the two young men in common pleasant pursuits: evenings at the theater, social visits, outings to such places of interest as the cottage once inhabited by Rousseau, the famed Hermitage, on the es-

136

tate of Montmorency. After several sentimental, bitter-sweet re-
unions with Mélanie, there was even a renewal of their
relationship, at least on a physical level. After an unsuccessful attempt to launch her career at the Comédie-Française, Mélanie
went on tour in French-occupied Europe, ending up in Russia,
where she met and married a Russian nobleman and general
named de Barcoff.[1]

Beyle's principal goal was now to convince Pierre Daru of the
seriousness of his desire to become a solid, respectable member of
the new establishment. Gone were the days when he dreamed of
leading a carefree life in Paris. In order to make himself more acceptable in the best circles, he followed Martial Daru's example
and had himself initiated as a Freemason, and became a member
of the exclusive Sainte-Caroline Lodge, to which his cousin belonged and which had recently been founded by no less a personage than Joseph Bonaparte, the brother of the Emperor.
When, no doubt as a result of Martial's intercessions, Beyle was at
last invited to visit Pierre Daru in his home on Sundays during
that summer of 1806, he was duly impressed. So much so that his
timidity came back and once more paralyzed him, making it impossible for him to question his gracious but evasive host about the
latter's plans for his future.[2]

Beyle's shyness was at first heightened by the disquieting presence of Pierre Daru's handsome young wife. In the summer of
1802, Pierre, at the age of thirty-five, had married Alexandrine-
Thérèse Nardot, sixteen years his junior and Beyle's contemporary.[3] A striking portrait of her by David immortalizes her regular,
wholesome, somewhat motherly features and pleasant smile. It
shows the good-looking, pleasantly buxom young matron in a low-
cut, Empire gown, her brown hair and eyes and her creamy complexion set off by a headdress of flowers and a magnificent parure
of emeralds and diamonds.

Countess Daru had a sunny, vivacious temperament. A bit
on the plump side and somewhat short of stature, she compensated for these slight defects with her expressive eyes, fetching
smile, and lively, friendly disposition. Beyle noticed that his host-

ess seemed to like him and when, overcoming his timidity, he displayed his quickness of mind in humorous repartees and shafts of wit, her sparkling brown eyes fastened on him with pleasure and approval. No doubt, she spoke well of him to her stern husband, for the latter began showing greater friendliness toward his young relative.

While Beyle was spending his time in agreeable pursuits, political events were accelerating their pace. Rumors of renewed war with Prussia filled the capital. On October 16, 1806, two days after Napoleon's victory over the Prussian army at Jena, Beyle left Paris with the younger Daru, who had been appointed intendant in charge of the finances of the French-occupied duchy of Brunswick.[4] Beyle's own functions were not defined; he had merely been told to accompany Martial and to assist him in his tasks. In this respect, his position was not unlike the one he had in 1800 when, in civilian clothes and without rank or commission, he had followed the Grande Armée in its conquest of Italy. He was once more a supernumerary in the Grande Armée as he had been six years earlier. Now, however, he felt better prepared for the role he would be called to play and he was determined to show his mettle to Pierre Daru.

Henri and Martial reached Berlin on the 27th of October, just in time to witness the triumphant entry into the city and victory parade of Napoleon and his army. Large crowds of Germans watched in glum silence the marching soldiers and the Emperor on his white steed. These onlookers were in marked contrast to the exuberant Italians who had so warmly greeted the victorious French in Milan.[5] On the 29th of October, Beyle received his official assignment: he was to be Provisional Deputy War Commissar in Brunswick, under the orders of Martial. The next two years would be spent in Brunswick. In 1807, Beyle was finally given the full title of War Commissar. At the end of the previous year, he had been sent on a mission to Paris about which little is known, except that it involved the war administration. His services were evidently deemed satisfactory, for in the beginning of 1808, he was entrusted with a more important assignment (left vacant by Martial

Daru who had departed for Spain): intendant of the imperial domains in the former duchy of Brunswick, recently annexed by Napoleon to the kingdom of Westphalia.[6]

He had at last succeeded in gaining a position of authority and power. That he derived a sense of pride and satisfaction from the significant role he had been called to play in the great Napoleonic epic is made amply evident by his letters, both official and personal, of that period.

The town of Brunswick was unlike anything Beyle had seen before. Its quaint old houses with their brightly colored, steeply slanted tile roofs and gaily decorated walls, its narrow but neat streets opening out into squares with their whimsical statues and ornate small fountains—all these naïvely fanciful features of German architecture were completely new to Beyle, who found them more curious and quaint than admirable.[7]

But always more interested in people than in buildings, Beyle spent much of his free time studying the natives and their customs. In general, he had little regard for the Germans, and those with whom he came into contact confirmed him in his belief that most were unenlightened and backward. As a disciple of the eighteenth-century *philosophes* and their liberal cosmopolitism, he was put off by the German provincial, tradition-bound ways, which he deemed feudal and primitive. Like so many of his contemporaries, he was reluctant to admire anything that smacked of Gothicism. Yet Brunswick and its surroundings were steeped in an atmosphere that strongly reminded him of a period he viewed through the prejudices of the Age of Enlightenment: "I don't know why," he wrote to his sister, "the Middle Ages are tied in my mind to the idea of Germany. The peasants in the Brunswick region still wear exactly the same costume as in Charlemagne's time." Yet he could be touched by the melancholy sight of a snow-covered old Gothic church and its surrounding wintry landscape. His letters to his sister testify to an awareness of a new range of perceptions and feelings. Images and symbols of a mysterious and tender quality invaded his consciousness. To his sister he wrote: "The Germans have perhaps a very touching poetry." And it was quite possibly under the impact of this new kind of poetry that he took notice of melancholy spectacles: "I have seen today a beautiful image of death in a young raven that fell and expired in the waters of the Ocker, a stream that flows through Brunswick. . . . I saw life desert that poor raven." [8]

While he thoroughly enjoyed the new importance he had acquired and mentioned, with obvious satisfaction, the fact that he was called *Monseigneur* as well as *Monsieur l'intendant*, and that French generals paid him courtesy visits, he had moments of nostalgia when he wished he was in Paris again, wearing a threadbare coat but free to come and go as he pleased, his mind filled with thoughts of love and literary plans. Monotony and boredom had all too quickly invaded his existence in Brunswick. And as always, when reality had failed to live up to his expectations, he turned to his sister for solace and comfort. Interestingly, it was when he had at last achieved the kind of success he had always dreamed of that he experienced the most acute feelings of melancholy and nostalgia, as is evidenced by his letters to his sister which had never been so filled with love and concern for her future and well-being. He urged her to marry, for a woman could not find any kind of happiness outside matrimony in contemporary society. He reminisced about their childhood in Grenoble and gave her all manner of advice of a practical nature which would help her survive in a world indifferent or hostile to women. [9]

Beyle's efforts at learning the German language and literature were only fitful at best and certainly not sufficiently sustained to give him a meaningful insight into the features of German mores and culture which Mme de Staël would soon extol in her controversial and epoch-making book *De l'Allemagne* (1810). Since he had recently determined to overcome his Rousseauistic sensibility as being injurious to his chances of success in the world, he was wary of the *Sturm und Drang* movement and the tormented romanticism of such works as Goethe's *Sorrows of Young Werther* or Schiller's dramas. Paradoxically, it was during his stay in Germany that Beyle assiduously perfected his knowledge of English and diligently pursued his study of Shakespeare. "I receive requests for favors, I write letters, I scold my secretaries, go to ceremonial dinners, take horseback rides and read Shakespeare," he reported to his sister, and wishing to pay her a compliment, he wrote: "You are a Portia in my eyes." [10]

While the German winters had a certain appeal for him, on the whole he complained to his sister about the rigors of the Northern climate. Gazing at the frosty, wind-swept scenery surrounding him, he fondly lingered over his memories of sunny Milan, its lilting music and spirited women, especially Angela Pietragrua, who now more than ever incarnated for him the very essence of womanhood. Interestingly, while the memory of the other women he had loved seemed to fade in his mind, Angela's face, form, and voice, haunted him on many a lonely winter evening. When he did go out, more often than not he was bored, for he found the local aristocrats and burghers slow-witted, excessively formal and stiff and too imbued with their own importance, too solemn in their speech and manner to be stimulating company. How different from the Paris salons, where he could be witty and tell risqué jokes and anecdotes without fearing to offend anyone! [11]

On one or two occasions, there were clashes between the German population and the French authorities. Beyle's description of one such bloody encounter, which he personally witnessed and during which he saw French soldiers shoot into the crowd and charge it with drawn swords, is curiously detached in tone. Beyle observed the dramatic scene as an artist would look at a painting, noting a magnificent full moon shining down on the street and its frantic, screaming mob. [12] But Beyle's approach in depicting this scene—matter-of-fact and spare yet vivid and with a touch of poetry as well as gallows humor—foreshadows quite clearly his later technique as a novelist when dealing with battle scenes.

Beyle's rise in the administrative cadre of the imperial regime was not due entirely to his family connections. A tireless worker himself, Pierre Daru exacted a great deal from his associates and subordinates, and even more from his relative and protégé, lest he be accused of nepotism. While finding his duties not exactly inspiring, Beyle, for his part, acquitted himself of his official tasks with conscientiousness, diligence, and even resourcefulness. As his responsibilities and experience grew, he demonstrated a real talent and ability as an administrator. His constant study of human nature and psychology bore fruit, for it gave him useful insights on how to exercise authority with skill and dexterity. With his growing self-assurance and the prestige attached to his position, he shed the last remnants of the timidity and gaucherie that had plagued him for so long. He was treated with deference and respect in the best social circles of Brunswick, and while he found the Germans he frequented too sluggish on the uptake and incapable of emulating the sallies of his quick, satiric mind, he took some pleasure in attending the glittering balls and gala functions that brought together the local notables and the ranking French officers and important officials.

To escape from the pressures of his duties and from the constant threat of boredom, Beyle went on frequent excursions and hunting trips to the nearby woods, stopping off at rustic outdoor cafés where he could meet and flirt with buxom, fresh-complexioned Fräuleins of the lower classes. At one of these open-air cafés with a Tivoli-type garden enlived by an orchestra, a short distance from the town and named the Green Huntsman, he heard Mozart for the first time. It was a warm, soft summer evening, and seated at a wooden outdoor table under a lofty elm, he was charmed by the composer's gentle, elegant music, so perfectly in harmony with the setting. Cimarosa had thus far been his favorite composer. Soon Mozart, especially his operas, would rank and rival with the Italian musician in his affections.[13] As for the evenings at the Green Huntsman, they became indelibly etched in his consciousness, for as Le Chasseur Vert, the outdoor café and its musicians and picturesque décor reappear in Stendhal's fictional works, in scenes of love and tenderness in Lucien Leuwen and The Pink and the Green.[14]

To keep himself intellectually occupied, Beyle embarked upon new literary projects. History as a genre now tempted him, and he began gathering materials for a study of the duchy of Brunswick as well as for a history of the War of the Spanish Suc-

cession. He also took a keen interest in Pauline's impending marriage to François Périer-Lagrange, a Grenoble neighbor who, like
his father, was a cloth merchant who had recently invested in an
important piece of real estate near the town, the château of Thuellin and its surrounding land. Périer-Lagrange was a good-natured,
likeable man, and Beyle obviously thought that he would be an
ideal husband for Pauline. To his future brother-in-law he wrote
friendly, affectionate letters in which his concern for his sister's
well-being and happiness is apparent.[15] On May 25, 1808, at the
age of twenty-two, Pauline became Madame François Périer-
Lagrange, and Beyle breathed a sigh of relief. He had recently
been preoccupied with his sister's fate, as is evidenced by his letters
to her, for he had been fearful that her sensitive, idealistic, and
proud nature, so akin to his own, would make her unfit for a normal role in contemporary society. His main fear, where Pauline
was concerned, was that she would be doomed to spinsterhood and
become another Aunt Elisabeth, or worse still, another Aunt Séraphie, that demon of his childhood who had once been an attractive, desirable young woman. After her marriage, he gently chided
her for not writing to him: "I can't get accustomed to not receiving
your letters. I am well aware that in marrying, one sacrifices half
of one's friendship for friends; but I want my half and you give me
nothing."[16] Unfortunately for Pauline, her husband's shrewdness
and business sense left a great deal to be desired; his pleasant
disposition could not very long hide the fact that he was a rather
mediocre person with limited capacities, and before long his business ventures, especially his heavy investment in the Thuellin
property, were dangerously straining his finances.

Beyle had become friendly with some of the oldest and most
aristocratic families in Brunswick, notably the Münchhausens, the
Strombecks, the Boethmers, and the Griesheims. He was invited
to their country estates and castles, supper parties, balls, outings,
and hunting expeditions. He dressed like a dandy and took great
pains with his clothes and appearance. The members of these ancient families all spoke fluent French and could appreciate Gallic
wit and liveliness. It was in this very exclusive Brunswick high so-

ciety that Beyle felt most at ease. As always, his attention focused on the women. One in particular soon struck him with her superb good looks and aristocratic charm. Wilhelmina von Griesheim, born into one of the aristocratic German families and the daughter of a general, was, as befits a northern beauty, blonde, fair-skinned, and blue-eyed. Beyle called her Mina or Minette and tried in vain to win her heart.

Mina was about to be married, and while she allowed Beyle to flirt with her, to court and amuse her, she kept him at a respectful distance. Beyle's passionate feelings had to be tamed in view of the circumstances. Soon a coquettish game, a playful, amorous stratagem of hide and seek between two sophisticated people, was established, and Beyle even tried to arouse Mina by giving her a rival in the person of another charming young lady of high birth who was also her friend, a Fräulein von Treuenfels. But Mina skilfully eluded all his attempts at seduction. He realized that if she was one of the most fascinating and beautiful women he had known, she was also one who made him waste a considerable amount of time. He found a measure of consolation with more humble German Fräuleins, such as Charlotte Knabelhuber, who were willing to satisfy his sexual needs without making unreasonable demands.[17]

It was also during his stay in Brunswick that Beyle, forgetting his ardent republicanism, decided that his career would benefit if his name was preceded by the noble particle de. With an aplomb worthy of Voltaire and Beaumarchais, who had similarly ennobled themselves through this procedure, he simply had himself called "Monsieur de Beyle," a form he held onto until the fall of the Empire. To Pauline whom he asked to send a print of the family coat of arms (which was doubtful at best), he justified his sudden interest in such matters by saying that Germans attached great importance to these trifles.[18]

All in all, despite occasional bouts of depression and boredom, Beyle's stay in Brunswick was one of the pleasantest times in his life, thanks to the diversions with the local nobles and the gemütlich if somewhat flat ambience of the burgher town of

Brunswick. With the exception of Mina von Griesheim, whose name would consistently appear in *Henry Brulard* alongside those he had truly loved but had not possessed, German women would always be evoked with a touch of humor and casual condescension.

Beyle's sojourn in Brunswick not only made his entry into the world of aristocracy possible, an experience that completed his alienation from his bourgeois origins, it also broadened his human outlook. For the first time, he had to deal with men from a position of authority. He now felt himself fully a man of the world.

After the defeat of Prussia and the Peace of Tilsit in July 1807, the Austrians attempted to reopen war against France. Each Napoleonic victory brought about new movements of men and matériel, necessitating a constant reorganization of the administrative cadres to which Beyle now firmly belonged. After two years in Brunswick, he was beginning to get restless when, in the beginning of November 1808, he received the order to return to Paris and await further instructions there. With eager anticipation he sped back to the French capital where, for four months, he gave himself over to his favorite pursuits. Since Martial Daru had been assigned to Spain, where Beyle expected to rejoin him before long, Spanish lessons were in order. Beyle also regularly called at the home of Pierre Daru, where Alexandrine received him with warm cordiality and a kindness that prompted him to play a role he relished, that of the assiduous, attentive admirer. He was beginning to become seriously enamored with the Countess and seemed totally oblivious to the loyalty he owed his protector.

The Austrian campaign was about to begin; on March 28, 1809, Beyle was ordered to Strasbourg. There, with the other War Commissars, he was to hold himself at the disposal of Pierre Daru and await further directives. On April 12, he was commanded to set out for Vienna. For a month he slowly made his way to the Austrian capital in the wake of the Grande Armée. It was by no means a leisurely, uneventful voyage. War Commissars had been assigned to duties that brought them close to the battleground, for they had to insure the subsistence, requisition, and billeting of the troops and secure temporary quarters as well as medical facilities for the wounded. The French army was engaged in a difficult campaign which was to culminate in the Battle of Wagram, on July 6, 1809, one of Napoleon's most brilliant victories.

Beyle, who traveled immediately behind the front lines, witnessed the scenes of horror and devastation that battles always leave in their wake. This was his first direct contact with the full extent of war and bloodshed. His experience of military action in Italy had been, on the whole, secondhand, and even the crossing of the Saint Bernard Pass had brought him only fleetingly under enemy fire. War, thus far, had meant the glamor of adventure, the exhilaration of coming close to the unknown, of facing danger, and of testing one's courage. Now he saw the other side of the picture: the desolate spectacle of a battlefield on the morrow of a fierce military engagement; the villages laid waste, the dead and wounded, the debris of matériel cluttering burned-out fields in helter-skelter fashion.

Showing little concern for his personal safety and well-being, Beyle accomplished his difficult, exhausting tasks with energy and dispatch, going without sleep for days on end. Not everything he saw was war and carnage. Between battle scenes, there were picturesque villages, lovely landscapes, green forests, and lofty mountains. Springtime was evident everywhere. Whenever time permitted, Beyle jotted down impressions and descriptions of what he saw in his letters and especially in his diary. Gone was the detachment with which he had thus far approached scenes of violence and bloodshed. The sight of corpses, both French and German, burned beyond recognition and piled up in heaps gave him nausea; perhaps even more moving were those dead soldiers who seemed to be merely sleeping or whose youthful, handsome features still retained an appearance of life.[19]

On May 13, Vienna capitulated and opened its doors to Napoleon and his army, and an elated Beyle rode into the Austrian capital with the victors. The legendary charm of Vienna soon worked its magic upon him. Mozart's music, which he had discovered in Brunswick, could be fully savored here. With a delight equal to that experienced when he first heard Cimarosa in Italy, he listened to Mozart's *Don Juan*. Joseph Haydn had recently died, and in his honor all the musicians of the city gathered and performed Mozart's requiem, an occasion that drew a large crowd, including Beyle in full military regalia.[20]

On July 6, the date of the Battle of Wagram, Beyle who had fallen ill, partly as a result of his recent exertions and partly because of a flare-up of the illness he had contracted in Italy, was confined to a chaise longue and unable to take part in the evacuation of the wounded, thereby missing one of the most awesome spectacles of the Napoleonic wars. On the whole, however, despite bouts of fever and dizzy spells which caused him recurring discomfort throughout the summer of 1809, he was in good spirits and willingly yielded to the sophisticated, romantic ambience of Vienna, his mind occupied with thoughts of love and music. After experiencing so directly the horrors and exhaustions of war, he was more eager than ever to savor life fully and, as might be expected, he took a lively interest in the alluring Viennese women. One of these, whose identity has come down to us only by the nickname of Babet, responded to his advances, but while she aroused his amorous feelings, she never stirred a deeper passion.[21]

Martial Daru had been called back from Spain and Pierre had also arrived in Vienna, where Alexandrine rejoined him in October. With the Countess' reappearance on the scene, Beyle once again became her constant companion and cavalier servant. Pierre Daru was always away, working harder than ever on the details of the negotiations which were to result in the Treaty of Vienna as well as on the impending marriage of the Emperor (who had finally decided to divorce Josephine) with the Archduchess Marie-Louise of Austria.

Beyle escorted Alexandrine on excursions and promenades through the Prater and the Wiener Wald. They went to the theater and opera and pursued their intimate if ambiguous relationship. Alexandrine openly showed her preference for Beyle as a companion and guide in the large, strange city. These flattering marks of interest coming from a desirable, handsome young woman aroused his highest hopes and expectations. When in an intimate tête-à-tête, which happened not infrequently, she allowed him to assume a tone of tender gallantry, and there were exchanges of confidences. Conveniently putting out of his mind the fact that she was his protector's wife and the mother of several children, Beyle liked to think that she had not yet known true passion, for how could she, a still youthful, lively woman with a zest for the pleasures of life, love her elderly taskmaster of a husband? He was soon convinced that he had only to declare himself to win the Countess' affections and become her lover. But his timidity, which invariably paralyzed his will when his feelings were truly involved, prevented him from being more than the ardent, respectful admirer.

Alexandrine Daru left Vienna with her husband on November 20, heading back to Paris. As a melancholy Beyle noted in his diary, just before stepping into the carriage she had turned around and kissed "her dear cousin" goodbye, and it seemed to him that her hurried but tender embrace had expressed something more than mere affection; and he chided himself for failing to put into practice the rules of his strategy of amorous conquest.[22] As a compensation no doubt, he would later endow most of his fictional heroes with a determination and aggressiveness in love which he himself possessed only in theory.

Soon after Alexandrine's departure, Beyle also left Vienna. The city, now entering the chilly winter months, was being deserted by the French and looked forlorn with its naked trees and empty avenues and streets. Beyle was eager to be in Paris once more, partly to be reunited with Alexandrine and also because he expected and wished to be transferred to Spain. After a fortnight in Linz, he was back in the French capital. A new year, 1810, had just been ushered in, and Beyle settled down to a new round of social activities while confidently expecting further benefactions from a man whose wife he was now more resolved than ever to conquer.

X

The Taste of Success

WITH BEYLE'S RETURN to Paris, in January 1810, the brightest and most successful period of his life was about to begin. Eagerly he resumed his courtship of Countess Daru and organized his existence in the capital as befits a dandy and important personage. Ambition was still his foremost passion and he took all the necessary steps to further his career in Napoleon's cadre of talented, eager young men who were shaping the Empire. The nucleus of this administrative structure was the Council of State, composed of three hundred Auditors selected from among the most capable officials. One of the most interesting features of the Napoleonic regime, created by decree as early as 1803, was that of the Auditors. These were the most talented young men from the old nobility and higher bourgeoisie. From the original sixteen nominated in 1803 they grew to sixty in 1809 and three hundred in 1810.[1] The Auditors benefited from a number of privileges and advantages and were strongly supported by Napoleon, who took an interest in them and encouraged them to display ability and independence of mind.

This favored position as a higher civil servant in Napoleon's governmental structure, with all its attendant honors and opportunities, soon struck Beyle as a most enviable and desirable rank, far more preferable to the continuation of his duties as War Commissar in some occupied foreign land or near the chaos of the front. As an Auditor, he would earn a handsome income, frequent the most exclusive social circles, eventually obtain a title of nobility, and be in a good position to marry into wealth and aristocracy.

Count Pierre Daru no longer expected to be sent to Spain and Beyle quickly gave up his former project of serving there himself. How much more pleasant was life in Paris! The Count was finally well disposed toward his young cousin, for the latter had at last convincingly demonstrated his reliability and seriousness of purpose. To be sure, their relationship remained impersonal and somewhat strained, but Pierre Daru was now certain that Henri was no longer the scatterbrained youth who had caused him so much trouble in Italy. Consequently, on August 1, 1810, Beyle read with exultation an official letter notifying him of his appointment as Auditor of the Council of State.[2] Napoleon had signed the decree adding one hundred and thirty-four new auditorships to the Council of State, and Henri Beyle was among those selected for this high post. On August 22 of the same year, moreover, he was named Inspector of the Accounts, Buildings, and Furniture of the Crown, a responsibility that involved the supervision of the Palaces of Versailles and Fontainebleau and the inventory of the Louvre, renamed Musée Napoléon.[3]

Beyle looked upon his success as the well-earned reward for four years of patient and careful planning and strategy. By dint of effort and cunning, he had managed to win his demanding, punctilious cousin over to his side. He could now savor the fruit of his toils and live on a scale commensurate with his dreams.

He hastened to set himself up in an elegant flat in a fashionable district of the Right Bank, near the Place de la Concorde and the Tuileries Gardens. He worked in an office with a superb view over the tree-lined alley of the Invalides Esplanade and extending as far as the woods of Meudon,[4] a view that made the hours spent at the desk more pleasant, for Beyle needed the proximity of a natural setting in one form or another to feel happy.

His official work, however, was not overly demanding. In the afternoon, he made courtesy calls to the right persons and he spent his evenings at the theater or the opera. With his new position came the usual unmistakable signs of social success and importance: "People I hardly knew pay me visits. Every evening I cull at least sixty smiles more than three months ago." [5] Blithely disregarding the extremely precarious state of his finances, he set up a household as he felt should befit a personage of his rank and dignity, hiring two servants and acquiring personal vehicles of transportation: a light cabriolet for his daily use and a carriage with coachman for the more formal occasions.

A special uniform went with the rank of Auditor. Beyle had his made by the most fashionable tailor in Paris: it was a formal suit of coat and trousers of blue velvet embroidered with blue silk and adorned with a sash. It was worn with a plumed hat; a sword was also de rigueur. With his short and portly build, Beyle must have cut a somewhat incongruous figure in this elaborate outfit, and his cousin Martial good-naturedly teased him about his dandy's taste for flashy clothes. Beyle, for his part, however, put great store by sartorial elegance, hoping to gain thereby feminine approval and admiration.

His duties frequently enabled him to combine business with pleasure. There were inspection tours of Fontainebleau and Versailles. There were also frequent supervisory visits to the Louvre, an experience that deepened Beyle's appreciation of the plastic arts. His taste, in these matters, however, reflected his predilection for the High Italian Renaissance and the French classical painters of the seventeenth century. All his life, he remained impervious to the Dutch and Flemish schools. He praised to the sky Raphael's idealized portraits and suave Madonnas, admired Leonardo, Correggio, and Titian, approved of Poussin and Lorrain, but found Rubens' female figures vulgar in their lusty fleshiness and had little to say about Rembrandt.

Stendhal's artistic criteria would change very little over the years: he judged a painting on the basis of its subject-matter, literary and psychological content, and purity of design and line. He was never able to appreciate a composition for its purely painterly values. For him an artist's excellence depended upon his ability to represent the human passions by means of attitudes, gestures, and facial expressions. Hence his preference for those masters who had focused on the human figure and on what is called "historical painting," which portrays famous episodes from the Bible, the New Testament, literary or political history in compositions that reveal human character in moments of stress or high drama. When he undertook to write a *History of Painting in Italy* (1817), Leonardo's *Last Supper* became the focal point of his concern with psychological content and tension and with the portrayal of contrasting expressions and attitudes.

Beyle had embarked upon his new existence firmly resolved not to allow anything to deter him from securing for himself a solid position in the world and from pursuing his search for personal happiness. Two obstacles, however, still stood in the way of achieving his goal: the lack of financial independence and the still unfulfilled need for a loving female companion. In his desire to make an impression in the right quarters, Beyle had spent recklessly and he was now in debt, a most embarrassing and humiliating circumstance for one who, like him, looked with disdain upon money matters and found it extremely irksome to have to devote a great deal of time and energy to scheme and borrow and write repeatedly to his sister and even to his brother-in-law in order to mollify his father through these sympathetic mediators.[6] As always, however, his appeals fell on deaf ears.

His longing for a young woman who would be more accessible than Alexandrine Daru, on the other hand, was fairly easily satisfied. A man in his position was entitled, almost obligated, to have an official mistress. And where could he find a suitable, attractive person if not in the world of the theater and opera, where aspiring and eager young girls would welcome such an opportunity?

Beyle's choice fell upon Angélina Bereyter, a member of the Opéra-Bouffe, which was part of the Théâtre Italien. She was pretty and had a lively, cheerful disposition as well as a pleasing singing voice. Before long, she shared Beyle's apartment and they lived in a quasi-matrimonial state. Her even temper, her eagerness to please her lover, and her compliance made her a highly satisfactory companion and a very good lover. A competent musician, she

sang for him his favorite arias by Mozart and Cimarosa.[7] Thanks
to her sunny presence, Beyle felt for the first time that he had a
real home, and her loyalty and attentiveness were a source of keen
gratification; she appealed both to his sensuality and to his amour-
propre. That he found this arrangement a convenient one is borne
out by the fact that, for the ensuing three years, until the fall of
the Empire in 1814, he maintained his relationship with her, at
least whenever he was in Paris.

Yet, of all the women who played a significant part in his life
Angélina Bereyter is the one who least appealed to those deep,
complex emotions that make up romantic love, at least as Stendhal conceived this passion. From his comments in his diary, correspondence, and later autobiography, it is obvious that, from the
outset, he looked upon her as no more than a charming, easy-going mistress whose main purpose was to fulfill his need for sexual
pleasure and for diversion and companionship. Unfortunately for
her, she was not sufficiently haughty, demanding, and unpredictable to satisfy his subconscious desires and complexes. Yet she was
far from uncultured or unintelligent and may well have been more
worthy of love than some of the women for whom he pined so desperately.

Beyle was pleased to have Angélina Bereyter around whenever it proved feasible, but never missed her when they were separated. When, in his *Henry Brulard,* he listed the names of the important women in his life, he included hers but added this rather
cruel qualification: "Angélina, whom I never loved (Bereyter)." [8]
Perhaps because her character was too predictable, because living
with her had quickly become a convenient habit, she failed to
evoke in him those feelings of anxiety and longing without which
there cannot be true passion.

At the end of May 1811 Beyle spent a week at the château of
Bècheville, the country estate of the Darus on the banks of the
Seine near Meulan. The time had come, Beyle thought, to declare himself to Alexandrine. Once more, he deployed in his mind
an elaborate scene, preparing in advance his every word and
move. As might be expected, reality did not live up to his strategy.

Taking advantage of a tête-à-tête, he seized her hand and breath-
lessly whispered that, whereas she had only had friendship for
him, he loved her passionately. To which the apparently stunned
and embarrassed countess replied by protesting the sincerity of her
friendship and by gently but firmly advising him to keep their relationship on a proper level.[9]

After this episode, Pierre Daru himself seemed to have at last
suspected something, for he spoke to Beyle with distant hauteur
and once or twice gave him fixed looks that made him feel uneasy.
But the Count was too discerning a judge of human character and
too loyal a relative to ruin his young cousin's career because of
pique or jealousy. Invitations to the Daru home, however, became
scarcer, and when Beyle, by now restless, bored, and eager for a
change of scenery, asked for a leave of absence to visit his family
in Grenoble, his request was promptly granted. Italy, and especially Milan, rather than Grenoble, were uppermost on his mind.

On August 29, 1811, Beyle happily set out for Milan. Before
his departure, he had paid a courtesy farewell visit to Alexandrine
and had done his best to comfort the tearful Angélina Bereyter.
After a ten-day journey by coach through Montbard, Dijon, and
Geneva, Beyle set foot once more on Italian soil.

There is nothing like a change of scenery to uplift one's spirits
after a disillusioning experience. Following Beyle's rebuff at the
hands of Alexandrine Daru, a return visit to his beloved Italy was a
particularly welcome opportunity to renew himself spiritually. His
expectations were more than fulfilled when, after more than a ten-
year interval, he found himself seated in a box of the Scala. A rush
of memories, emotions, and sensations surged in his consciousness, filling him with nostalgia and delight. After all that had happened to him since his first stay in Italy, it was somehow reassuring and comforting to know that, in Milan at least, life went on as
before. So little had changed there and, in the last analysis, he
too, despite all his adventures and disappointments, had retained
the essential traits, beliefs, and hopes that had characterized the
eager, timid youth who, in 1800, had found in Milan the earthly
answer to his dreams and aspirations. To his sister he confided:

"Milan offers me very tender memories. I have spent there the sweet years of my adolescence. It is here that I have loved the most. It is here too that my character was formed. I realize every day that my heart is Italian. . . . This wild love of gaiety and music, this freedom of mores, this art of enjoying life with serenity, etc., all this is the character of the Milanese." [10]

Ever since he had left Paris, Beyle had thought and dreamed of beautiful Angela Pietragrua for whom, as a shy and inexperienced lover, he had sighed in vain. He had never forgotten her during the intervening years and, in spite of other amorous involvements, would now and then evoke her full, voluptuous figure and dark, expressive eyes. No wonder then that, one of the first things he did upon arriving in Milan was to rush over to her father's shop near the Piazza del Duomo. With a trembling hand he opened the door and hesitantly asked to see Angela. When she emerged from the living quarters, he was once more struck by her regal beauty. If she had lost some of her sprightliness, she was now more majestic and handsome than ever, her facial features more firm and forceful, her manner more assured and self-confident. Having introduced himself as Beyle, the friend of Lieutenant Joinville (her lover in 1800), he was more amused than peeved when she at first did not recognize him. [11]

Despite this initial contretemps, an easy, warm relationship was soon established. To be sure, Angela, in addition to her husband, also had admirers and lovers. But she quickly managed to have tender, intimate conversations with her French visitor, either in her box at the Scala or in her father's house. Between visits to Angela, who had by now rekindled his old passion, Beyle set about rediscovering Milan and its artistic treasures. His recent experience as Inspector of the Louvre had deepened his appreciation of art, and he was especially eager to look at paintings and to study his favorite masters, Leonardo and Correggio.

Angela's full-blown beauty and generous proportions not only reminded Beyle of the female figures he admired in Italian paintings, she also bore a certain physical resemblance to Alexandrine Daru to the extent that both incarnated a motherly type of woman-

hood that must have had irresistible appeal for one who, like
Beyle, had experienced the trauma of losing a mother at a very
early age. Unlike Countess Daru, however, Angela Pietragrua did
not keep her enthusiastic admirer at a safe distance. Taking the
initiative, the knowledgeable Angela relieved her lover of the necessity of engaging in a long, elaborate courtship. In less that two
weeks she was his mistress. But this easy victory somehow damp-
ened his love for her. As always, in order to love a woman passionately, Beyle needed the ingredients of mystery, suspense, uncertainty, and distance. Milan itself, after the initial excitement of
the first few days, failed to retain his interest and to quiet his restlessness. He was now eager to take advantage of his leave to acquaint himself with other Italian towns and their artistic treasures.

On September 22, 1811, Beyle was in a coach rattling away
on the road to Modena.[12] In order to prepare himself properly for
this artistic tour, he had equipped himself with Vasari's famous
Lives of the Painters, with the *Letters from Italy* by the eighteenth-
century magistrate and peripatetic scholar Charles de Brosses, and
with Winckelmann's epoch-making *History of the Art of Antiquity*.

In Bologna Beyle visited the famed university, ancient pa-
lazzos and churches and museums filled with antiquities and masterpieces of the Italian Renaissance and of the Manneristic and
Academic schools. In Florence, which was next on his itinerary,
he haunted the Uffizi Galleries and the Pitti Palace and spent
hours in the art-filled churches of the Tuscan capital.

It was in the course of this tour that Beyle conceived the idea
of writing his own book on Italy, its culture and art. His erudition,
to be sure, left much to be desired, and in writing his *History of
Painting in Italy*, he borrowed heavily, to the point of plagiarism,
from such authorities in the field as Vasari, Luigi Lanzi, and
others.[13] But the tone of his work and his ideas would be distinctly
his own, and between passages lifted from other books are personal
observations and reflections which are the essential tenets of the
philosophy of "Beylism": exaltation of the individual of superior
will, energy, and sensitivity, and quest for those passions and spiri-

tual experiences that enable us to rise above the common level of mediocrity and vacuity.

Beyle's tour also included a stay in Rome and a visit to Naples.[14] Although he had less appreciation for architecture than for painting, Beyle duly admired Saint Peter's and its imposing colonnade, but was more impressed by the ruins of ancient Rome, a hardly surprising reaction from one who was reading so diligently the works by such influential promoters of antiquity and the classical revival as Winckelmann. Furthermore, as one who considered himself a disciple of the eighteenth-century *philosophes*, he was convinced that he had a natural affinity for the pagan message of the Greeks and Romans, if only because it negated so thoroughly the religious values he associated with his Catholic and bourgeois upbringing. Naples, in particular, puzzled and fascinated him. Here religious faith, reduced to superstitious beliefs and practices, coexisted with unbridled passion. A poor yet lusty populace gave itself over to the immediate satisfactions of the senses. Murders were fairly common here, but they were generally crimes of passion or vengeance, something that appealed to Beyle's preoccupation with human emotions at their paroxysm.

But the time allotted for his leave of absence was drawing to a close, and he now grew impatient to return to Milan and rush into the arms of Angela. By October 22, he was back in Milan, where he was informed that Mme Pietragrua was out of town. Impetuously, he decided to follow in her footsteps and try to rejoin her in the mountain village in the Lake region where he was told that she was to be found. When he at last came face to face with her, she gave him a cool, elusive reception, invoking her husband's jealousy to keep him at arm's length.[15] Angela's disappointment at her lover's rapid loss of interest may have had a great deal to do with her sudden inaccessibility. But she was not an over-complicated and difficult woman, and before long the lovers made up. Beyle's leave, however, was about to expire, and he had to prepare for the journey back to the French capital, with an obligatory detour to Grenoble in order to visit his family. He stayed with his sister Pauline and her husband on their estate at Thuellin where they had settled. It was during this visit that he saw for the last time his beloved Grandfather Gagnon, now eighty-three years of age and with declining faculties.

On a bleak afternoon of November 27, he was once more in Paris. During his absence, there had been some reshuffling in the Napoleonic administrative organization and Beyle's new superiors greeted him with marked reserve. His police files and personal reputation had by now created the picture of an unreliable hothead. His escapades in Italy had, moreover, been diligently traced by the police. It is also likely that Count Daru had again grown weary of protecting a relative who invariably managed to get himself in hot water.

The ever-affectionate and accommodating Angélina Bereyter, however, readily resumed living with Beyle. Furthermore, his newly conceived project of writing a *History of Painting in Italy* kept him occupied during the winter months and helped to ward off moments of boredom and nostalgia when he longed for sunny Italy and the voluptuous Angela Pietragrua. As for his infatuation with Alexandrine Daru, it was quite extinguished by now. In his rare private meetings with the Countess, she consistently showed marked reserve.

For a while Beyle hoped for a diplomatic post in Italy which would enable him to supervise the transfer of Italian art treasures to France, a mission that might make it possible for him to return to his beloved Italy and to rejoin Angela. But his bad reputation, as he now realized, would preclude such an appointment.

Beyle had become accustomed to a life of action, movement, and adventure. Even his need for study and intellectual effort, which he presently satisfied with the research and gathering of material for the *History of Painting in Italy*, could not fill the emotional void that made everything look flat and monotonous in Paris.

In the meantime, Napoleon had made up his mind that a showdown with Russia was inevitable, and Pierre Daru was involved in the gigantic task of helping to organize and provision the Grande Armée for the secretly planned campaign and invasion of

Russia. Immense preparations had been under way since the second half of 1811.[16]

Beyle, who had participated in the conquest of northern Italy, who had followed the triumphant entrance of Napoleon and his army in Berlin and Vienna, now felt the irresistible urge to be part of the Emperor's greatest challenge and adventure. He requested and was granted permission to be transferred to active duty with the Grande Armée and its march into Russia. On July 23, 1812, he was accorded the privilege of an audience with Empress Marie-Louise, who honored him with a few minutes of conversation.[17] She also entrusted him with a personal letter for the Emperor. This was not a sign that his superiors had forgiven him the liberties he had taken in Italy with his leave of absence. It merely meant that communications with Napoleon in far-off Russia were difficult to maintain and every opportunity was taken to entrust departing officials with letters and messages.

So confident and optimistic was Beyle about the outcome of this expedition that he equipped himself for the long journey not only with necessary personal effects and with two portfolios filled with official papers, but also with books and manuscripts, including his projected play *Letellier* and his more recently launched work, the *History of Painting in Italy*. He fully expected to have the kind of leisure in Russia that would enable him to make significant progress on these literary endeavors. And he was by no means alone in envisaging the invasion of Russia as yet another foreordained victory for France. Napoleon and everyone else on the French side shared the belief that this would be a short, easy war.[18]

XI

The Russian Campaign

FOR THREE WEEKS, Beyle rode eastward by coach through Germany and Poland. On August 14, 1812, he rejoined the Emperor's headquarters at Boyarinkowa. As he advanced closer to the front, he saw, for the first time, utter confusion in the French army..In the tangled mass of soldiers, horses, cannons, and supply vehicles that cluttered the roads, Beyle soon had to give up traveling by carriage. Continuing on horseback, he reached Smolensk, which had just surrendered and was in flames. It was such a spectacular sight that, at the risk of being killed by one of the shells which the Russians continued to fire at the French-occupied sector, Beyle neglected to take cover and remained outside in order to get a better picture of the panorama.[1] In this disregard for his personal safety, he was entirely consistent with himself. Equally true to form was his fascination with the esthetic emotion or pleasure a situation, no matter how dreadful or dangerous, could afford him. In this respect, unbeknownst to himself, he was already behaving like a true novelist, culling sights and impressions that would enrich his inner storehouse of those compelling images and visual details that are a necessary part of a writer's fictional world.

To the dismay of the French, the Russians avoided joining battle with the adversary, pursuing instead a strategy of retreat and systematic "scorched earth." Throughout the Russian campaign, the notes and observations Beyle hurriedly jotted down in his diary and the letters he managed to write offer us a lively if at times sketchy picture of the dramatic scenes he witnessed. Character-istically, the tone is deliberately detached, even light-hearted and humorous. But it was no doubt this ability to view the most mo-mentous events with a sense of emotional uninvolvement that en-abled Beyle to survive the perils that awaited him. Contemporaries who found themselves with him in this disastrous campaign have all testified to the fact that, in the most dangerous and exhausting circumstances, he never lost his sang-froid and clear-headedness.

On August 25, 1812, the French resumed their advance to-ward Moscow. The elderly Kutusov had been appointed Com-mander-in-Chief by Czar Alexander, who had at last yielded to public opinion. After the humiliating experience of the Austerlitz campaign, in which he had taken part, Kutusov knew his oppo-nent well and did not make the mistake of underrating him. Re-sisting pressure to fight a battle for Moscow, he determined to avoid a decisive confrontation and to use instead the vast Russian land and harsh climate as his best weapons.[2]

After the battle on the River Moskva at Borodino (September 7), during which Napoleon failed once more to pin the Russians down in a frontal, decisive assault, Kutusov retreated while the French troops, depleted by heavy casualties, entered the capital on September 14. The euphoria of the conquering army was of short duration. Only a few thousand civilians had stayed behind and soon fires broke out all over the city, kindled on the order of Ros-topchine, Military Governor of Moscow.[3]

Beyle entered the Russian capital with the Grande Armée on September 14. That same evening, however, the great conflagra-tion began and for four days and nights the city consumed itself in flames. Beyle, who had somehow managed to flee from the city proper, watched the awesome spectacle from the villa of Ros-topchine, two miles outside the limits of the capital.[4] His account of this historical event, although matter-of-fact and undramatic, vividly suggests the looting and incredible scenes of confusion and panic he witnessed. Even though he was exhausted and feeling ill, he stayed up at night, hypnotized by the extraordinary sight of the huge flames that rose from the burning city like some immense pyramid, setting the whole dark sky ablaze with incandescent colors. While around him French officers and soldiers drank, chatted, and made coarse jokes, he stood in silence, meditating on the beauty of the spectacle and the perverseness of human nature.

After a few days, Beyle and his companions were able to return to the devastated city, which had been reduced to a charred ruin. Only the Kremlin remained intact amid smoldering and abandoned dwellings, mansions, and palaces. Looting and pillaging resumed, unchecked by the French authorities. The first snows and frosts announced the approaching cold northern winter. Napoleon belatedly ordered the retreat and decided, after waiting in vain for peace overtures from Czar Alexander, that winter quarters for the army had to be set up. Appointed Commissioner of War Supplies, Beyle was ordered to proceed to Smolensk, Mohilov, and Vitebsk to organize provisions and living quarters for the rear. The title of Commissioner of War Supplies was, as Beyle ironically pointed out in a letter to his sister, an impressive one, but he no longer harbored any illusions about such matters and the only thing that sustained him was the hope of "ending up one day in my happy Italy." [5]

On October 16, Beyle left Moscow with a convoy of soldiers and started on the difficult journey back to Smolensk. Harassed at night by Cossacks and peasants, hampered by snowstorms and slowed down by their wounded and baggage, the French straggled into Smolensk on November 2. It had been a harrowing journey during which their ranks had been pitifully decimated. Troops that had arrived earlier had exhausted the supplies of food and provisions that could still be found in the ruined city. Discipline had completely broken down and, once more, Beyle saw widespread plundering. Pausing briefly in Smolensk, Beyle hastily penned a few letters which, despite their apparent light-heartedness, vividly suggest the dangers and physical discomforts with which he had to contend. There is even a brief but affectionate and good-humored letter to Angélina Bereyter. And to his friend Félix Faure he confided: "I have seen and felt things that a sedentary man of letters would not be able to guess in a thousand years." [6]

Events moved so swiftly that after leaving Smolensk on November 11, Beyle could not pursue his mission to Mohilov and Vitebsk. Matters had rapidly worsened for the freezing and famished French troops and the retreat was becoming a rout. In the utter confusion that prevailed, Beyle lost nearly all his personal effects and papers. Yet he retained his presence of mind and even his sense of humor. Neither did he lack in resourcefulness, for he managed to have some bread distributed to the soldiers of his convoy between Smolensk and the Berezina River, no mean feat in view of the fact that the French were retracing their steps over devastated territory.

Despite the fearful cold and lack of food, utterly exhausted and plagued by bouts of fever, Beyle endured the ordeal in a praiseworthy manner. Upon reaching the Berezina in a carriage he shared with a wounded officer, he was quick in sizing up the situation. The pontoon bridge was jammed with huge columns of soldiers, horses, and vehicles. He immediately resolved to drive downstream to look for a passable ford, a decision that probably saved his life and that of his companion.[7]

After fifty days on the road, Beyle reached fortified Vilna on December 7. He hastened to write a reassuring, cheerful note to his sister, quipping that an unexpected benefit from this whole adventure was that his waistline had considerably receded. When he had somewhat recovered, he wrote her at greater length, and having had some time to reflect about the whole extraordinary experience, concluded that he had survived through sheer force of will: "I have often seen total exhaustion and death close-up."[8] At Königsberg, where he stayed during the second half of December, he was able to regain some of his strength. He then proceeded to Danzig, Berlin, Brunswick, and Frankfurt, and at last arrived in Paris on January 31, 1813. About a week earlier (on January 23), he had reached his thirtieth birthday.

All in all, Beyle was not displeased with the way he had endured this supreme test of his character; he now knew for certain that, in the face of imminent death, he was able to remain clearminded and decisive. That he valued this particular trait very highly is made abundantly clear in his writings and by the fact that his fictional heroes would be endowed with the same kind of moral fortitude. In Stendhal's ethical and esthetic system, an individual can be worthy of true inner freedom only after he has proven to himself his readiness to accept self-sacrifice. Henri Beyle's eagerness to expose himself voluntarily to situations that tested him to the very limits of endurance may seem to be merely an infantile form of braggadocio if one does not keep in mind the crucial role an individual's ability to overcome his own mortality played in his concept of the superior being. The ideal of self-realization was of course part of the whole set of creeds he had inherited from the Age of Enlightenment as well as from the revolutionaries. But he transformed it into a more personal and self-centered notion of individual nobility of behavior and spirit.

Despite the frightful hardships he had withstood during the Russian campaign, Stendhal never regretted the experience. On the contrary. As the retreat from Moscow became part of a legendary saga, he took growing pride in having been personally involved in this epic and felt it had immeasurably enriched his insight into human nature. He had not only seen extraordinary spectacles, but had also learned what extremes of suffering human beings are capable of sustaining. To be sure, he had also seen acts of human savagery and stupidity, and he had at times been more exasperated by the insensitivity of his companions than by the actual ordeals he had to endure. But he was not embittered, although there were no tangible rewards for his courageous behavior. He had left behind in the vast spaces and snow-covered plains of Russia his last youthful illusions and ambitious dreams.

An overwhelming sense of apathy and general indifference followed the weeks of extreme strain and exertion. The Paris salons, the theater and opera, friends and even women found him curiously detached and unresponsive. The initial excitement of being reunited with the lively Angélina Bereyter quickly wore off, and she failed to dispel his mood of listlessness and despondency. "I am now," he noted in his *Journal* on February 4, 1813, "in a state of perfect insensitivity, I have lost all my passions. . . . I feel dead at the present moment; an old man of sixty is probably not more spiritless." [9] Attempts to resume work on what he could salvage of his manuscripts taken along to Russia and largely lost during the retreat from Moscow were equally futile. Any sustained intellectual effort was impossible and everything around him struck him as boring and trivial.

Beyle was suffering from a fairly common psychological ailment typical of demobilized soldiers trying to readjust to civilian life. His *History of Painting in Italy*, begun with such enthusiasm in Italy, now left him cold, and he could not muster the kind of élan and verve necessary to write new scenes for his play *Letellier*. [10] He was now more preoccupied with general observations on human character made by theorists and moralists, and he interspersed his readings with brief but penetrating comments based upon his own recent experiences. What especially intrigued him was comedy as a dramatic genre, and more specifically the whole question of the comic and the exclusively human phenomenon of laughter. That he had observed both in himself and in others the capacity to see the ludicrous side of things and events in the more stressful situations no doubt greatly enhanced his curiosity about these matters. Once more he reread Molière with a heightened appreciation of this great master's insight into those subtle and complex psychological forces that trigger in us a sense of release, satisfied vanity, or feeling of superiority which express themselves in laughter. That this phenomenon varies according to social and cultural factors was not overlooked by Beyle, who in this respect as in so many others remained a disciple of Montesquieu. The Englishman, he noted, had a different sense of the comic than the Frenchman, and a member of the *peuple*, or lower class, would laugh at situations that would not strike a more literate and sophisticated person as funny. Similarly, individual character also entered into the picture: one could not expect the same reactions from all individuals. Some people hardly ever laugh, and others break up at the slightest provocation. [11] All these perceptions would eventually enrich Stendhals' art as a novelist and endow his fictional works with a multitude of specific observations.

In a more general way, Beyle's personal involvement in the Napoleonic saga would directly affect his inspiration as a novelist. Fabrice del Dongo of *The Charterhouse of Parma* is a participant in the fateful Battle of Waterloo and both Julien Sorel of *The Red and the Black* and Lucien of *Lucien Leuwen* face the same frustrating predicament of being born too late to fulfill their dreams of glory and heroism on the battlefield.

As the German campaign got under way, Beyle fervently hoped that he would not be called back to active duty, for he was thoroughly weary of war. But on April 16, 1813, he received the orders to rejoin the army and, with a heavy heart, he crossed the Rhine once more and set out for the front.

He quickly discovered that this new adventure had the unexpected effect of restoring his zest for life. He eagerly took in the sights and admired the German countryside and villages awakening to springtime. After a brief stop at Erfurt, he rejoined the French general headquarters at Dresden and proceeded to Bautzen, which he reached on May 19 and where the constant cannonade announced an imminent battle. Witnessing the battle of Bautzen from a nearby hill on May 21, he made an observation which he would put to effective use in the celebrated battle scene of Waterloo as seen by Fabrice del Dongo, the hero of *The Charterhouse of Parma*: a participant or eyewitness can actually make out very little in the general confusion of such an event; he can only sense that something awesome is taking place.[12] To be psychologically authentic and truthful, a literary depiction of a battle scene should be discontinuous and in flashes, as it would be experienced by a combatant, an insight that would not be overlooked by Tolstoy in his *War and Peace*.

After the battle of Bautzen, Beyle was proceeding from Reischenbach to Görlitz with a convoy of supplies escorted by about one hundred and fifty soldiers, when, on May 24, the rear guard was attacked by a band of about thirty Cossacks. Panic and confusion momentarily overtook the French column. Some soldiers and even officers started fleeing, but the attackers were eventually driven off. Later, an inquiry was instituted, owing to the poor showing of the men entrusted with the protection of the convoy. Upon arriving at Görlitz, Beyle was questioned about the incident, apparently by Napoleon himself, who listened to his report (which was later put in writing) [13] with an expression of concentrated wrath. That a mere handful of Cossacks should have thrown a French column into near panic greatly upset and infuriated the Emperor.

Some biographers have expressed doubt that this dramatic tête-à-tête between Stendhal and Napoleon actually ever took place. [14] Yet, in a short and obviously hurried letter to his sister dated June 9, 1813, Beyle proudly informs her that "eighty days ago, I had a long conversation with His Majesty." [15] This "conversation" is most likely the one that took place in Görlitz. That this meeting, which was his most intimate encounter with Napoleon, made a strong impression upon him is attested by the fact that he later liked to recount it and that, in dedicating in 1817 his *History of Painting in Italy* to the by then deposed and exiled Emperor, he identified himself as "the soldier whom you buttonholed at Görlitz," a gracious and nostalgic reference to past glories and adventures.

A few days after these events, an armistice was signed. On the sixth of June, Beyle had been appointed Intendant of the German province of Sagan, in Silesia. [16] His stay in Sagan, however, turned out to be of short duration, from June 10 until July 26. His health, already sorely tested during the Russian campaign, now completely gave way. He contracted a high fever, probably of a contagious nature for there was an epidemic of typhus in the area. As he quipped in a letter written when he was beginning to recover, he thought he would have the honor of leaving his bones in Sagan. [17] He was granted a leave of absence and permitted to complete his convalescence in Italy. But he was not yet capable of undertaking the long journey. Meanwhile, he continued his recovery in Dresden, familiarizing himself with its famed art treasures and attending its opera as soon as his health allowed such activities.

By August 20, Beyle was back in Paris for a short visit and in order to get his affairs straightened out for his forthcoming stay in

Italy. He was still feeling weak and feverish and eagerly looked forward to being once more in Milan, a city that had occupied his thoughts and dreams throughout the disastrous Russian campaign and the weeks of illness in Germany. On September 7, he was at long last in Milan. The emotion of finding himself in his favorite city was so overwhelming that when at the Café Nuovo he picked up his first cup of coffee with a trembling hand, he spilled it all over a brand new pair of expensive trousers.[18]

The Milanese climate and atmosphere had immediate beneficial effects on Beyle's health and morale. Before long, he had resumed his relationship with Angela Pietragrua, but remained sufficiently clear-headed to pursue other interests and activities. In short, while he enjoyed Angela's company, he was no longer in love with her.[19] But their secret rendezvous, necessarily spaced because of her husband and family obligations, were still highly prized by Beyle for their easy-going tone of intimacy, confidence and affection, something he had not experienced in his days of frantic passion. He soon felt well enough to undertake trips and excursions to Lake Como and to Venice.

But the rapidly worsening situation of the French Empire was affecting northern Italy and Beyle's leave of absence was reaching its end. At the Battle of the Nations at Leipzig (October 16–19), Napoleon, outnumbered by a vastly superior enemy, had to retreat despite his brilliant defense. By the end of November, Beyle was back in Paris, but not without having stopped off at Grenoble to visit his family. Grandfather Gagnon had died shortly before, and with his disappearance Beyle's strongest tie with the past was broken.

Dr. Gagnon had illumined Beyle's difficult and lonely childhood and early adolescence with his scholarly grace and wit, his urbane taste, his intellectual curiosity, and his eighteenth-century skepticism and tolerance. It was in his well-stocked library, dominated by the bust of Voltaire, that young Beyle had spent some of the happiest days of his youth, and it was in his grandfather's company that he had found the kind of personal warmth and intellectual stimulation so sorely lacking in his father's gloomy household.

Now Dr. Gagnon was gone, and with him a most appealing embodiment of a whole era of French thought and culture which, in Stendhal's eyes, would always be endowed with special significance.

XII

From Soldier to Writer

AT THE END of 1813, Beyle had settled down in Paris, still hoping to return to his literary studies and to his writing and to secure a permanent assignment in Italy. He resumed reading Shakespeare, went to concerts, and bought a subscription to the Comédie Française. The art of writing comedies was still one of his foremost preoccupations and he diligently attended performances of Molière's plays, scribbling comments on the text precariously balanced on his knee. While waiting for the moment of inspiration and "genius," he worked on the notes he had been gathering on the subject for the last ten years.

Around him, the Napoleonic drama was drawing to a close, but his greatest wish now was to avoid further involvements in campaigns and battles. He was utterly tired of war, of its futility and wastefulness. Events, however, did not yet allow him to return to the life of a man of letters. The Grande Armée had been decimated and France was threatened by invasion. Before the end of the year, he was assigned to assist Comte de Saint-Vallier in organizing the national defense in the Dauphiné, one of the most exposed and threatened provinces.

By January 5, 1814, Beyle was once more in his native Grenoble, where Saint-Vallier had been sent on the urgent mission of speeding up the conscription, building up the morale of a frightened population, and evacuating food and goods that might otherwise fall into the hands of the enemy.

To have to deal with the Grenoblois, whom he had always loathed, in the hour of their greatest need was one of those twists of fate whose irony did not escape him. The elderly Saint-Vallier relied heavily on his energetic assistant. When the Austrians began to invade the pass leading from Geneva to Chambéry, Beyle rushed to the scene of action to supervise the deployment of the defending army and to advise General Marchand, in charge of the operations for the region.

Beyle's exertions took their toll on his impaired health and, before long he again fell ill. His patriotic fervor had been reawakened and he had worked hard, meeting for days on end with representatives of the local bourgeoisie and peasantry, writing proclamations and decrees countersigned by the helpless Saint-Vallier, showing once more the sang-froid that had enabled him to survive the rigors of a Russian winter and the disasters of the retreat from Moscow. He felt he had fulfilled his mission and his state of health demanded a rest. He obtained a leave of absence and permission to return to the capital.

Some of Stendhal's biographers have pointed out that, once more, he failed to show what the French call "esprit de suite" by giving up his duties at a time of such grave national crisis.[1] Whether it was illness or utter frustration that prompted him to ask to be relieved of his post is, of course, impossible to tell. It was most likely a combination of both. To deal with a nearly senile superior, with the naturally mistrustful and petty-minded provincials, and with the inertia of bureaucracy in the midst of yet another campaign was no doubt more than he was capable of handling, both mentally and physically, after his eventful and exhausting years in the service of the Emperor.

As the Allies advanced on French territory, Beyle, still unwell and above all sick at heart, made his way back to Paris in time to see, on March 29, the carriage bearing Empress Marie-Louise and the infant King of Rome cross the Pont Royal. They were leaving the Tuileries Palace and the French capital while the Senate debated the question of the Emperor's abdication. With his friend Louis Crozet he wandered through the streets, observing the

reaction of the Parisians to these dramatic events. On the following day, the hill of Montmartre was assaulted and taken by the
Russians. Before long, the Champs-Elysées were lined with their
bivouacs. Beyle was gripped by intense and conflicting emotions as
he watched these spectacles, and he noted in his diary that the uncertainty of his own fate somehow sharpened his sensibilities. He
who had witnessed the conquering and plundering of cities had at
least the consolation of seeing that, as he wrote to his sister, "everyone behaved correctly, not the least disorder," and, in an indirect reference to Moscow, that "nothing was burned or scorched." [2]
At the Comédie Française, performances continued as usual,
and one evening, while watching Beaumarchais's *Barber of Se-
ville*, he found himself seated next to a very handsome Russian
officer who, he mused, must have been irresistible to women, all
the more so since there was an aura of naturalness and forceful
dignity about him that his more sophisticated French peers lacked:
"Had I been a woman, I would have followed him to the ends of
the earth." [3] This casual observation, recorded in the diary, testifies to the future novelist's ability to identify with members of the
opposite sex, to this unique androgynous sensibility shared by
writers of fiction endowed with a keen imagination and a capacity
to empathize with others. To conclude from this, as well as other
similar notations, that Stendhal had latent homosexual tendencies
would, of course, be tempting for a biographer eager to interpret
his sexuality in light of the latest post-Freudian theories. The
truth, however, is far simpler. Stendhal had few prejudices, sexual
and otherwise. His broad-ranging intellectual and human curiosity, his vast cultural frame of reference enabled him to refer,
without undue self-consciousness, to many cases, in history, literature, and art, of homosexual love. His own inclination, in this
matter, however, was decidedly and unequivocally heterosexual.

Beyle knew that with the fall of the Empire his own world
was also coming to an end. His greatest desire now was to leave a
France that would be turned over to the reactionary forces he
loathed and to obtain a post in Italy that would permit him to
dedicate himself to his favorite pursuits. Finding himself without

any income or position, he had to give up his fine apartment, sell his furniture, carriage, and horses, and move into a small hotel room.

Assuredly, Beyle could have intrigued and maneuvered, as so many others did, in order to extricate himself from his impasse. Such tactics, however, were foreign to his temperament. His mood was calm and detached as he went about selling his possessions and, as he recorded in his diary, he even experienced joy when he found himself in a small, furnished room, for it reminded him of the truth of the old axiom for finding happiness, or at least contentment and peace of mind: *"Hide your life."* [4] Doubtless, this unexpected feeling of cheerfulness had something to do with the realization that this disastrous dénouement to his exertions, hopes, and dreams had at least one important advantage: he had now regained the kind of freedom he had known as an obscure young provincial in Paris, with the crucial difference, however, that he was better equipped to deal with his independence. Henceforth, he would dedicate himself to refining his philosophy of life, this very personal outlook on men and events that would come to be associated with *beylism*. In the general debacle that accompanied the fall of Napoleon, he aspired above all to find a small niche for himself in Italy, where the cost of living was advantageous and where he would be able to settle down to a modest but unencumbered existence. In his *Life of Henry Brulard*, he tells his reader simply and tersely: "I fell with Napoleon in April 1814." [5]

During the Napoleonic campaigns in which he had participated, and especially during the retreat from Russia, Beyle had had ample opportunity to observe human nature in stressful situations. What he had seen did not enhance his respect for the majority of men and for the passions that motivate their behavior. That these passions were, for the most part, base and selfish was now reinforced by what happened after the Battle of Waterloo and the Restoration of the Bourbons.

In the process of severing his ties with the French capital, Beyle broke off with Angélina Bereyter. On the other hand,

Mélanie Guilbert, now Madame de Barcoff, was in Paris, and the two former lovers briefly resumed their relationship.[6] But nothing held back Beyle; he was impatient to be once more in his adoptive homeland, which, in the midst of the collapse of all his hopes and ambitions, beckoned to him like a haven of peace and beauty. Paris had lost its magic for him: "I have had my fill of Paris," he noted in his *Journal*, "I was rather disgusted with the job of Auditor and with the insolent stupidity of the powerful. Rome, Rome is my homeland, I can't wait to be on my way." [7]

It was during this fateful year of 1814 that he brought out his first book, *The Lives of Haydn, Mozart and Metastasio*, dashed off while he was waiting for events to follow their course and probably as an escape from his own sense of uncertainty. Published in Paris at his own expense and under the cryptic pseudonym of Louis-César-Alexandre Bombet (all his life Beyle, in his private life as well as in his career, would evidence an irresistible penchant for aliases), the book failed to sell or attract critical attention, except for the dubious distinction of causing a minor uproar over its obvious plagiarisms. Beyle was no musicologist and his appreciation of the composers analyzed in his study was primarily an emotional one. Mozart, for him, was great because of his aptitude to evoke in us tender, melancholy thoughts and feelings.

Written in the form of letters, a genre favored by eighteenth-century authors, it contained not only heavy and unacknowledged borrowings,[8] but also showed the future novelist's unmistakable stamp in its aphoristic and witty digressions and anecdotes, reminiscent of one of his favorite stylists, Montesquieu. Stendhal's method of lifting whole passages from experts may seem cavalier, to say the least, to the modern reader, and much effort has been expended by scholars on tracing the sources of his critical essays on music, art, and tourism. It is obvious, however, that Stendhal himself felt little compunction about making such a free use of what he considered merely raw material.

Yet it is this curious book, largely made up of disparate elements, published under such inauspicious circumstances and greeted with such general indifference, that marks the official beginning of Stendhal's literary career. It is as though some inner compulsion had driven Beyle, helplessly witnessing the end of the Napoleonic dream, to assert his own existence to himself and the world by rushing into publication a book which, for all its brazen borrowings, faithfully expressed its author's profound passion for music and its liberating, uplifting influence on man's soul.

In July 1814, shortly after Louis XVIII had been restored to the throne by the Allies after their entry into Paris, Beyle quietly left the capital and made his way back to Italy, but not without having paid a visit to his sister Pauline, whose financial situation was beginning to suffer as a result of her husband's speculative bent and poor business sense. On August 10, 1814, Beyle arrived in Milan, where he was to remain until the spring of 1821, with several trips, two of which were to Paris and one to England (1817) during the intervening years. He resumed his relationship with Angela Pietragrua and gave himself over to the life of a dilettante and man of letters, relying for sustenance on the small income of a retired official's half-pay.

This self-imposed exile suited him so well that not even the flight of Napoleon from Elba and the Hundred Days could lure him back to France. But if he had lost all his enthusiasm for Napoleon's militaristic adventures, the news of Waterloo filled him with bitter, melancholy thoughts: "Everything is lost, even honor." If anything, the humiliation of the French at the hands of the Allies and the reestablishment of the monarchy confirmed Beyle's determination to remain in Italy, despite the precautions he had to take with the Austrian police and censorship and the financial and personal difficulties he was experiencing there as a foreigner with a suspect record of association with a regime now in disrepute. The question in his mind was, in what part of Italy should he settle down? He opted, not surprisingly, in favor of Milan. It had the advantage of being a big city and a great cultural center; Naples was too backward, Rome was too dominated by the Church, "one has to be too hypocritical," Florence was over-sophisticated and reminded him too much of Paris and its social rituals and rigid conventions.[9]

Exile, no matter how pleasant, always exacts a heavy price. Even though he loved Milan, Beyle was an isolated foreigner there, one moreover whose meager financial resources constantly forced him to content himself with a mode of existence far below his aspirations. And his appeals to his father, through the intermediary of his sister Pauline, fell once more upon deaf ears.

Angela Pietragrua, moreover, probably none too happy about the prospect of having to cope with a lover without influence or power, was becoming increasingly difficult and unpredictable. After several quarrels and tentative reconciliations, the inevitable occurred. By the end of 1815, their tumultuous relationship was over, but not without scenes and complications that left Beyle irritated and distressed.[10] Angela had played a cunning and maddening game of deception and evasion. If her behavior had at last killed his passion for her, it took him several months to recover from the emotional stress she had caused him. Ruefully calling her a *catin sublime*, a sublime strumpet, he had to admit to himself that, once more, he had been unlucky in love. Yet, despite this disappointing dénouement, something of Angela's unpredictable willfulness and capriciousness, tempered by her cheerful affability, would be transmuted into his more imperious fictional women. For Angela Pietragrua undoubtedly embodied for Beyle an ideal of womanhood that corresponded with some of his deepest needs: she was both the queen and the harlot capable of making her lovers experience ecstasy as well as despair.

As usual, Beyle found the most effective antidote for his sentimental misadventures in his activities and endeavors as an amateur, dilettante, and littérateur. Visits to museums and evenings at the Scala alternated with short trips to neighboring places of cultural interest and with furious bouts of work and study. He was again engrossed in a project undertaken in 1811, his *History of Painting in Italy*.

In 1815 Beyle learned, while on a short stay in Turin, that Alexandrine Daru had died, at the age of thirty-three, of complications after giving birth to her eighth child.[11] Under the impact of this sad news, which he had come across while casually reading a

French newspaper, he wrote a dedication to her on the cover of his manuscript of the *History of Painting in Italy*, replacing the one he had originally written for Angela Pietragrua.

Increasingly, Beyle felt at home in Italy and thought that his decision to exile himself there had been a wise one. He found the Italians, their casual naturalness and outgoing ways to his liking. Whenever possible, and as much as his meager *pension* allowed, he traveled to various cities and art centers of northern Italy and, as the news from France confirmed his premonitions and fears about what was happening there, congratulated himself on his self-imposed expatration. In Italy at least, he could find delight and comfort in a mild climate, lovely countryside, beautiful blue skies, a lively and cheerful people, and inexhaustible riches of art and music, Here, moreover, he found that he could work well on his literary projects. In his letters to his sister Pauline he reiterated his intention of remaining permanently in Italy. "The Seine will never see me again, except in passing," he quipped.[12]

Italy allowed Beyle to develop as a writer and critic after the chaotic, exhausting years in the service of Napoleon. In Milan he was able to convert his rich experiences into an esthetic and moral philosophy that would form the basis of his subsequent works. Admittedly, he continued to view himself as an eventual dramatist, but his absorption in the great Italian masterpieces of art at last bore fruit when, in 1817, he published, at his own expense, his *History of Painting in Italy*, under the initials M.B.A.A. (*Monsieur Beyle, ancien Auditeur*, Mister Beyle, former Auditor). The manuscript, taken along on the Russian campaign, had been lost with Beyle's other effects during the disastrous retreat. As a result, he had had to piece the work together again from notes and drafts fortunately left in Paris.

Once more, Beyle did not hesitate to lean heavily on previous authors, especially the treatises of Vasari, Lanzi, and Condivi.[13] But between borrowed passages, Beyle initiated the reader into his own philosophy of life and art through anecdotes, digressions, personal observations, and aphorisms. Art historians have refused to take the work seriously, and admittedly Stendhal cannot be considered a specialist or an authority on the subject of painting. But the originality of his outlook and approach has too frequently been overlooked.[14] One of the strongest sections of the book is devoted to Michelangelo and the Sistine Chapel. Under the impact of recent events, Beyle transformed what might have been a theoretical, academic treatise into a manifesto asserting his political and esthetic creed. But characteristically, Beyle gave expression to his beliefs not in a dogmatic, ponderous manner, but rather in light-hearted, frequently ironical or satirical asides. The lesson of a Montesquieu and a Voltaire, who preferred to deal with serious subjects in an entertaining way, had not been lost on their loyal disciple. To be effective, a moral or political message has to be couched in a diverting, ingenious form. In this respect, as in so many others, Stendhal remained closer to the spirit of the Age of Enlightenment, which so successfully combined playfulness and intellectual content (also a major characteristic of the Rococo style), than to the solemn, self-conscious and emotionally charged approach typical of the Romantics.

At a time when nationalism, monarchism, and pre-Revolutionary values were reasserting themselves on the European scene, Stendhal openly defied these currents by flaunting his cosmopolitism, anticlericalism, liberalism, and skepticism.

Yet it was also during these years that he became increasingly interested in the German and English manifestations of Romanticism. One evening in October 1816, at La Scala, he was introduced to Byron, who had just arrived in Milan with his whole retinue and was invited to dine with him. In a letter written soon after this meeting, Beyle described the controversial English poet, whose personality and looks had obviously impressed him: "I dined with a handsome and charming young man, with the face of an eighteen-year-old, although he is twenty-eight, profile of an angel, the most gentle expression. It's the original of Lovelace, but a thousand times better. . . . When he enters an English salon, all the women depart instantly. He is the greatest living poet, Lord Byron." [15] He also added that Greece was to Byron what Italy was to himself.

While Beyle was at first fascinated by Byron and felt a real kinship with the English expatriate, he was somewhat put off by his arrogance and his unpredictable swings in mood. Yet Byron's personal charm compensated for his aristocratic haughtiness and egotism and the two men struck up a friendly relationship. Two later short but pithy essays by Stendhal, written in 1829 and 1830 respectively and entitled "Recollections of Byron" and "Lord Byron in Italy," provide further information on Stendhal's impressions of the English poet in 1816. Stendhal was well aware of Byron's notoriety and was intrigued by his complex, self-centered character and personality, which he found reminiscent of Jean-Jacques Rousseau's. Yet he noted, with some amusement, that the comparison with Rousseau angered Byron, and he attributed this reaction to the English nobleman's secret annoyance at being put on the same level as an artisan's son who, moreover, had for a while earned his living as a mere lackey.[16] These observations, however, in no way diminished Stendhal's enthusiastic admiration for Byron's genius as a poet and for the power, range, and satiric verve of his *Childe Harold* and other works. As for Byron, he was eager to learn more about Napoleon and his campaigns from a veteran who had been a participant in the famous Moscow retreat. Several years later, in 1823, a cordial exchange of letters briefly reestablished contact between the two men before Byron's tragic and premature death in Greece in 1824.[17]

In the salon-like atmosphere of La Scala, Beyle made several friends among the Milan literati and through them became acquainted with the new Italian romantic movement.[18] A particularly influential figure in a group composed of liberals and young poets and such writers as Grossi, Foscolo, Leopardi, Monti, and Manzoni, was Monsignore Ludovico di Breme, former chaplain to the king of Italy under Napoleon and scion of a noble Piedmont family. A handsome but pale and thin young man, he had a spiritual intensity not unlike that of Fabrice del Dongo, the hero of the *Charterhouse of Parma*. Breme was editor of the new *Il Conciliatore*, a literary review whose contributors were proponents of the Risorgimento.

Beyle felt welcomed and in his element in the company of these idealistic, passionate young men. He had a great deal in common with the circle of friends that faithfully attended Ludovico di Breme's gatherings: they believed in freedom in literature and politics, but had to be wary of the close surveillance of the Austrian police and agents.

The struggle for Italian national unification and independence and for a revolution in literature greatly appealed to Stendhal's own rebelliousness and sense of conspiracy. He therefore closely identified with the ideals and aspirations of his Italian friends and espoused their political and literary causes. The cult of energy and of powerful emotions, which constituted the essential tenets of the new literary movement of Italian romanticism and Risorgimento, coincided perfectly with Beyle's natural predilections and current preoccupations.

In 1817, barely one month after bringing out his *History of Painting in Italy*, Beyle published his third book, *Rome, Naples and Florence*, a voyage journal interspersed with personal reflections and observations. Here again a curious mixture of heterogeneous elements characterized the composition of the book. The style is aphoristic, lively, and playful. There are travel impressions, sprightly anecdotes, information of a practical nature, comments on music, the theater, and museums. The author's irreverence and political independence assert themselves under the guise of an innocuous travelogue and introduction to Italy's culture. The book obtained a measure of success, for a second French edition came out in London the same year, soon followed by an English translation.

For the first time, Beyle used the pseudonym of Stendhal, which he had borrowed, embellishing it with an h, from the name of a small Prussian town, Stendal, birthplace of Winckelmann, the famous classical archeologist and historian of ancient art. The Germanic sounding Stendhal also served to hide the true identity and nationality of an author who outspokenly criticized the consequences of the Congress of Vienna, which reduced Italy to a geographic entity and dashed all its hopes for political unity and independence.

Buoyed by the unaccustomed pleasure of seeing one of his works receive a favorable reception, Beyle embarked in the winter of 1817–18, upon a new project, a *Life of Napoleon*. This was obviously an inauspicious time to bring out such a book. When he showed the manuscript to his friends, they cautioned him not to publish it. Beyle was to return to this project intermittently, reworking and enriching it with further observations. It was never completed. When, twenty years later, he undertook a new version, *Memoirs on Napoleon*, it too remained unfinished. Both manuscripts would see the light of day long after Stendhal's death.[19]

Beyle's attitude toward Napoleon was never one of uncritical adulation. But as the most reactionary elements got the upper hand under the Restoration, as Beyle saw the *ultras* (the extreme royalists) speak scoffingly of the fallen Emperor, derogatively calling him "Buonaparte," he was filled with sentimental nostalgia as well as with compassion for the prisoner of Saint-Helena. Napoleon became in his eyes a symbol of transcendent energy and drive. It is characteristic of Stendhal's uncompromising individualism that, once more, he found himself out of step with his times. He now took great pride in having served the man who had single-handedly dominated the European scene through his daring and genius, in having been a soldier in the Grande Armée, and in having personally experienced the hardships of the Russian campaign.

Stendhal's two unfinished works on Napoleon present a revealing and consistent picture of his political philosophy. While they give eloquent expression to their author's revulsion at the representatives of the new French regime and solidarity with young General Bonaparte as the natural heir to the French Revolution and to the ideals of democratic republicanism, they don't hesitate to point out the corrupting influence unlimited power had on the Emperor and his eventual betrayal of the principles associated with the Enlightenment and Revolution.

The year 1817 was also marked by journeys to England and France. The trip to London was primarily motivated by Beyle's literary interests. A detailed and favorable review of *Rome, Naples and Florence* had appeared in the influential *Edinburgh Quarterly Review.* Beyle's cosmopolitan, liberal, and anticlerical views, his unvarnished criticism of certain traits of the French character appealed to the English reading public.

Beyle arrived in London on August 3 and stayed there until the middle of the month. We are ill-informed on this first visit to the English capital, except that, with one or two companions, he made the rounds of the museums, theaters, and concert halls.[20] During the six-week stay in Paris that followed, he made the personal acquaintance of an ideologist he had long admired, Destutt de Tracy. Works were exchanged and a friendship was cemented which would last for many years to come. Relations with old school friends such as Louis de Barral were also renewed.

On his way back to Milan, Beyle stopped off at Grenoble and stayed with his sister until the middle of November. Her husband had recently died, leaving his financial affairs in a serious tangle and his widow in straitened circumstances. As for Beyle's father, he was ruining himself with ill-conceived business schemes. More than ever Beyle felt stifled and depressed by the atmosphere of his hometown, and he was eager to return to Milan. But he also wanted to do something for his sister, the only surviving member of his family he loved. A stay of a few months in Milan would cheer her up, he thought, and he therefore took her with him. In Milan, he got her separate lodgings, provided a box at La Scala, and introduced her to suitable lady friends. Whether out of necessity or choice, after four months Pauline returned to Grenoble.

As for Beyle, he knew that Milan was now the only place on earth for him. If anything, his recent stay in Paris had strengthened his determination to remain an expatriate. In the French capital he had watched in frustration and disgust the first results of Napoleon's demise. Everything the Enlightenment and Revolution stood for was now being reversed. The return to the throne of Louis XVIII had ushered in an era of reaction, hypocrisy, and mediocrity. While the social and political progress accomplished by the Revolution had slowed down under the Empire, many positive gains had taken root in France and gradually spread throughout Europe. The Congress of Vienna undid all these accomplishments, and the party of the "candle-snuffers," as Beyle scornfully called the new leaders, had triumphed.[21] In his *History of Painting in Italy* as well as in his *Rome, Naples and Florence,* Beyle made many barely veiled references to these recent events, references whose boldness alarmed his friends in Paris. His allusions in his *Journal* express in concise but unmistakable terms the full extent of his disenchantment and loathing.

Stendhal had taken too active and intimate a part in the political and military upheaval of post-Revolutionary France and Europe to resign himself, now that he had opted for permanent exile and a literary career as a mode of existence, to the role of a detached and benign spectator. His first published books clearly show that the dilettante, esthete, and amateur in him could not repress the keen political observer and critic. His later works would, if anything, reveal even more forcefully that literature and politics, for Stendhal, were inextricably interwoven.

Ever since his lonely and rebellious childhood, Stendhal had been fond of secrecy. An abiding mistrust of all the figures that represent authority, a penchant for conspiracy, fostered by his alienation as a young Jacobin in the midst of a fiercely Royalist and Catholic milieu, were to grow over the years, especially after Waterloo when, once more, he found himself isolated in a world that had returned to the beliefs he had abhorred ever since he had learned to reason for himself. While the leading writers of the age, especially Chateaubriand, championed a new spirit closely identified with Christianity, legitimism, and anti-Bonapartism, Stendhal remained true to the spirit of the age of Revolution and Napoleon and felt only contempt and hatred for the political and religious principles that were now fashionable and officially advocated.

His situation as a Frenchman with Jacobin and Bonapartist convictions living in Italy after the Congress of Vienna was, inevitably, a difficult one. But his stubborn, tenacious nature, his determination to be true to himself, enabled him to remain firm in

purpose and steady in his devotion to a political and philosophical
creed that was now out of favor and deemed outmoded. It was
Stendhal's lifelong conviction that to achieve greatness in whatever
endeavor one undertook, it was necessary, above all else, to be authentic and consistent with one's nature, a deceptively simple
credo which required, he felt, a kind of self-knowledge and self-
awareness that few people could achieve.[22] Stendhal's diary during
these years of voluntary exile is a clear testimony to his constant efforts in order to gain greater insight into his own character.

Not too surprisingly, his paranoiac tendencies, his sense of
being surrounded by hostile or indifferent people, which he had
experienced so vividly as a youth in Grenoble, now reappeared in
various forms, but especially in his compulsive need for secre-
tiveness, concealment, and mystery. As an adolescent, he had
closely identified with Rousseau partly because he viewed the
famous writer as a victim of both his own exacerbated sensibilities
and of the misunderstanding and cruelty of his contemporaries.
Although his enthusiasm for Rousseau had somewhat diminished
since then, he would continue to look upon Jean-Jacques as the
symbol of the man of genius who, in the face of every possible ob-
stacle, follows unswervingly his own path.

Beyle's desire to escape Rousseau's tragic fate, to avoid persecution and thwart the efforts of those who could harm him now
assumed the guise of an obsessive preoccupation with police surveillance. He had always been fond of using pseudonyms or cryptic initials when referring to himself or intimates in his letters and
diaries or when signing his works. This mannerism now became a
mania. His most frequently used pseudonym, the one by which he
would be immortalized by posterity, is of course Stendhal. In his
personal writings he also liked to call himself Dominique. There
were other, and sometimes childish, subterfuges to which he
would resort through the Restoration years in order to dupe the
authorities and Austrian police in Italy and to indulge his penchant for role-playing.[23]

All these stratagems and artifices rested upon one basic as-
sumption and had one common purpose: the man of talent and

originality, if he wants to survive in a hostile and incomprehending world, has to hide his true self behind a deceptive and misleading mask. Stendhal carried over this obsession in his personal behavior, frequently concealing his deep feelings and beliefs even from those close to him. The image he taught himself to project was one of a debonair, jaunty, light-hearted and cynical wit and bon vivant, and he played this part with such gusto and conviction that even the most perceptive of his contemporaries were often fooled, mistaking the assumed personality for the real one and concluding that this funny, talkative, casual and carefree bachelor was not to be taken with excessive seriousness. Hence a misunderstanding, for which Stendhal is himself partly responsible and which was fostered by early critics and contemporary authors, that could be corrected only when devoted Stendhalians, no longer under the impact of hasty, superficial impressions, would learn to distinguish the facets of a complex and sometimes elusive and baffling personality.

XIII

Métilde and *De L'amour*

IN THE SPRING of 1818, on March 4, to be precise, an event took place in Stendhal's life which was to have a profound and lasting impact on his sensibilities. On that day he was introduced to a young woman, Mathilde Viscontini Dembowski, whom he would always call Métilde.

Métilde made an immediate and overwhelming impression on Stendhal, and his fascination with her quickly became the most passionate and shattering love of his life. For the following three years, as he confides in his autobiographical writings, she was the center of his universe, his sole and exclusive preoccupation and the cause of such torment and anguish that, when at last he had to admit defeat, he left for Paris in 1821 in a suicidal mood. So obsessed was he at that time with a desire, as he put it, to blow out his brains that he kept drawing revolvers in the margins of his notebooks.[1]

What manner of a person was this Métilde who wrought such havoc in Stendhal's emotional life and whose memory would haunt him with greater poignancy than that of any other woman he loved?

Métilde was a native Milanese, and her family, the Viscontinis, formed part of the most highly regarded circles of the old and wealthy upper bourgeoisie in that city.[2] She had married young, at the age of seventeen, Jan Dembowski, a Polish officer who had decided on a military career in Italy and who eventually rose to the

186

rank of brigadier general. He was twenty years her senior and whatever happiness and glamor there may have been in this union, which produced two sons, must have been of fairly short duration. After years of abuse at the hands of her unfaithful and ill-tempered husband, Mme Dembowski took her children and separated from him, an unusual act of independence for a woman of her times and social background. When Stendhal made her acquaintance, in the spring of 1818, she was twenty-eight years old.

From all accounts, Métilde was a cultivated, beautiful woman, with an oval-shaped face, fine features, an aristocratic, slightly aquiline nose, melancholy, pensive brown eyes, and a delicately drawn mouth. Her dark auburn hair, parted in the middle, accentuated a smooth, rounded forehead. What no doubt immediately attracted Stendhal to Métilde was her proud, pensive expression and the nobility, reserve, and gracefulness of her manner. An air of mystery and self-contained aloofness added fascination to her person, and Stendhal saw her as the perfect living counterpart of those northern Italian beauties he so greatly admired in his favorite paintings.

That Métilde's ambiguous position as a woman who had left her husband made her more vulnerable to gossips and scandalmongers endeared her even more to Stendhal, who had always felt a special sympathy for women victimized by men and ostracized by society. In this respect, she must have reminded him of another great love in his life, Mélanie Guilbert. For her part, though, Métilde had been so deeply scarred by her unhappy marriage and was furthermore so conscious of the precariousness of her present status as a woman living alone that she was especially on her guard in her relations with members of the opposite sex.

After years of misery and humiliation, proud, serious, and self-reliant Métilde prized her hard-won freedom and independence and was determined to safeguard her honor against society's malevolence toward women like herself. She sympathized with the cause of the liberal patriots who were secretly engaged in the struggle against the Austrian occupation. Just as she had revolted against the oppression of a tyrannical husband, she passionately identified with those courageous Italians who wanted to throw off the yoke of Austrian rule and establish the independence of their motherland. Her political beliefs and activities were well known to the Austrian agents, who regarded her as a dangerous, subversive troublemaker. While her association with the leaders of the Carbonari movement did not help her position in the social circles in Milan, it only intensified Stendhal's respect and admiration for her character and spirit.

Hearing her speak with eloquence and passion about the cause of Italian independence, Stendhal fell completely and hopelessly under her spell. Here was a lovely woman who also possessed a noble soul and who did not fear to espouse a just but hazardous cause. Stendhal had always sought in women spiritual qualities that endowed them with a poetic, even heroic aura.

Of all the women he had so far loved or been attracted to, Métilde was the one who combined, in the most exemplary fashion, those attributes of mind and sensibility that coincided with his ideal of perfect womanhood: passion held in tight control by pride and reserve, independence of mind, strong convictions, courage and generosity. There was, moreover, a more indefinable quality about Métilde that struck the most secret chords in Stendhal's sensibility. This quality can perhaps best be intimated as being of a poetic and elegiac nature, for Stendhal's references to her all conjure up tender, affecting images.[3]

From the outset, Métilde assumed with Stendhal a severe, stern attitude and repulsed his ardent advances and declarations of love. In vain he tried to persuade her of the sincerity of his feelings; not even his most eloquent and pathetic letters and appeals succeeded in allaying her suspicions.[4] He found totally baffling her sudden and unexpected changes of mood, from warm cordiality to icy reserve. Of all the women he had loved, she was indeed the most incomprehensible and unattainable. But the more she proved difficult and elusive, the more he humbled himself in sorrowful letters which she answered perfunctorily or not at all.

In early May of 1819, Métilde left Milan for several weeks in order to visit her two sons who were boarding at a school in Volterra. Unable to face her absence, Stendhal impulsively decided to rejoin her. Had she been apprised of this, Métilde would, of course, have sternly forbidden an enterprise that could not but damage further her already compromised reputation and position.

An ancient and rather isolated small town situated in the hills of Tuscany, where every newcomer was bound to be noticed, Volterra was not exactly an ideal meeting place for a secret love tryst. Stendhal's arrival startled and alarmed Métilde. She received him coldly and rebuked him severely for following her. Stendhal's ill-considered adventure ended in bitter disillusionment. In order to get him to leave Volterra, she made vague promises to meet him in Florence, where he waited in vain for her arrival. Proceeding to Bologna, he found there several letters from Grenoble informing him of his father's death on June 20.[5]

Of all of Chérubin Beyle's ambitious business ventures and agricultural enterprises only debts, complicated litigations, and very little else remained. Stendhal was not unaware of his father's penchant for high risk projects and of the serious difficulties that had resulted from his speculations in land, real estate, and experimental farming. That his father died a ruined man, however, came to him as a shock. He spent the whole month of August and the first two weeks of September 1819 in Grenoble trying to sort out the financial tangle left by his father. The land, houses, sheep, all had come to naught.[6]

Stendhal took this new disappointment very hard, and his long-standing enmity toward his father turned into embittered contempt. In addition to the vexing problem of several ensnarled lawsuits which were to take several years to settle, there was the heavy burden of accumulated debts. Stendhal regarded this enormous fiasco as a personal betrayal on the part of his father. He never forgave him for having indulged his speculative proclivities at the expense of the financial security of his children. The supreme irony was that Chérubin Beyle had always been an avaricious man who had repeatedly refused to part with any of his money, even to help his only son. It was Chérubin Beyle's greed, his overwhelming desire to make great and quick profits that had been the cause of his ruin and of the state of impecuniousness in which he left his heirs.

Stendhal's mental state, already deeply affected by Métilde's intractability, was further aggravated by the consequences of his father's death and by the renewed uncertainty with which he now faced his future and meager prospects. Once more he had to reexamine his financial situation and was not even sure whether he would be able to continue living in Milan. As he confided to Pierre Daru, he might have to go back to Paris and look for employment and some source of income. In his reduced circumstances, however, he had a consolation. Thanks to his powerful relative, he was not just another *petit bourgeois* struggling for a living and hopelessly ensnared in a life of mediocrity and pettiness: "I owe it to you . . . to have seen Europe and enjoyed the advantages of important posts."[7] At a time when Stendhal felt that he might have to depend once more upon Pierre Daru's influence and good will, he thought it politic to pay him this flattering compliment and to inform him of his own difficult situation. The letter, dated August 30, 1819, and written from Grenoble, was all the more timely since Pierre Daru, who had been ordered to retire and had had his own difficulties after the fall of the Empire, had evidently recovered a measure of his former importance since he had recently been elevated to the rank of Peer of France by Louis XVIII.

Stendhal's journey to Grenoble at least enabled him to visit Paris, where he stayed for about a month. But despite the distractions afforded by the theater, opera, and social life, he felt the irresistible pull of Italy and especially of Métilde. He would not stay on in the capital trying to solicit some post or sinecure. By the end of October, he was back in Milan, paying renewed homage to the ever intransigent Métilde.

Despite his passion, which made it difficult for Stendhal to evaluate his situation vis-à-vis Métilde objectively, he was too perceptive an observer of human nature not to recognize that she was determined to keep him at arm's length and did everything to prevent their relationship from becoming intimate. She spaced his visits, imposed harsh conditions for the encounters she reluctantly granted, and showed displeasure, even anger, when he dared break her rules and tried to catch her by surprise or see her outside the specific appointments.[8]

As always when his feelings were deeply involved, Stendhal's customary clear-headedness somehow deserted him. He committed error upon error with Métilde and, in her presence, was paralyzed by his overwhelming emotions. What he refused to admit but is clear from all evidence is that it is doubtful that Métilde ever loved him. It is more than likely that, had she had for Stendhal a truly passionate attachment, she would have thrown caution to the winds, or at least treated him differently. She most likely regarded him as a good but rather importunate friend, one whose impetuousness could complicate her life and with whom it was best to maintain a reserved, aloof demeanor.

While Stendhal continued to be under Métilde's spell, he had to turn to more accessible women in order to satisfy his sexual needs. The result was a renewed bout with a syphilitic infection which he mentioned rather light-heartedly, as was his custom when referring to this sort of mishap, in a letter dated February 8, 1820, and which he treated according to the medical lights of the day.[9] And to make matters worse, his position in Milan was becoming more precarious, for as a French expatriate with unorthodox, if not eccentric, opinions he aroused the suspicions of all, of the Austrian police, who considered him an undesirable foreigner and a dangerous radical, and even of his friends and of Métilde herself, who looked upon him as an unreliable sympathizer to the cause of Italian independence and liberalism.[10] That Métilde did not trust him left Stendhal disconsolate; in vain he tried to dispel her fears. She remained adamant, and all the more so since she not only distrusted him as a political ally, she had also been darkly warned about his character. He was, she had been told, one of those cynical Frenchmen entirely dedicated to the pursuit of their selfish gratifications, in short a heartless Don Juan who would think nothing of seducing and bringing disgrace to an honest woman.[11]

At last, Stendhal had to resign himself to the inevitable. Métilde would never be his. They parted on June 13, 1821, and Stendhal, sick at heart, set off for Paris.[12] His departure from Milan was dictated both by his desire to learn to live without Métilde and by considerations of prudence, for he was being so closely observed by the Austrian occupation authorities that a continued stay in Italy was no longer advisable under the circumstances. His situation in Milan, for these personal and political reasons, had become even more intolerable than the unpleasant alternative of struggling to survive in Paris under the Restoration.

During his last meeting with Métilde, she had asked him when he would come back to Milan: "Never, I hope," he had answered somberly. There had been some awkward attempts at explanation and justification on both sides, but not the words from Métilde that might have changed Stendhal's life. The journey was a gloomy one and Stendhal felt as though everything was over for him, since he was leaving behind a woman he adored and the city he loved most in the world. Yet even then a thought lingered on that Métilde had repulsed him not because she did not love him but out of pride and an inability to ignore the local gossips, scandalmongers, and busybodies and to live up to her unusual position as an emancipated woman.[13] Many years later, when writing his autobiographical *Henry Brulard*, he still speculated about her true feelings toward him: "Métilde absorbed my life totally from 1818 to 1824. And I am not cured yet. . . . Did she love me?"[14] It is not inconceivable that Métilde had not been indifferent to her passionate admirer but, not unlike the proud and uncompromising heroine of *La Princesse de Clèves*, the famous seventeenth-century novel by Madame de Lafayette, had steadfastly refused to give into feelings of love and tenderness out of a general distrust of men, a sense of her own self-esteem, and a desire to remain irreproachable in the eyes of the world.

Four years after Stendhal's sad departure from Milan, in 1825, Métilde died prematurely. But by then Stendhal's all-consuming passion had had time to turn into a tender, wistful memory, and her image had lost much of its unbearable intensity. It lived on, however, until Stendhal's own death, and that he cherished that image dearly is made amply clear by his gentle, loving, elegiac evocations of her in his personal writings.[15]

A direct, immediate outcome of Stendhal's unrequited love for Métilde was his essay *De l'amour*, the idea of which had occurred to him at the height of his passion. *De l'amour* is both a treatise and a veiled personal confession. It was written during the winter of 1819–20, and appeared in 1822. Métilde's haunting presence in Stendhal's psyche and imagination as a creative writer can also be detected in his most touching, vulnerable, yet unattainable heroines. Perhaps Madame de Chasteller, in *Lucien Leuwen*, is the closest fictionalized recreation of Métilde.

De l'amour has frequently been misunderstood. Its very title holds the alluring promise of a manual on physical love and its techniques. It is neither that nor an abstract, philosophical disquisition on the subject. There are, to be sure, anecdotes in the book, but they are not of the salty variety. The emphasis, throughout, is not on the physical but on the psychological workings that cause what Stendhal calls "crystallization," the complex process by which a man or woman endows a member of the opposite sex with those qualities that exemplifly a subjective ideal of perfection. The term is an analogy deriving from an observation Stendhal made when visiting the salt mines in Salzburg.[16] A naked branch left in the depths of a mine is in time covered with the most beautiful, dazzling crystals.

De l'amour presents a curious mixture of impersonal, cerebral analysis and subjective self-revelation. As a disciple of the ideologists, themselves partisans of a strictly mechanistic and determinist theory of human behavior, Stendhal endeavored, in *De l'amour*, to reduce the complex psycho-physiological phenomenon of love to a rationalistic, predictable process. He divided love into four broad categories: 1) love-passion, the strongest and highest form of love, such as that of Héloïse and Abélard; 2) *amour-goût*, an untranslatable expression signifying a sophisticated form of attraction based upon an affinity in culture, background, taste, and predilection, the best examples of which could be found in Paris in the eighteenth century and which embody the kind of delicacy and refinement identified with the Rococo style and spirit; 3) physical love, the most elementary and basic form of love which is entirely dependent upon sexual attraction; 4) love-vanity, a product of the most artificial values and which consists in equating love with power, status, and wealth.[17]

Stendhal further divided love into stages of evolution which encompass admiration, desire, hope, jealousy, and the final crystallization. These divisions and categories may appear rather arbitrary and pedantic. But they are a synthesis not only of eighteenth-century ideology and psychology, but also of Stendhal's own experience and first-hand observations of human behavior. The chapters are very brief, in the manner of Montesquieu's *Spirit of the Laws*, and the style is pithy and deliberately unadorned. "I make every possible effort to be *dry*," writes the author in one of those personal statements that stand out amid the more analytical passages.[18] There are also detached *pensées*, aphorisms, and maxims reminiscent of the moralists and writers of the seventeenth and eighteenth centuries, and love is not only analyzed in its various manifestations, but also in its relation to climate, social and political institutions, literature and art. Throughout the book one feels, behind veiled allusions, the presence of Métilde, here renamed Léonore, and it is love-passion, its intense spirituality, that the author analyzes at greatest length.

De l'amour, with its peculiar amalgamation of lyricism of feeling and matter-of-factness of form, is a somewhat disconcerting work, even to the modern reader. Yet it has charm, simplicity, and naturalness, and if it cannot be ranked with Stendhal's masterpieces, it nevertheless bears the unmistakable stamp of his literary personality and genius. At the time of its publication, however, it completely failed to sell or to impress contemporary critics.

XIV

Paris under the Restoration

UPON HIS ARRIVAL in Paris from Milan, on June 21, 1821, Stendhal tried his best to cope with his suicidal frame of mind. "In 1821," he later wrote in his *Souvenirs d'égotisme*, "I had a lot of trouble resisting the temptation to blow out my brains." But with characteristic self-deprecatory irony, he added this explanation for not taking his own life after all: "It seems to me that it was political curiosity which prevented me from ending it all; perhaps, without my suspecting it, it was also the fear of hurting myself." [1]

Even though he had dreaded returning to the French capital, Stendhal was to remain there until the end of the decade and the establishment of the July Monarchy. Little by little, he came to reconcile himself to life in Paris, even under a political regime he loathed. There were also journeys that provided the cultural enrichment and diversion he so highly prized. Because of his literary interests, he was becoming increasingly eager to familiarize himself with the land of Shakespeare. [2] No sooner had he settled down in Paris than he set off for England, where he spent October and most of November 1821, and where he slowly emerged from his depression over leaving Métilde and Milan. He was to visit England again in the summer of 1826. And there was one sentimental trip to his beloved Italy in 1827–28.

His years as an expatriate harboring political views that were considered radical and subversive and his experience with the Austrian police had taught Stendhal the value of secrecy and concealment. In a reactionary society the liberal-minded individual had better learn to disguise his real beliefs and keep his own counsel if he is to elude persecution and harassment. This philosophy of duplicity and hypocrisy, of which Julien Sorel of *The Red and the Black* would be such an exemplary exponent, coincided with a significant aspect of Stendhal's own philosophy and strategy, which he adopted largely as a result of pragmatic necessity.

Thus circumstance and intimate conviction combined to reinforce Stendhal's determination to cultivate a light-hearted persona. Throughout his years in the Paris of the Restoration he consistently adhered to this strategy. As a sparkling conversationalist and raconteur, he was soon made to feel welcome in the leading salons, where he met writers, artists, political figures, and intellectual as well as social luminaries. His new acquaintances and interests helped him to emerge from his downcast mood.

Once he was able to overcome the state of depression that had followed his disastrous adventure with Métilde, he plunged eagerly into the lively intellectual and artistic life of Paris in the 1820s, taking an active part in the great literary debate between the classicists and romanticists.

The controversy had centered on the theater, and with his special interest in dramatic theory and practice, Stendhal soon focused on the relative merits of Racine and Shakespeare as a means to expound his own views on the subject. In 1823, he published his by now famous manifesto, *Racine and Shakespeare*. The essay, although not systematic or scholarly, is lively, entertaining, and original in that it rejects the notion of any permanent artistic ideal or canon of beauty and defines romanticism as the most contemporary, modern expression of beauty, a definition which was to make a great impression upon Baudelaire.[3] With time romanticism becomes classicism. Racine was a romantic for his age. Following such eighteenth-century writers and theorists as Montesquieu and Dubos, Stendhal had a relativistic esthetic theory and envisaged literature and art as conditioned by cultural and geographic factors.

Stendhal extolled Shakespeare as a free, creative, and untrammeled genius at a time when the English Bard continued to be viewed in most French literary circles as an undisciplined, unschooled talent whose example it was dangerous to follow. Nineteenth-century man, Stendhal proclaimed, was entitled to a new concept of tragedy, freed from the prescribed models and from the stifling neo-classical rules. Shakespeare offered a liberating example of a kind of theater that responded to the needs and aspirations of the modern Frenchman, who could hardly identify with the courtier-like, polite seventeenth-century heroes and heroines who spoke in alexandrine verse and expressed the esthetic ideal of pre-Revolutionary monarchism. Stendhal, in short, advocated a theater of actuality and realism.

Stendhal's nostalgia for Milan, La Scala, and Italian opera found expression in another book on music, also published in 1823, a *Life of Rossini*. Aside from his own predilection for Italian music, Stendhal had a more immediate, practical reason for devoting a book to Rossini. Such a study, he felt, would be timely, for Rossini was still little known in Paris. Aside from a small devoted following, Parisians, when exposed to his music, failed to respond in a manner showing a proper appreciation of the composer's greatness and originality. Here again, Stendhal had an opportunity to denounce the traditionalistic and conservative tendencies of his contemporaries. Like *Racine and Shakespeare*, the *Life of Rossini* is a manifesto exalting romanticism as the most progressive expression of modernity. [4]

Despite his Rousseauistic tendencies, Stendhal had a sociable, even gregarious side to his nature. He had always prized the intellectual stimulation that good conversation can provide, and he therefore quickly found himself in his element in the Paris salons, where he could match his wits with equals and find an appreciative audience.

Among his old friends and acquaintances, two became constant companions: Romain Colomb and Adolphe de Mareste. [5] Romain Colomb was a cousin on his mother's side and a schoolmate from the Central School in Grenoble on whose loyalty and sound advice, especially in literary and publishing matters, Stendhal had come to rely heavily. Level-headed and a middle-of-the-roader in his outlook and tastes, Colomb was a trifle too down-to-earth and stolid to fathom the depths of Stendhal's sensibility. But he was a devoted, fastidious friend and a valuable, steadying influence, and in his autobiographical *Henry Brulard*, Stendhal makes it clear in his references that Colomb was his most reliable and faithful confidant.[6]

Adolphe de Mareste, who also hailed from Grenoble, was more aristocratic in his temperament and personality than Romain Colomb. Highly cultured, refined, sophisticated, and shrewd in his judgment of men, he became Stendhal's favorite companion. Whereas Colomb had an unglamorous career as a supervisor in the administrative cadres of the department of taxation for the city of Paris, Adolphe de Mareste had, like Stendhal, embarked upon a military career under Napoleon. But he fared better than his friend after the fall of the Empire and managed to rise to a high post in the Paris police prefecture under the Restoration and July Monarchy. This was perhaps a factor in the cooling off of their relationship at the end of the 1820s.

One of Stendhal's new friends, on the other hand, was Prosper Mérimée, the novelist and short-story writer, today known outside of France mainly as the author of *Carmen*, the basis of Bizet's famous opera. A scholar and linguist as well as a man of the world, Mérimée shared many interests and attitudes with Stendhal. Like Stendhal, he disliked effusiveness in manner and speech and, in his writings, was a practitioner of the sober, concise style. Despite their considerable difference in age (Mérimée was twenty years Stendhal's junior), the two men became inseparable.

With their sharply critical intellects, they spared neither each other nor those with whom they came into contact and allowed few inhibitions to hamper their lively discussions and comradeship. Stendhal advised his young friend to familiarize himself with the eighteenth-century writers and thinkers and told him to avoid the turgid, high-flown style then in vogue. Stendhal, who regarded most men of the younger generation of writers as cunning practitioners of what he harshly called literary "charlatanism," paid his friend what to him was the highest form of compliment: he placed. Mérimée in the very select and small company of those rare authors (including himself) who had steadfastly remained "noncharlatans" in their style of writing.[7] Stendhal's esteem and affection for Mérimée were repaid in kind, for at a time when so few contemporaries were able to penetrate our author's true nature and unique literary merits, Mérimée showed perspicuity in his evaluation of both the man and the writer, and in his personal comments stressed his friend's gentleness, sensitivity, tact, and thoughtfulness, traits that were not easily discernible beneath the carefree and cynical manner Stendhal was wont to assume not only in society, but also frequently in his dealings with intimates.

It is to Mérimée's credit that he was quick to perceive that, underneath Stendhal's swagger and braggadocio, there beat a passionate, courageous, yet vulnerable heart and that, behind the dilettante and dabbler, there was a great and original literary artist. Mérimée also testified to his friend's character and to the fact that, with his generous, loyal, and proud nature, he would have been totally incapable of any base or mean act.[8] Theirs was to be a lifelong association; comrades in arms in the battle of romanticism, they frequented the same salons, had the same friends, and enjoyed an easy, intimate rapport.[9] Under the July Monarchy, they even became travel companions on journeys in France and Italy.

That this friendship between two writers must have had an impact on their work is entirely conceivable although well-nigh impossible to measure in quantifiable terms; and it is more than likely that, of the two men, it was the younger one who profited most from this relationship. With his vast personal experience, wide learning, and intellectual as well as emotional bonds with the Enlightenment, French Revolution, and Napoleonic era, Stendhal had much information and insight to impart to his gifted and quick-witted young friend.

Gradually Stendhal broadened his circle of acquaintances and eventually got to know personally or to resume contact with the most notable intellectuals, men of letters, artists, and scientists of his day: the writers Balzac, Benjamin Constant, Alfred de Musset,

Lamartine, and Sainte-Beuve, the painters Gérard and Delacroix, the sculptor David d'Angers, the art critic Delécluze, the historians Thiers, Mignet, and Count Ségur, the philosophers Destutt de Tracy and Victor Cousin, the naturalist Cuvier, the physicist Ampère, and many others a list of whom would constitute a who's who of the French capital in the 1820s.

Stendhal's gifts as a conversationalist and critic found an outlet in his steady contributions, which were particularly active in the 1820s, to English journals and, more occasionally, to French reviews.[10] In his light, bantering manner, he touched upon everything that he found interesting or significant in literature, politics, or social mores. Unabashedly subjective and partial in his judgments and views, he expressed his ideas and passions with force and daring, never deigning to veil his true convictions behind a show of impartiality or ponderous erudition. As a result, these lively articles are more than an exercise in intellectual and egocentric showmanship. They bear the distinctive impress of Stendhal's style and thought and present a vivid, revealing tableau of the European culture of the time as reflected by an extraordinarily acute, original, and well-informed mind.

Among the salons most assiduously frequented by Stendhal, there was the famous one presided over by the influential Countess Beugnot, wife of a high official under Napoleon who had successfully made the transition to the Restoration. Already in 1810, in his heyday as an Auditor to the Council of State, Stendhal had been one of the habitués of Countess Beugnot's salon. When his fortunes plummeted with those of Napoleon, Beugnot, himself a protégé of Talleyrand and a political ally of Bernadotte, tried to obtain a new post for him, no doubt at the instigation of his wife.[11] But Stendhal, in his impatience to leave France and too proud to accept favors, had hastened to Milan before anything could come of Beugnot's efforts on his behalf.

When Stendhal returned to Paris in 1821, Countess Beugnot, who had always had a liking for him, welcomed him warmly and made him feel at home in her salon. That Stendhal, for his part, was fond of Countess Beugnot is borne out by his references in his intimate writings and by the fact that he dedicated to her his first work, the *Lives of Haydn, Mozart and Metastasio.*[12] He was all the more eager to visit the Beugnots after 1821 since he had become aware of the existence of their lovely daughter Clémentine. Born in 1788, Clémentine had married in 1808 a nobleman and general, Count Curial, who had served Napoleon but subsequently switched his allegiance to Louis XVIII. The marriage was an unhappy one, for Curial was a notorious philanderer and Clémentine, for her part, was a headstrong, temperamental, and rather spoiled young woman.

Clémentine, or Menti as Stendhal liked to call her, was an elegantly tall young woman with expressive features, full, sensual lips, a rather strong nose, and magnificent eyes. At first, Stendhal was too filled with the haunting memory of Métilde to fall in love with the daughter of his patroness. Moreover, he had been too harshly rebuffed to expose himself to another humiliating rejection. He therefore remained on his guard, attentive, considerate, but reserved. It was finally the strong-willed Countess Curial who took the initiative. By the spring of 1824, she was Stendhal's mistress. In an autobiographical essay humorously composed in the form of a necrological article and dated 1837, Stendhal credits Menti with having pulled him out of the suicidal mood in which his unhappy love affair with Métilde had left him and with having restored his zest for life.[13] If he was at first understandingly reluctant to embark upon another liaison, he quickly made up for his initial hesitancy, and in his *Henry Brulard* he ranks Clémentine Curial among his four greatest passions, the other three being Mélanie Guilbert, Alexandrine Daru, and Métilde Dembowski.[14] He even felt that she surpassed the others in one respect, that of *esprit*, or liveliness of mind, a form of intelligence frequently referred to as wit. And it is no doubt because she herself was endowed with this eminently eighteenth-century intellectual attribute that she felt strongly attracted to Stendhal, to his sparkling conversation, and original, daring insights. When their liaison began, Menti was in her mid-thirties and no doubt conscious that this might well be her last opportunity for fulfillment through passionate love. As for Stendhal, he had reached his forty-first birthday, and his short stature, ample girth, and large head hardly qualified him as the ideal lover. Yet his personality was so arresting, his intelligence so evident, his manner so engaging that it is not surprising a discriminating woman like Menti found him irresistible.

The ardent, impulsive, and sensual Menti had this in common with some of Stendhal's boldest fictional heroines that she did not hesitate to take chances in making secret assignations and that the risks she took to meet her lover were in proportion to her amorous fervor. In July 1824, she kept him hidden for three days in the basement of her country house. While she admired his intellectual forcefulness, she was no less appreciative of his prowess as a lover, as her remarkably blunt letters to him testify.[15]

Stendhal's happiness with Menti, however, was not destined to be long-lived. Possessive, jealous, suspicious, temperamental, intense, and demanding, Menti sorely tried her lover's patience and forbearance, and there were frequent quarrels. In 1826, after two years of a stormy relationship, Stendhal had to face the fact that Menti had lost interest in him. Unpredictable, excessive, and strong-willed that she was, Menti was as swift and decisive about putting an end to her relationship with Stendhal as she had been about starting it. Mindful of the adage that distance makes the heart grow fonder, Stendhal had decided that a journey to England might help arrange matters. His anguish and unhappiness were acute, therefore, when in the late summer of 1826, while he was visiting London and touring the north of England, he was informed in no uncertain terms that everything between them was over.[16] Of the women he had loved most passionately, Menti was the one, as he confides in *Henry Brulard*, who made him the most miserable by leaving him, with the notable exception of Métilde Dembowski, "who would not tell me whether she loved me."[17]

It took Stendhal no less than a year—from September 1826 to September 1827—to recover from Menti's defection: "On the day of that fearful anniversary [of the rupture of their love affair]. I was on the isle of Ischia; and I noticed a marked improvement; instead of thinking about my misfortune directly, as I did a few months earlier, I only thought of the *memory* of the unhappy state in which I was plunged in October 1826 for instance. This observation greatly comforted me."[18] Stendhal and Countess Curial were to remain good friends, however, and ten years after their breakup, in 1836, he was to make one last but futile attempt to recapture her love.[19] In his *Henry Brulard*, Stendhal, musing about this relationship, made a general psychological observation based upon this particular experience: "And what is singular and rather regrettable, I said to myself this morning, is that my *victories* (as I then called them, my head being full of military ideas) never gave me a pleasure half as strong as the profound unhappiness I experienced in my defeats. The astonishing victory over Menti did not give me a pleasure one hundredth part comparable to the pain she caused me by leaving me."[20]

Having gradually recovered his emotional equilibrium, Stendhal once more plunged into literary and artistic endeavors. Work, in the last analysis, was always his best antidote and therapy against depression. In February 1826, he had begun writing his first novel, entitled *Armance*, but had interrupted his work to make a journey to England. It was partly in order to cure himself of his love for Menti that he resumed writing *Armance*, which was published in August 1827.

The theme Stendhal selected for *Armance* constitutes a fascinating twist in the novelistic tradition. The hero, Octave de Malivert, appears to have everything in his favor to achieve happiness: youth, social stature, good looks, intellect, and sensitivity as well as the passionate love of an intelligent, proud young woman, Armance de Zohiloff. Yet, Octave is moody, somber, and reluctant to marry Armance, even though the young couple is ideally matched from every standpoint. Such unpredictable behavior was by no means exceptional on the part of romantic heroes, and there is a Byronic aura about the handsome but morose Octave. Among the important and influential novelists of the eighteenth century who Stendhal had read with special interest were the abbé Prévost and, of course, Rousseau.[21] Their main protagonists had a brooding, hypersensitive nature and were given to introspection and self-analysis. Yet the reason for Octave's saturnine behavior is quite different. He is sexually impotent. Such a singular and delicate theme obviously constituted a challenge for Stendhal, who resorted to indirection and nowhere in the novel stated the cause of Octave's unhappiness in sufficiently clear terms to enlighten his reader. The latter can only rely upon vague hints and references to a dark secret in order to guess at the reason that retards Octave's marriage with Armance and that leads to the tragic outcome: the hero's suicide.

Stendhal was highly conscious of the fact that the subject of his novel was a dangerous one for several reasons, not least of which was that it closely bordered on the comic or the scabrous. He thought that he would avoid these pitfalls by using extreme discretion and understatement. In addition, precautions were in order in the prim and proper society of the Restoration and under the repressive and moralistic reign of Charles X. But as the freest and least tradition-bound of the literary genres, the novel lent itself to such a bold experiment. Moreover, Stendhal had read a recently published novel, *Olivier*, on a similar topic.[22] It had been brought out anonymously, but had been authored by a man of letters by the name of Hyacinthe Thabaud de La Touche, who in turn had borrowed the subject from a contemporary woman novelist who specialized in such controversial subjects, Madame de Duras.[23]

The result is a work which, to be sure, is not wholly new in its theme, but which is strikingly original in the way Stendhal probed the psychological workings of his two main protagonists and especially of his unlikely hero and lover. The novel is further enriched with lively vignettes of Parisian social manners and morals in the late 1820s. That the eccentric, enigmatic hero of *Armance* embodies some of Stendhal's own traits and his occasional failings as a lover has been demonstrated, and that the problem of sexual impotence rather preoccupied him is shown by his allusions in his intimate writings as well as by the chapter "Des Fiasco" in *De l'amour*.[24]

The theme of impotence, however, has broader, more symbolic implications in the novel. Octave is a Hamlet-like figure and an outcast who views society from the sidelines. His endless self-analysis and fastidiousness deprive him of the ability to act. He is the alienated intellectual, the eternal outsider and critic.

While all of Stendhal's fictional characters possess autobiographical elements, it would be a gross simplification to identify them with their creator. Octave represents one exaggerated facet of Stendhal's psyche: the masochistic, melancholy, hypersensitive misanthrope. Writing *Armance* was both an exercise and an exorcism. No wonder it has intrigued and captivated such discriminating writers and critics as André Gide and Albert Thibaudet.[25] It is a penetrating, compelling study in abnormal psycho-physiology, and it was novel and bold in its sympathetic, subtle treatment of a case which, by its very nature, tested Stendhal's resources as a budding novelist. It is also worth noting that, already in his first work of fiction, Stendhal rejected easy formulas and proven methods but preferred to experiment with a situation that would make unusual demands on his skills as a storyteller and analyst of human motives and behavior.

With *Armance*, Stendhal was to set another pattern. He composed quickly, even feverishly, writing at a furious pace and limiting drastically the process of revising and polishing. This approach was in keeping with his esthetics of unvarnished sincerity and truthfulness. Too much attention to style and form could easily become a convenient screen hiding the author's ideas or the absence thereof. It is precisely of this kind of literary mendacity, practiced in the name of formal, stylistic beauty, that he considered Chateaubriand and the other Romantics guilty.

Despite its titillating theme, *Armance* failed to attract the interest of the public and critics. It was indifferently, even coldly received. It both baffled and displeased most readers, and its matter-of-fact, terse style was not appreciated by a generation that was conditioned to expect fiction to be written in a sumptuous, richly orchestrated prose.

As a writer, Stendhal had thus far obtained best results with his journalism and with his essays as an art critic and touristic guide to Italy. He decided to augment his *Rome, Naples and Florence*, published in 1817 and almost simultaneously followed by a second printing in London, with a view to bringing out an enlarged, third edition of the work. From this project arose the idea of yet another book, *Promenades in Rome*, published in September 1829.

The cultural and artistic pilgrimage to Rome was, of course, a well-established tradition and it was an integral part of the grand tour, that essential feature of the education of young men of the British aristocracy. It was Stendhal's purpose to fill a need for a guide book to the Eternal City and its historic treasures. It is easy to guess, however, that he would not content himself with presenting merely practical, useful information and an accumulation of facts and dates. At the same time, however, one cannot reasonably expect him to be the most reliable and accurate of guides. Whatever defects and shortcomings are to be found in the *Promenades in Rome*, they are more than compensated for by the author's acuity of insight and perception, his vivacity of style, and his preoccupation with the larger questions of creativity and vitality in their interconnection with politics and social institutions.

As a disciple of Montesquieu and the Ideologists, Stendhal showed a special concern for the historic, geographic, and political factors that directly affect culture; and while he made earnest efforts to show impartiality and objectivity in evaluating different periods and their respective artistic contributions, it is obvious that his personal preference went to those privileged eras that witnessed the most spectacular bursts of creative energy. No wonder, then, that his favorite period was the Italian Renaissance, when a corrupt and therefore tolerant Church and a political atmosphere charged with ambition and intrigue contributed powerfully to the blossoming of strong personalities.

The great artists of the Renaissance reflect this individualistic culture which fostered men of fiery imagination and unbridled passion. This esthetic theory coincided perfectly with Stendhal's own cult of energy and with his loathing of the timorous, grossly materialistic, and hypocritical values of post-Napoleonic society. But while Stendhal, like the Romantics, exalted the passions, he was unremittingly out of tune with them on several counts. Their political and religious ideology went counter to his own Enlightenment philosophy and their stylistic flourishes and fireworks irritated and bored him. Chateaubriand and his epigones generally left him cold, partly because of their political and religious ideology, which he found both naïve and retrogressive, and also because of their literacy stance, which he deemed narcissistic and exhibitionistic. The Italian Renaissance, at least the way Stendhal envisaged it, presented an ideal combination of intellectual curiosity, idealism and cynicism, passion and calculation, and the *Promenades in Rome* is, among other things, an eloquent testimony to his love of his adopted country and its cultural heritage.

In the beginning of 1829, Stendhal became passionately if briefly involved with Alberthe de Rubempré, a cousin of the painter Delacroix, whom he saw fairly regularly since they both frequented the same salons. Madame Azur—the nickname he gave her—was twenty-five when Delacroix introduced her to Stendhal. The two men were on good terms since Stendhal, in his capacity as journalist and art critic, had praised the highly controversial painter.[26]

Madame Azur was a provocative, high-spirited brunette who liked to dress in colorful, exotic outfits. Hailing from a theatrical family, she had made an early and respectable marriage, but had afterwards indulged in her taste for men, astrology, and supernaturalism. According to some contemporaries, she was quite mad. She became Stendhal's mistress in June of 1829, but before long she deserted him for one of his closest friends, Adolphe de Mareste. In the *Life of Henry Brulard*, she has the dubious distinction of occupying the last position in two lists of women who played important roles in Stendhal's life, with the further qualification that his love for her had lasted "a month at most." [27]

Before resigning himself to middle age and permanent bachelorhood, Stendhal was to experience one more love affair. A noble and wealthy young Italian woman, Giulia Rinieri, from

Siena, Tuscany, had arrived in Paris in 1826, accompanied by a tutor, Daniello Berlinghieri, himself of aristocratic parentage and a close friend of the family. Giulia met Stendhal in the salon of Cuvier, the naturalist, and by the beginning of 1830, made it clear to him that, aging and homely though he was, he could still stir the heart of an attractive and desirable woman. Like Countess Curial, Giulia took the initiative and practically threw herself in the arms of her astonished and delighted lover. But unlike Menti, Giulia was not married and her liaison was a liability in the starchy Restoration society. Stendhal, as a man of honor, hastened to ask for her hand in marriage in a formal letter to her tutor and guardian, in which he honestly stated all his liabilities, both personal and financial.[28]

As might be expected, Stendhal's proposal was politely but firmly turned down and Giulia was eventually married off to a cousin, deemed a more appropriate match. That Giulia, for her part, was sincere in her attachment for Stendhal is demonstrated by the fact that she remained his good friend even after her marriage. In his testament, Stendhal bequeathed to Giulia a copy of Rousseau's *La Nouvelle Héloïse*. In view of the writer's lifelong and intimate involvement with the novel, of his admiration for its heroine and its lyrical and moving depiction of passionate love pitted against social convention, this was the highest tribute he could pay to the woman who had so generously given herself to him at a time when he no longer believed that such a miracle was possible.

XV

The Red and the Black

IN THE COURSE of writing his cultural and touristic guides to
Italy, Stendhal developed a keen interest in the folklore material,
legends, and chronicles revelatory of the character, customs, and
manners of Italians, especially of the Renaissance. While rum-
maging through old manuscripts, he came across tales and *causes
célèbres* that struck him as the perfect sources for freely interpreted
and adapted stories of doomed love and thwarted passion. He became an avid collector of these manuscripts.[1]

Here were colorful, dramatic examples of instinctive, unfet-
tered energy, of crimes of passion and jealousy showing violent,
primitive but also vital and creative natures in the throes of overwhelming emotions. Crimes of passion and their psychological and
sociological implications held a special fascination for Stendhal, for
they offered him an opportunity to test his deterministic philosophy of human motivation and to enrich his knowledge of human
behavior. Crimes motivated by mere greed, on the other hand, left
him indifferent, for he considered them as too simple and commonplace.[2]

Focusing on the short story with an Italian setting, Stendhal
found that it enabled him to combine his predilection for the
picturesque manners and mores of the Italians of old with short,
compact prose narratives loosely based upon historical or pseudo-
historical sources. Thus was born the idea of a number of short
stories, which appeared in the *Revue des Deux-Mondes* and the

209

Revue de Paris and which were posthumously published as a collection under the title *Italian Chronicles* in 1855. Here Stendhal could give free play to his idealized and dramatized concept of Italy and indulge his love of mystification by pretending that the stories were merely transcriptions and translations of authentic, original historical data retrieved from musty archives, a fictional device greatly favored by eighteenth-century novelists.[3]

Vanina Vanini, the first of the *Italian Chronicles* to be published, appeared in the *Revue de Paris* in December 1829. Like the other stories in the series, it was a somber tale of passion and violence, but it is uncharacteristically set in early nineteenth-century Italy and directly related to the Carbonari movement. This departure was probably meant to demonstrate that contemporary Italians were the worthy descendants of the energetic and daring men and women of the Renaissance. The heroine, Vanina Vanini, a proud, strong-willed young Roman aristocrat falls in love and gives herself to an outlawed Carbonaro. Unable to bear the thought that her lover is more committed to his political cause than to her, she turns informer on his underground friends in the mistaken belief that by isolating him she will succeed in bringing him back to her.

It is a story of feminine passion and tragic miscalculation, and as such it renews, albeit in a different setting, a French tradition already brilliantly practiced by a number of eighteenth-century novelists, who were also acute analysts of the female psyche. The theme of frustrated passion and vengeance was by no means unknown to Stendhal's predecessors—but it was his original conception to give his heroine patriotic fervor, rather than another woman, as a rival to her lover's affections.

But the character of Vanina is already the prototype of the Stendhalian heroine: ardent, proud, disdainful of the conventional standards of morality, more impressed by character than social status, and equally capable of acts of heroism and cruelty. With *Vanina Vanini* we already see the Stendhal of the great novels at work.

Unlike his romantic contemporaries, Stendhal did not exploit the external apparatus of historical, geographic exoticism in order to enhance the appeal of his fiction, even in his *Italian Chronicles*. Here as elsewhere in Stendhal's novels, the use of local color is minimal and the main focus is on motivation and the play of passions. Despite his rejection of classicism and espousal of romanticism in *Racine and Shakespeare*, Stendhal remained a classicist in many ways, not least of which are his tautness and sharpness of focus and his intense, tragic, and inward-directed vision of human behavior. His long experience and familiarity with the seventeenth-century French theater no doubt contributed to his profound insight into the complexities and ambiguities of the human psyche, particularly in moments of extreme stress and emotional paroxysm.

But if Stendhal's romanticism does not express itself in the outward trappings that make up the *Italian Chronicles*, it nonetheless permeates the plots and situations for which he had a predilection and which mingle tragedy with melodrama and horror. As in the Gothic novels of Ann Radcliffe and other practitioners of the genre, although in a far lesser degree, love in the *Italian Chronicles* is associated with death, and there are castles, prisons, tortures, and executions as well as criminal clerics.

The year of 1830, so momentous in the political history of Europe, was a remarkably productive one for Stendhal. In addition to publishing two short stories, *The Coffer and the Ghost*, dealing with the theme of jealousy and, interestingly enough, with a Spanish rather than an Italian setting, and *The Philter*, another tragic love story, Stendhal conceived and completed his first great novel, *The Red and the Black*, at first identified merely as *Julien*.

Having at last come to the realization that he was no dramatist, Stendhal turned with increasing confidence to fiction. His apprenticeship as a novelist had been a long and roundabout one, and he came to it indirectly, almost by accident. It is as a critic, journalist, psychologist, political observer and commentator, moralist and philosopher that Stendhal approached the novel. His intellectual and artistic equipment was impressive and wide-ranging, and his personal experience more diversified and richer than that of most writers.

But because Stendhal would frequently use actual events and cases or pseudo-historical sources as a basis for his fictional creations, he has been accused of lacking the powers of invention and imagination, supposedly the unmistakable marks of the really great novelist.[4] If it is true that Stendhal is not, like a Balzac, the creator of a whole army of fictional characters and that his main protagonists either reflect aspects of himself or of the men and women who had made a certain impact upon his sensibilities,[5] his originality resides elsewhere, particularly in the way in which he imbues his novels with an intensity, freshness, and spontaneity of emotion, with an element of unpredictability and vivacity and with an understated style that no doubt account to a large extent for their enduring appeal to the modern reader.

Some commentators have even gone so far as to suggest that Stendhal's works of fiction should be regarded less as novels than as disguised essays in autobiography.[6] While this represents an extreme point of view, one is justified in being careful to distinguish Stendhal from such novelists as Balzac, Flaubert, or Zola, for storytelling was never his primary concern. He viewed the novel, rather, as a means of illustrating and testing, by way of narrative examples, psychological, moral, and political ideas and beliefs that were close to his heart. Like Diderot, one of the eighteenth-century authors he most respected, he was impatient with the purely technical, mechanical aspects of novel-writing, and also like Diderot he preferred to work on a canvas of existing facts and data in order to feel freer to improvise and experiment.[7] Another eighteenth-century novelistic feature frequently used by Stendhal concerns the active role played by the narrator, who does not hesitate to make humorous, critical, or ironical comments at the expense of the main protagonists.[8] This gives both characters and action an aura of greater believability and immediacy, and draws the reader more directly into the plot and situations, since these are no longer recounted by an omniscient, distant, and God-like witness.

Rather, they are related by a more informal, familiar figure who, by virtue of his unabashed editorializing, becomes a quasi-participant in his own fictional creation. No doubt, Stendhal's life-long interest in the theater also had something to do with this irrepressible desire to share the limelight with his fictional characters.[9]

The position Stendhal occupies in the evolution of the French novel is a rather solitary one. He differs from the Romantics and came to look upon them with mingled feelings because, in their preoccupation with the reader's reaction, they tended to overstate and overdramatize their perceptions and emotions, to resort to hyperbole; and he is at variance with his immediate nineteenth-century successors in his disregard for "realism," for the minute recording of external settings and data. Concerned above all that any attempt—no matter how well-intentioned or spontaneous—at stylistic embellishment was betrayal of truth and sincerity, and equally disdainful of the exact, meticulous verbal reproduction of outward reality, he preferred to focus upon the inner workings—the mental and emotional processes and vagaries—of his central characters. At the same time, he was very consistent in his belief, exemplified both in his personal and fictional writings, that the writer should take his reader into his confidence, treat him on an equal footing, give him credit for imagination and creativity, and therefore leave some things unsaid or state them in a shorthand language comprehensible to a perceptive mind and keen sensibilities. That Stendhal was fond of maintaining this relationship of mutual trust and quasi-complicity with the privileged souls he considered his ideal readers is evidenced by his discreet but insistent appeals to that small band of kindred spirits he liked to call the "happy few." [10]

Much has been written about the sources of *The Red and the Black* and about the way in which Stendhal used and adapted the Berthet case in writing what probably is his most famous novel.[11] The title of the novel has also been explicated both for its historical and symbolic message, the red signifying the values embodied by the French military uniform under Napoleon and the black referring to the priestly garment which Stendhal saw as the emblem of post-Napoleonic France: in other words, the conflict between liberal, dynamic, forward-looking values and the reactionary forces brought to the forefront by the Restoration.[12] Not to be overlooked is the subtitle of the book: *Chronicle of the Nineteenth Century.* Neither is the message of the French Revolution forgotten, since Danton, one of the most notorious representatives of Jacobin radicalism, is quoted in an epigraph to the novel: "Truth, truth in all its harshness." If Julien Sorel is above all an ardent admirer of Napoleon, he also gives his due to the leaders of the French Revolution; like most of them he, too, will meet an untimely and unjust end under the guillotine.

Had he been born earlier, Julien Sorel would—like so many young men whose humble origins did not prevent them from achieving positions of national leadership—have found a proper outlet for his intelligence, drive, and ambition. But in his own time, only the priesthood was open to a youth in his circumstances.

Always fascinated with criminal cases exemplifying the conflict between the energetic, strong-willed individual and societal institutions, Stendhal had come to the realization that Italian folk history, mores, and legends were not the sole source of examples of the kind of human behavior he found worthy of special study. Two contemporary trials held in France in particular, those of Adrien Lafargue and Antoine Berthet, both reported in the *Gazette des Tribunaux,* revealed to him that crimes of passion also occurred in Restoration France. It is not our purpose to dwell upon the details of these two sensational trials. Suffice it to say that, of the two cases, the one that particularly struck Stendhal was that of the former Dauphinois seminarist Antoine Berthet, accused, convicted, and guillotined for the crime of shooting down, in the midst of a religious service, a woman who had been both his benefactress and mistress. Antoine Berthet, like his fictional counterpart, was a social misfit, a drifter, both unstable and resentful, endowed with a lively intelligence but quickly embittered by the way in which society, he felt, had ignored his ability.

Julien Sorel, of course, is a far more complex and interesting

Portrait of Dr. Henri Gagnon, Stendhal's maternal grandfather and favorite relative (1728–1813). Unsigned painting, perhaps by Joseph Le Roy, young Stendhal's drawing teacher
Musée Stendhal, Grenoble. Photo Piccardy

The Jardin de Ville of Grenoble, view of the upper terrace and chestnut lane.
This painting by Joseph Le Roy was originally owned by Stendhal.
Musée Stendhal, Grenoble. Cliché du Musée

Portrait of Pauline-Eléonore Beyle (Mme François Périer-Lagrange), Stendhal's
beloved sister and loyal confidante (1786–1857). Anonymous painting
Musée Stendhal, Grenoble. Photo Piccardy

Anonymous portrait of the abbé Jean-François Raillane, young Stendhal's hated
tutor (1756–1840)
Musée Stendhal, Grenoble. Photo Piccardy

Portrait of Jean-Gaspard Dubois-Fontanelle, Stendhal's professor of French literature at the Central School of Grenoble. Painting by Louis-Joseph Jay, who taught
drawing and art history at the Central School
Musée Stendhal, Grenoble. Photo Piccardy

Portrait of Count Pierre-Antoine Daru (1767–1829), by Baron Antoine-Jean Gros. Relative of Stendhal on his mother's side and powerful administrator and statesman under Napoleon. It is primarily to Count Daru's influence and protection that Stendhal owed his military assignments and administrative posts in the vast European Napoleonic cadre.
Musée de Versailles. Cliché des Musées Nationaux—Paris

Portrait of Countess Alexandrine-Thérèse Daru (1783–1815), by Jacques-Louis David. Wife of Count Pierre Daru and good friend of Stendhal until he tried to become her lover
Copyright The Frick Collection, New York

The Crossing of the Great Saint Bernard Pass, May 1800. Watercolor by Joseph-Pierre Bagetti
Musée de Versailles. Cliché des Musées Nationaux—Paris

Lake Como. Lithograph, by Mazzola
Musée Stendhal, Grenoble. Cliché du Musée

Napoleon in his study. Portrait by Jacques-Louis David
National Gallery of Art, Washington. Samuel H. Kress Collection

The Crossing of the Berezina River (November 26–29, 1812). Anonymous gouache
Cliché et Collection Musée de l'Armée, Paris

The Retreat from Russia. Anonymous watercolor
Cliché et Collection Musée de l'Armée, Paris

The Great Fire of Moscow, as seen from the ramparts of the Kremlin Citadel (September 14–18, 1812). Watercolor by Faber du Faur

Cliché et Collection Musée de l'Armée, Paris

Last portrait of Stendhal, executed at Civitavecchia, August 8, 1841, after the author's first stroke and seven months before his death. Pencil drawing by Henri Lehmann

Musée Stendhal, Grenoble. Photo Piccardy

character than Antoine Berthet, if only because Stendhal endowed him with his own experience, insight, and sensibility. One of the reasons why Stendhal eventually gave up the theater as a means of literary expression was no doubt his awareness that only in the novel could he give full play to his love of facts firmly grounded in reality and his need for painting broad canvases encompassing the whole social and political spectrum of an epoch. It is worth noting that, while he had written his plays laboriously and with painful self-consciousness, he dashed off his major novels with an extraordinary facility of execution.

Julien Sorel is not only a projection of Stendhal's innermost dreams and obsessions, he is also the symbolic incarnation of a period in history which encompasses many contradictory trends. More than anything else, Julien Sorel embodies within himself the conflict between opportunistic hypocrisy and passionate impulsiveness. Mme de Rênal and Mathilde de La Mole, on the other hand, may be envisioned as two facets of the feminine dilemma: compliance and tenderness on the part of Mme de Rênal, and rebellion as well as headstrong action on the part of Mathilde de La Mole. The novel, on the whole, is built upon a binary and antithetical construction: the individual versus society, man versus woman, the Napoleonic red versus the Restoration black. The political implications of the novel are crystal clear.

If Stendhal used his own experience to impart depth and substance to Julien Sorel, it should not be inferred from this that one can identify the novelist and his fictional hero. Julien Sorel, unlike Stendhal, reasons and acts, at least until his impulsive attempted homicide defeats all his careful plans and calculations, like the very type of scheming, unscrupulous opportunist, bent upon achieving his ends by every means at his disposal. The early readers and critics of the novel, shocked by the character of Julien, have been mainly responsible for this gross oversimplification.[13] Temperamentally, Julien Sorel, with his single-minded, obsessive desire for success and recognition, could not be at greater variance with Stendhal who, throughout his life, evidenced a remarkable lack of consistency and purposefulness, a lackadaisical detachment, in his purely mundane endeavors. Admittedly, he admired ambition backed by drive, self-confidence, and single-mindedness. But, as he readily conceded with characteristic candor in his personal writings, he was too "lazy," too frequently troubled by diffidence and self-doubt, also too fond of indulging in his favorite pastime, which was to give himself over to the delight of dreaming over a beautiful musical composition, a great painting, a fine landscape, or a lovely woman, to make more than erratic, impulsive efforts in order to achieve immediate renown and success.[14]

To be sure, Julien Sorel, unbeknownst to himself, is at bottom more passionate and impulsive than ambitious and calculating, as his tragic and self-redeeming end amply demonstrates. But when, in his bitter resentment against a society which refuses to give him what he considers to be his due, he sets out to emulate Tartuffe and experiences no compunction in manipulating ruthlessly those who cross his path, and especially the two women who love him, he is at the opposite pole of his creator. But despite all his machinations and reprehensible scheming, Julien Sorel remains essentially a victim, a youth whose overheated imagination, stirred by the Napoleonic myth, made him look at the world, not as it really is, but as a field of battle where, thanks to his own elaborate strategy of deception and subterfuge, he would overcome all obstacles to his self-fulfillment. He who prides himself on his lucidity and perspicuity is at the mercy, not only of an indifferent or hostile society, but also of his own self-delusions and hypersensibilities. A young man endowed with a less active imagination, a less acute perception, a less troublesome dose of pride, would undoubtedly have fared better in a world where insensitivity and intellectual mediocrity, and above all a willingness to conform, are the prerequisites for approval and acceptance. Try hard as he might to wear a mask, to conceal his inner thoughts and feelings, Julien Sorel remains an outsider to the others, an odd sort of fellow, one who through an ill-repressed glance, tone of voice or gesture inspires distrust in his elders and superiors. And it is in this respect that Julien Sorel compels our interest and compassion and transcends the ordinary social climbers and cynics that people the eighteenth-century novels that had delighted Stendhal. The lesson of Rousseau's *La Nouvelle Héloïse* had not been forgotten. And it is precisely this odd mixture of quixotic fantasy and ruthless scheming, this combination of cynicism and idealism in a fictional hero which unnerved, and still occasionally does today, Stendhal's readers.

There is also humor in *The Red and the Black*, but of a sharp, satirical, Voltairean nature. It is rather paradoxical that Stendhal, who professed to dislike Voltaire for what he called the latter's meanness of outlook, should have learned so much from the literary comic devices so brilliantly used in *Candide*. He greatly admired Voltaire's pithy style, his ability to reduce a portrait to a caricature, and to simplify human character to the quintessential psychological elements that go into the making of a type. In *The Red and the Black*, the secondary protagonists in particular, but even occasionally the main characters, are given the Voltairean treatment.

But what makes Julien Sorel an essentially Rousseauistic and romantic character is his basic isolation and alienation. All his schemes and calculations fail pathetically and he is ultimately unable to repress, despite his constant self-surveillance, the intensity of his emotions and the powerful surge of his subconscious drives.

Julien Sorel has this in common with Vanina Vanini that he tries to do away with the one being, Mme de Rênal, that he loves the most, as he belatedly realizes in prison. And that she, in turn, loved him the most sincerely and completely is also a truth he sadly ponders in jail, while awaiting his execution. Mathilde de La Mole, on the other hand, had conceived for him an *amour de tête*, an attachment that brings into play the intellect as well as what the French call *amour-propre* (a combination of self-esteem, pride, and vanity), and what she found irresistible in this proud young plebeian who prickled so easily and whose haughty, cold demeanor only disguised an exacerbated sensibility and seething resentments was her conviction that he was the living embodiment of the fearless revolutionary and leader of men that she had been fantasizing about in her boredom with the proper and colorless noblemen who frequented her parents' home.

What Julien, in his remorse over shooting Mme de Rênal and in his resurgence of passion for her, fails to recognize, however, is that Mathilde de La Mole's emotions undergo a drastic change after his arrest and imprisonment. Her love for him has become transformed into true passion, but Mathilde's spell over him is broken. He yearns only for the kind of tenderness he had experienced with Mme de Rênal and is weary of Mathilde's difficult, demanding ways. Above all, in the face of a society that has branded him as a criminal and has imposed upon him the ultimate penalty, he is determined to preserve his dignity as an individual.

But with characteristic restraint, Stendhal leaves it up to the reader to speculate about the complex psychological motivations that cause Julien's aborted homicide and precipitate his sudden downfall. Perhaps the basic explanation is a simple one: the constant tension and self-control that regulated his every word and ac- action were bound to snap. That he was able to find serenity and inner peace only in a dark prison cell and under the shadow of the guillotine is of course the supreme irony in a work that abounds in unexpected situations and unpredictable twists of fate. Perhaps it was Stendhal's way of asserting his freedom as a storyteller and that of his protagonists. Events, no matter how tragic, have a way of resolving themselves, and it is a Julien reconciled with himself, if not with a world that spurned and rejected him, who calmly and without undue dramatics meets his untimely and unjust death. Here we rejoin Stendhal's essential epic vision of man's fate, his ideal of what a critic has aptly called the "âme généreuse." [15] An embittered, resentful, erratic, cunning, and deceitful young man has been metamorphosed, through suffering and introspection, into a moving, heroic figure.

From Stendhal's afterthoughts and comments on *The Red and the Black*, we know that, in depicting the manners and mores of middle-class provincial milieux and of Parisian aristocratic circles, Stendhal had deliberately steered clear of the elaborate descriptive techniques then so fashionable.[16] Yet, he himself was keenly aware that his refusal to give his reader what the latter expected and delighted in, vast tableaux of landscapes and interiors and scrupulously detailed catalogues of the physical characteristics of his protagonists as well as of their apparel would baffle and displease the contemporary public. His esthetic ideal, throughout the work, he insisted, had been naturalness, *le naturel*.[17] Curiously enough, however, it is in the name of this ideal that he justifies the presence in the novel of such extraordinary scenes as that, reproduced on the cover of the first edition of the novel, of Mathilde de La Mole cradling her lover's severed head in her lap.[18] It is evident, therefore, that for Stendhal naturalness does not mean the faithful description of the instincts, desires, appetites, and drives of the average person. In one way or another, each of his main characters, Julien Sorel, Mme de Rênal, Mathilde de La Mole, is outside the sociological norm, and it is obviously the novelist's intention to demonstrate that French society in particular, with its rigid codes and stress on conformity and on appearances, all based upon the psychological motive of vanity and *amour-propre*, is hardly the ideal milieu for the blossoming of strong, individualistic personalities. And in this respect, as in so many others, Stendhal was reinterpreting and reshaping the moral message of Rousseau's *La Nouvelle Héloïse*.

Stendhal, who greatly valued poetry, yet in his own writings shied from it in the name of truth and veracity, had gnawing and persistent doubts about *The Red and the Black*. In this work, he felt, he had too consistently endeavored to be truthful. The result had been that his style in the novel was too dry, too elliptic, that not enough allowance had been made for the reader's desire for a leisurely pace and for restful, reassuring scenes. But in good eighteenth-century tradition, Stendhal resorts to the explanation that his novel was not fiction, that everything recounted in it had actually happened.[19] This explanation was supposed to justify the harshness of tone of the novel, its lack of poetry. Yet there is poetry in *The Red and the Black*; there are elegiac moments, brief to be sure, but all the more intense because of their fleeting quality. Julien Sorel, despite his preoccupations, is not insensitive to a beautiful landscape, especially a mountainous one.[20] Contemplating a lofty panorama, Julien is able to achieve, if only momentarily, a sense of supreme independence and detachment. Here again, Julien turns out to be the spiritual heir to Saint-Preux, the hero of *La Nouvelle Héloïse.*

With his eighteenth-century predecessors Stendhal shared the belief that fictional art is a superior form of mystification. He also agreed with the novelists of the pre-Revolutionary era that a character is best depicted when he is shown in action. Hence his theory of the revealing feature, quirk, or idiosyncrasy, and his rejection of description in favor of selection. Description reduces the reader to a passive, numbing role; the selection of striking, revealing features, on the other hand, stimulates the reader's creative faculties and forces him to become an active participant.

Opinion varies, among readers and critics of Stendhal, as to which of his novels is his masterpiece, preference generally going to *The Red and the Black, The Charterhouse of Parma,* or even the unfinished *Lucien Leuwen.* But if *The Red and the Black,* perhaps because of its relentless and generally somber depiction of French society during the last years of the repressive regime under Charles X, is not everyone's favorite, it must be recognized as Stendhal's most strongly unified work, the one where the basic ingredients of the writer's esthetic and moral philosophy are welded with the most striking and dramatic results. Here we find the most characteristic Stendhalian themes, images, and metaphors within a novelistic structure that fuses passion, rebellion, hatred, tenderness, prison, and death by the guillotine. Here, too, are some of the most fundamental Stendhalian paradoxes and ambiguities: a hero who thinks he knows what he wants and acts with ruthless determination, only to discover, when it is too late, what it is that he truly needs in order to achieve happiness; the misunderstandings, doubts, and suspicions that complicate the relations between the sexes; the self-delusions and rationalizations that impel the most perceptive and keenly intuitive individuals such as Julien

Sorel to reach totally false conclusions about their own nature and needs; the kind of inner freedom and insight that can be achieved in a prison cell and in the face of impending death.

The novel as a whole is an eminently successful construction upon inner tensions and the play between opposites. It is also a strongly satirical work in which controversial opinions concerning contemporary religious, social, and political institutions are unabashedly aired. And it is a work that offers to the attentive reader many a lesson on human nature, but not stated directly and straightforwardly. It is through indirect clues, ironic both in meaning and intent, that the lesson is conveyed. If irony is a method of expression in which the opposite of what is explicitly stated is actually intended, then, of course, *The Red and the Black* is rich in this kind of satirical, sarcastic humor. And the liberties Stendhal as narrator took in editorializing freely upon the discrepancies between the real motives of his protagonists on the one hand, and their self-justificatory lines of reasoning on the other, provide some of the most ironic touches on what lengths an intelligent but misguided individual can go in order to suppress his natural inclinations in favor of what he considers to be his duty and moral obligation to his better self.

Stendhal was correcting the proofs of *The Red and the Black* when the July Revolution broke out. He was ideally located to see the action at first hand since his lodgings were on the rue de Richelieu, near the famed Palais-Royal and the Théâtre-Français.[21] From his window or from the less safe vantage point of the colonnade of the Palais-Royal he watched, in a mood of quiet jubilation, the dramatic unfolding of the successful insurrection. Once more, the people had taken over, and the effect of this momentous event upon Stendhal was comparable, by his own admission, to that of a great natural phenomenon, such as the enormous mass of the Mont Blanc seen from its base.[22] The overall impression was one of sublimity, of unleashed natural forces. The sight of the first tricolor flags filled him with renewed hope for the regeneration of France as a truly democratic nation.

XVI

An Unconventional
Diplomat

THE FALL OF Charles X marked the demise of the Bourbon
monarchy in France. With the advent to the throne of Louis-
Philippe, the son of Philippe Égalité, duc d'Orléans, who had supported the Revolution and voted in favor of the death of his cousin
Louis XVI, middle-class liberals and intellectuals felt that a constitutional monarchy, modeled on the English system, had at last
been established. Louis-Philippe himself had also joined the Revolutionary army and played a part in the battles of Valmy and
Jemappes (1792), had known hardship and obscurity as an émigré
during the Terror, and had subsequently returned to France,
where he played a significant role in the opposition to Louis XVIII
and Charles X. That he was proclaimed, on August 7, 1830, King
of the French, rather than of France, was considered a significant
symbolic change, for it meant that he was above all accountable to
the French people and answerable to its collective will.

Once more, Stendhal had taken to the streets and boulevards
of Paris in order to savor fully the impact of these stirring events
upon the mood and behavior of the people.[1] To be sure, he had
observed the Revolution from the sidelines, and while his sympathies had gone to the insurrectionists, he had remained an approving spectator rather than an actual participant. Even while directly involved in the Napoleonic military campaigns, Stendhal

had always evidenced a fascination with scenes of violence as "spectacles." Other reasons probably caused him to watch the July Revolution without giving it his immediate and wholehearted endorsement in the form of a total and personal commitment. By inclination, Stendhal tended to be the analyst, observer, and critic, rather than the man of action. Furthermore, his profound disappointment with the turn of events in France since the fall of Napoleon had gradually led him to the conviction that the French character had degenerated. He had always been critical of French manners and customs, reflecting in this as in so many other respects, an eminently eighteenth-century and Rousseauistic attitude. The Revolutionary and Napoleonic periods had restored his confidence and faith in the ability of his compatriots to be bold, energetic, and enterprising. After Waterloo, however, he had grown skeptical about the possibility of establishing a more democratic regime in a nation that seemed to lack the necessary nerve to fight for its basic political rights as defined by the *philosophes* and enacted by the leaders of the Revolution.

The July Revolution, therefore, took him somewhat by surprise, engrossed as he was at the time with the final preparations for publication of The Red and the Black. His initial doubts that the French people would support the insurrectionists quickly gave way to enthusiasm, for he was too profoundly a liberal not to become jubilant over the downfall of the repressive regime of Charles X. That he himself had been by-passed and snubbed by the men who held the reins of power during the Bourbon Restoration could only heighten his enthusiasm over the success of the July Revolution and the subsequent change in government.

On August 15, 1830, Stendhal formally expressed his willingness to serve the new regime by writing a letter to Count Molé, Minister of Foreign Affairs. Reviewing his past experience and citing his credentials, he expressed the hope that his qualifications would permit him to put his knowledge of foreign affairs to good use. He then went on to express his preference for a post as Consul General in Naples, Genoa, or Livorno. If none of these were available, however, he was ready to settle for the next best thing:

the position as First Secretary in the French embassies of Rome or Naples.[2]

By a Royal Ordinance of September 25, 1830, Stendhal was appointed Consul at Trieste with commensurate remunerations for this important post. In his state of euphoria he hastened to invite friends and such influential figures in French letters as the critic Sainte-Beuve to be his guests in his new home, to enjoy the lovely natural setting and the mild climate.[3]

Stendhal's eagerness to return to Italy and assume his new responsibilities was such that he left Paris on November 6, without having completed the proofreading of *The Red and the Black*. A rather perfunctory letter to his publisher Levavasseur informed the latter of this decision and entrusted to him all decisions concerning the sale of the book.[4]

Having reached Trieste on November 25, Stendhal lost no time in notifying the authorities of his arrival and demonstrating officially his zeal for his new functions.[5] Trieste, an important port at the head of the Adriatic Sea was, with its population of nearly fifty-thousand, a center of commerce where diverse cultures and ethnic groups freely commingled. Stendhal was nevertheless uneasy, and for good reason. He had left for Trieste without waiting for the official exequatur, which had to be approved by the Austrian authorities, for Trieste was under Austrian rule.

Unfortunately for Stendhal, Austria had not forgotten, thanks to the reports of its police, his past association with the subversive Carbonari in Milan. Neither did it escape the notice of the Austrian Foreign Ministry that M. de Beyle was none other than Stendhal, the author of highly suspicious works in which the most heretical political and religious opinions were freely aired. In short, the Consul that the new French government had appointed was a notorious liberal and agitator and a dangerous, undesirable individual. This adverse report having reached Metternich, the latter promptly informed Paris that the Austrian government had refused to grant its exequatur to the new Consul. Stendhal's appointment, as he was soon informed through official channels, had been bluntly rejected: "Mr. Metternich . . . has given the order to the ambassador of Austria in Paris to protest against my nomination." [6]

Stendhal was understandably stunned by the news when it reached him in Trieste. While he had at first been pleasantly surprised by his good fortune, he had quickly and happily adjusted to the idea of settling down in the port of Trieste, although it had not been one of his own choices. Living in the city in a kind of limbo and waiting for the Austrian confirmation of his new post had not been a gratifying experience. To his friend Mareste he had confided that he was put off by the northern climate and "the abmonible *Bora*," a glacial wind that made the winter months painful to endure, by the strong Germanic influence noticeable everywhere he went, and by the high cost of living. Sunny Italy seemed depressingly remote in this northern town: "Imagine that I am in Hamburg and you will have the correct picture," he complained to Mareste. There was, to be sure, some redeeming local color, but the inhabitants of this bustling commercial center knew only one religion, that of money. One feature of the port that Stendhal responded to favorably was its proximity to the "Orient" and to such exotic lands as Greece and Turkey, which Stendhal hoped to visit before long. In the meantime, he enjoyed watching and chatting with the handsome Turkish sailors: "I treat them to drinks; they are amiable half-savages. . . . Their language is continuous poetry." The port itself and its beautiful surroundings offered to an incorrigible stroller like Stendhal many a lovely sight. Yet, he grew increasingly restless. He did his best to fight tedium and while away the time and, above all, to escape, whenever he could, from the stifling atmosphere of the city's proper and prim society. Thus he managed to spend a week in Venice, from December 17 to 23, and returned to Trieste only to receive, on the 24th of that month, official notification of the Austrian refusal to approve his appointment. [7]

If Stendhal's immediate reaction was one of anger and dismay, all the more since he was convinced that he had acted with commendable prudence and caution and had done everything to demonstrate his good will, the seriousness of his intentions and his eagerness to serve the new French regime, his mood soon became one of philosophical resignation. He had been naïve once more, he reasoned, in believing that France was capable of regeneration. The new men in power were, after all, not so different from their immediate predecessors, and it was obvious that they were more interested in pleasing such reactionary but powerful figures as Metternich than in recognizing the ability and past services of a controversial individual like himself. The best he could hope for, under these circumstances, was another post as Consul in one of the southern Italian cities which were not under the Austrian rule, such as Palermo or Naples.[8] The more he thought about these alternatives, the more they appealed to him for, with their warm climate and truly Italian character and culture, they might offer him the kind of mild, pleasant, and secure haven that he increasingly yearned for as he felt the burden of years and approaching old age.

In the meantime, he waited for his new assignment, making short trips and revisiting Venice in order to get away from the boredom of Trieste's social life. At last, on February 11, Louis-Philippe signed a decree nominating Stendhal French Consul at Civitavecchia, a small port town near Rome, on the Tyrrhenian Sea. Civitavecchia was under Papal rule and Pope Gregory XVI, more accommodating than Metternich, made no particular difficulty in approving the appointment.

Stendhal, for his part, was none too pleased when he got official word of his transfer to Civitavecchia. The whole arrangement struck him as a demotion. Not only was Civitavecchia a far less important city than Trieste, his salary would also be reduced from fifteen thousand to ten thousand francs per year. The fact that he was a man of letters, and one with resolutely independent ideas and a forward-looking philosophy, had done him a disservice: "They have a rather strong grudge against any writing animal," he bitterly confided to Mareste. "Why write? If all scribblers were hat-makers or stone-cutters, we would be undisturbed," he ironically added.[9]

In leisurely fashion, Stendhal set out for Civitavecchia, which he reached on April 17, 1831.[10] On his way he had spent a week in Florence, one of his favorite Italian cities.

The population of Civitavecchia numbered 7,500 and Stendhal was determined to discharge his duties conscientiously. One of his first observations was that the town completely lacked an intellectual and social life, that it was uglier than a Paris suburb such as Saint-Cloud, but that, on the other hand, the common people there liked the French and were devoted to the memory of Napoleon.[11]

Stendhal's somewhat fatalistic and detached outlook on the vagaries and unpredictability of human events enabled him to accept without undue bitterness this last blow to his ego and vanity. Civitavecchia, besides, had some redeeming features. As the ancient and main port of Rome since Emperor Trajan's times, it handled an active maritime traffic and boasted a picturesque harbor, dominated by a fort which was supposed to have been partly constructed by Michelangelo. The city itself, however, was, as Stendhal justifiably complained, hopelessly provincial, with a maze of narrow streets, alleys, and courtyards where the sun hardly ever penetrated, with musty old houses, some of which went back to the Middle Ages, and with more recent but unattractive administrative buildings. For several months of the year, the town was in the grip of a stifling heat, and it was furthermore not immune to the fierce sirocco winds. All in all, however, Stendhal found this climate a definite improvement over that of Trieste.[12]

The new consul's office was located on the Piazza San Francesco, in the heart of the city, and he lived nearby, in a house handsomely situated on a height near the Fort of Michelangelo. From his windows he had a sweeping view over the harbor and sea and could watch the vessels and steamships constantly entering and leaving the busy port.

If the papal authorities had thought it politic to approve Stendhal's nomination as Consul at Civitavecchia, they did not for that reason renounce their deep suspicions regarding this rather unconventional diplomat. Stendhal's reputation as a "radical" harboring dangerous opinions and political ideas had preceded him. And to make matters more difficult, shortly after his arrival, he fell ill and did not recover his health and strength before several weeks had elapsed in enforced idleness.[13]

Before long, Stendhal was able to befriend a few intellectuals and liberals in Civitavecchia itself, notably the amateur archeologist Pietro Manzi, the lawyer Benedetto Blasi, a lover of music, and especially the antiquarian Donato Bucci. The latter's art shop was only a few steps from the French Consulate, and hardly a day passed when Stendhal did not drop in to chat with his friend about matters of common interest and concern. And when he was out of town, it was Bucci who was entrusted with the authority to deal with all diplomatic matters of some significance.

Despite his laudable intentions concerning his duties as Consul, Stendhal quickly grew bored and restless with his thankless, monotonous work. He therefore found various excuses to escape from his office duties and to leave routine responsibilities in the hands of subalterns. One of his favorite pastimes was to excavate, under the guidance of his archeologist friends, the old Etruscan tombs in the region. More than anything else, however, he sought to spend as much time as possible in nearby Rome. In one of his autobiographical essays, he states, with some humorous exaggeration, that while at Civitavecchia he spent half of each year in Rome.[14]

The social, intellectual, artistic, and diplomatic circles of Rome had of course far more to offer to Stendhal than the small port of Civitavecchia. But Rome was not Milan, and Stendhal felt that the Romans, despite their satirical and individualistic spirit, were unreliable friends of France and of the liberal cause.[15] Rome, however, was a welcome place of escape from the dreariness of Civitavecchia. Its convenient location enabled Stendhal to make frequent and prolonged stays there and his witty conversation, wide learning, and colorful personal background made him a welcome guest in the salons of the city. The French ambassador, Count Sainte-Aulaire, and especially his charming and vivacious wife, appreciated his company and were willing to overlook his biting sallies and unorthodox political opinions, for among their guests he was the one who possessed the richest store of information about a vast range of subjects, and especially about Italian history, art, and literature.

Another frequent host was Horace Vernet, an immensely successful French painter who specialized in military life and battle scenes and who occupied the prestigious post of Director of the Villa Medici, the Roman branch of the French Academy of Painting where promising young artists from the Ecole des Beaux-Arts pursued their studies. Stendhal also struck up acquaintanceships, if not friendships, among Romans of cultural and social status. And one of the distinguished foreign visitors with whom Stendhal established an amicable relationship and to whom he served as guide to the historical and artistic treasures of Rome was Count Alexander Turgenev, the Russian scholar and writer whom he had already met in Paris.[16]

At the local cafés, inns, and restaurants, where Stendhal was a regular customer, he had further opportunities to meet travelers and tourists as well as natives whose interests coincided with his own. There were, furthermore, the distractions afforded by the theater, by such popular festivities as the carnival, and by the spectacle of religious processions.

Despite his prolonged stays in Rome and trips to Siena, Florence, Naples, and other places of historical and cultural interest, Stendhal missed Paris. By an ironical twist of fate, he who had always dreamed of settling permanently in Italy found his assignment there increasingly tedious. He yearned for the kind of intellectual stimulation that only the Paris salons could offer. And he also missed his long conversations with French writers, scientists, and artists. His recent involvement in the exciting battle between the staunch upholders of neo-classicism and the fiery Romantics had sharpened his taste for controversy and argumentation. Life in Rome and Civitavecchia seemed to him to be stagnant, and even those French and Italian luminaries he met there failed to alleviate his growing boredom and sense of isolation. And as always, Stendhal did not succeed in concealing his real feelings, an unlikely characteristic for a diplomat. But then, the author of *The Red and the Black* was hardly a conventional Consul!

One of Stendhal's favorite occupations, while in Rome, was to rummage through and transcribe old manuscripts which furnished the themes of the *Italian Chronicles*. His correspondence reflects some of the literary ideas and projects with which he filled his leisure time and which helped him fight ennui and loneliness. He was not convinced that his decision to give up writing plays in favor of fiction had been a correct one. "A taste for reading novels," he observed in a letter of November 1832, "has replaced in England and France the taste for the theater. . . . Why is that? It's because literary pleasure is largely made up of *novelty*: The great playwrights have exhausted all the dramatic situations. A man, for instance, can only be a son, father, lover, brother, citizen. When you have pitted love against civic duty and every passion against a duty, it will be impossible to give a new drama." This pessimism concerning the limited number of dramatic situations echoes some of Diderot's arguments against the classical theater and its limitations.[17] What is more striking about Stendhal's statement is that it was expressed at a time when the Parisian public was under the spell of the Romantic dramas in verse, of such plays full of history and local color as Alexandre Dumas's *Henri III and his Court* (1829) and Victor Hugo's *Hernani* (1830). But then, Stendhal had never, in spite of the role he himself had played in the Romantic battle, been a great admirer of these new melodramas, which he considered inferior to the tragedies of Racine and to the plays of Shakespeare.[18]

What Stendhal sought in the theater and was unable to find among his contemporaries, with their fascination for rhetoric, picturesque exoticism, and big effects of contrast and antithesis, was psychological truth and nuanced character study. Dissatisfied though he was with certain aspects of his *Red and the Black*, especially its "dry" style,[19] he felt he had been able to accomplish things in this novel which would have been impossible in a play: "Conventions forbid many dramatic developments. . . . Everything, on the other hand, can be said in a novel. Another reason: the author of a drama can only depict things that are a bit *obvious*, he must not have more wit than the majority of the spectators. Many nuances of feeling given by the author of the *Red* to Mme de Rênal, his provincial heroine, would not have been understood in the theater." [20]

Reflecting upon the differences between drama and fiction, Stendhal, who had so stubbornly clung to the hope of making his mark as a playwright, at last came to the firm conviction that the novel, which for so long had been regarded as an inferior genre unworthy of a writer's best efforts,[21] in fact offered a wider range of possibilities than any other literary form. It was as a novelist that he could best bring into play the full scope of his thought and expression, that he could be at once chronicler and historian of his age as well as analyst of the human soul. The novel was not only the most modern and flexible literary medium, it had also supplanted the theater as the genre that attracted the most original and creative minds among writers.

Stendhal's thesis concerning the superiority of the novel over the theater was to find its most vigorous and straightforward expression four years after the November 1832 letter, in an article for the *Revue de Paris* entitled "Comedy is impossible in 1836." [22] Here the emphasis is on the social, economic, and political conditions which have, since the French Revolution, caused standards of conduct and cultural values to evolve so rapidly as to annihilate the kind of homogeneous theater-going public on which the playwright of the Old Regime could confidently rely. Granted the contemporaries of Racine or of Voltaire were not uniformly intelligent, perceptive, and sensitive to literary excellence. But they had in common the same breeding and language. Court and salon life under Louis XIV and Louis XV had produced a unique elite that shared a heritage of customs, traditions, and beliefs. This facilitated the playwright's task, for he knew how to provoke certain reactions on the part of his audience. A Molière in 1836, on the other hand, would have to deal with a mixed bag of people with a wide assortment of sympathies and backgrounds.

The novel, on the other hand, had the advantage of dealing with the public on a one-to-one basis. Balzac, in particular, had elevated the novel to the exalted level of history and, in his detailed and convincing recreations of a whole society, had surpassed Walter Scott, his master and the creator of the historical novel. At the other end of the spectrum, Benjamin Constant, in his acutely introspective and quasi-autobiographical *Adolphe,* was brilliantly perpetuating a novelistic tradition that Mme de Lafayette had originated in *La Princesse de Clèves,* a novel Stendhal admired enormously.

In a short but brilliantly provocative article entitled "Walter Scott and *La Princesse de Clèves,*" published in *Le National* in 1830, Stendhal compared these two opposite poles in fictional technique, the British novelist then at the acme of his popularity and reputation and the courtly French woman writer of the seventeenth century, and it is obvious from his analysis that his personal preference goes to Mme de Lafayette: "Should one describe the costumes of the characters, the landscape in which they move, the contours of their faces? Or would one be better advised to paint the passions and various sentiments that agitate their souls?" Once more, Stendhal knew full well that he was out of step with his times and was willing to take his chances: "My observations will be badly received. An immense troupe of literary people are interested in praising to the sky Walter Scott and his style. The clothes and the copper collar of a serf of the Middle Ages are easier to describe than the movements of the human heart." [23] The realism and verisimilitude that interested Stendhal concerned far less external reality and the circumstantial trappings of a given society than the complex and dynamic play of powerful human emotions pitted against rigid laws, customs, and traditions. In another revealing critical essay on the novel, which was a project of an article on *The Red and the Black,* Walter Scott is again taken to task for making an overly descriptive style fashionable and for overloading his own novels with a clutter of unnecessary details and with too many static tableaux. [24]

Having by a long and tortuous route at last come to a full and clear realization of what his true vocation was to be henceforth, Stendhal, in characteristic fashion, was careful to avoid a solemn and self-important tone when referring in his letters to this crucial insight. But his light-hearted, self-disparaging manner should not fool us about the seriousness of the thought he wished to convey to his friends. Time was growing short and he had to choose his priorities with care: "The animal's real job," he quipped in a letter dated November 5, 1832, "is to write a novel in an attic." [25] Stendhal's fear of sounding bombastic, pretentious, and affected when writing about his innermost thoughts and feelings, his aversion to the kind of dramatic posturing he frequently criticized in his contemporaries, caused him to take refuge either in discretion or in humor. In his desire to be both truthful and lucid, Stendhal carefully and consistently steered clear of grandiloquent statements about himself. Hence the deceptively casual, even flippant tone of some of his most intimate and significant revelations.

That Stendhal's interest in the novel and in the autobiographical form should have developed simultaneously is no mere accident. The central and constant preoccupation of Stendhal was the psychological, esthetic, and moral instruction life offers the exceptional individual. That his heroes and heroines are, in one way or another, projections of his own experiences, insights, and feelings is evident to any fairly attentive reader. But the relationship between autobiography and fiction is never a simple linear one with Stendhal. His taste for subtleties, nuances, ironic indirections, and shifting perspectives, and his corresponding dislike for lengthy, ponderous descriptions and obvious moralizing, endow both his novels and autobiographical essays with a unique lightness of touch and with a highly personal tone which are all the more elusive when one attempts to dissect them in purely analytical terms. Be that as it may, even as a novelist, Stendhal "was driven," as a critic aptly put it, "by an essentially autobiographic urge." [26]

Like the Jean-Jacques Rousseau of the *Confessions*, Stendhal was impelled by the need to unravel the baffling mysteries and contradictions of the self and to trace their origins in his past experience. But unlike Rousseau, he was less eager to recount in picturesque and compelling details his experiences, discoveries, and disappointments than to scrutinize, without the benefit of stylistic embellishment and literary dramatization, the motives for his actions and decisions and the evolution of his consciousness as a man and as a writer. He was keenly aware that in order to achieve truthfulness and self-knowledge, sincerity is not enough.[27] One can prevaricate unconsciously, and a writer, with his ego, vanity, and love of words, is especially vulnerable to the temptation of depicting his past in advantageous, flattering colors, of confusing fact with fantasy.

Despite his misgivings, Stendhal was eminently well prepared to tackle the difficult task of the autobiographer. His diaries, letters, essays, and works of fiction had been one long lesson in self-analysis. And his very diffidence and self-doubts are a tribute to his acute perception of the pitfalls that await the writer, no matter how gifted, who embarks upon this dangerous voyage of self-discovery. Rousseau had placed the spotlight upon himself as an unjustly persecuted victim, had described with great lyricism and feeling both his admirable and despicable deeds, and had appealed to the future generations of readers in eloquent, stirring terms. Stendhal, for his part, approached autobiography in a far more tentative, skeptical spirit.

Whereas Rousseau, in the famous preamble to his *Confessions*, proudly addressed himself to the collective conscience of posterity, Stendhal unassumingly expressed the hope of being read some day by a few kindred souls. Neither would he allow the artist in him to distort for dramatic effect those flaws of character, failings, and mistakes in judgment that had been the main causes of past misfortunes and misadventures. Far from shifting the blame to circumstance or to others, he straightforwardly recognized that he had been the principal architect of his own failures and disappointments. With characteristic wry self-mockery, but also with blunt frankness, he attributed his inability to make his way in the world to his incorrigible insouciance, and above all to his lack of ambition and to his devotion to pursuits which held no tangible rewards but which he had always found irresistible because of the less substantial yet irreplaceable gratifications they afforded him. He would always remain at heart an inveterate traveler, a habitual dreamer, an enthusiastic amateur of the arts, a lover of music, and an ardent if frequently unhappy suitor.[28]

Stendhal's first venture as an autobiographer was an essay, *Souvenirs d'égotisme*, covering the most recent events in his life: "To spend my leisure time in this foreign land, I feel like writing a little memoir of what happened during my last stay in Paris, from June 21st, 1821 to November 6, 1830." To write exclusively about oneself, he averred, was an enterprise fraught with danger. To begin with, there was the monotony of the constant repetition of I's and me's. But sustained by the thought that he might be read by sympathetic souls, he went on with his self-analysis and with his attempt to answer these baffling questions: "Have I drawn all the possible advantages for my happiness from the positions chance offered me during the nine years I just spent in Paris? What sort of man am I? Do I have good sense? Do I have good sense with depth? Do I have a remarkable mind? In truth, I don't know." [29]

Stendhal dashed off the *Souvenirs d'égotisme* during the summer of 1832. But that he was not yet quite ready to commit himself fully to autobiography is made clear by the fact that he selected, for his first endeavor, a period of his life that was closest to the present and that therefore involved his most recent memories rather than those subterranean layers of one's early experience that are crucial to a full understanding of the self.

The essay was executed with spontaneity and brio. It contains forceful sketches of contemporaries and affords us revealing glimpses into French society during the Restoration. Its sharpness of style reflects Stendhal's wish to avoid wordiness and his admiration for such eighteenth-century masters of the concise phrase as Montesquieu and Voltaire.

More and more Stendhal's thoughts turned to Paris and, having applied for a leave of absence, he was delighted to depart for the French capital, where he spent nearly three months, from

September 11 to December 4, 1833. It was during his return journey to Italy that, on a steamship going down the Rhône river, he met Alfred de Musset and George Sand on their way to Venice. At Marseilles, he and the famous couple went on their separate ways. Two humorous sketches of the portly Stendhal by Musset record this encounter.[30] One of the drawings shows a jolly Stendhal dancing a jig in his ample winter overcoat, top hat, and boots while George Sand observes him with a bemused smile.

In reality, however, Stendhal's mood was far from cheerful as he made his way back to the boredom and isolation of his Civitavecchia post. His show of high spirits to Alfred de Musset and George Sand was, as always in such circumstances, a façade to protect his inner thoughts and feelings. Ironically, Italy was no longer for him a haven of freedom and happiness. As he left behind him the French capital, its salons, theaters, and cafés, he felt like a man banished to a perpetual exile, with nothing to look forward to save loneliness, ennui, and oncoming old age.

XVII

Two Unfinished Works:
Lucien Leuwen and
The Life of Henry Brulard

ON JANUARY 8, 1834, Stendhal was back in Civitavecchia, at least officially, for he continued to spend as much time as possible in nearby Rome. His journey from Paris had been a leisurely one, and he had spent the last days of 1833 in Florence. Stendhal's melancholy upon resuming his unexciting and undemanding diplomatic duties was offset, at least partially, by the news that he had been awarded the Cross of the Legion of Honor for his accomplishments as a man of letters. Probably out of considerations of political prudence, the government of Louis-Philippe had decided to recognize Stendhal's services to France not for the role he had played under Napoleon, but rather for his contribution to French literature. Ironically, his sponsor for this distinction had been a man with whom he had always had an ambiguous relationship, François Guizot, the French statesman and historian who, as Minister of Instruction under Louis-Philippe, had achieved a high degree of political influence. Stendhal did not like Guizot as a man, politician, and author, and this is made plain by his consistently derogatory remarks in his intimate writings. The basic reason for this antipathy was perhaps Guizot's conservative sympathies and complacent acceptance of the established order.

Stendhal's official letter of thanks to Guizot, dated February 16, 1835, is therefore understandably short and formal in tone and language.[1]

In order to relieve the boredom of Civitavecchia and to keep himself occupied, Stendhal decided to write another novel. He had, after all, made a final commitment to the novel as the literary genre best suited to express the needs, aspirations, and creative urges of modern man.

Lucien Leuwen, which was supposed to present a broad panorama of contemporary society, owed its inception, like Stendhal's other novels, to an apparently incidental circumstance. It was begun in May 1834, after Stendhal had read an unpublished contemporary novel entitled *The Lieutenant*, whose author, Mme Marie-Jeanne-Julie Gaulthier, nicknamed Jules or Aricie by her friends, hailed like him from the Dauphiné and had known him for many years. She was a woman of sensitivity, intelligence, beauty, and charm and, since she lived in Paris, Stendhal understandably sought out her company and her conversation whenever he was in the French capital. Their relationship had grown more intimate during the 1820s and especially in 1833, on Stendhal's last visit to Paris.[2] It was then that Mme Gaulthier had entrusted to her friend the manuscript of a novel that she had just completed, *The Lieutenant*. Stendhal took it back with him to Civitavecchia and by May 4, 1834, he had read it and was writing a letter to the author in which he rather severely criticized her florid style and advised her to rewrite the whole thing and to make greater use of the dialogue form. At the same time, he recognized that there was truth in the characterization and that the basic idea was both interesting and original; but these qualities were spoiled by her flowery, labored style.[3]

Stendhal's critique of Mme Gaulthier's manuscript is of course highly significant, for it faithfully reflects his own esthetics of the novel. Unfortunately, the work has been lost, and it is therefore impossible to establish what Stendhal has retained of it in embarking upon a novel with a similar theme.[4] It is likely, however, that working on his friend's rather amateurish effort kindled his own imagination and enthusiasm and had the beneficial effect of alleviating the state of depression and ailing health that had dogged him since his return from Paris. His immense faith in eighteenth-century novelists as models of good style and accurate observation of social manners and mores is once more borne out by the fact that, in the two letters to Mme Gaulthier of May 4 and November 8, 1834, in which *The Lieutenant* is the main subject of discussion, Marivaux's *Vie de Marianne* is warmly recommended to the would-be authoress. A daily dose of twenty pages of this work of fiction, which so vividly and faithfully portrays contemporary social types and at the same time analyzes the human heart so penetratingly, would be the best medicine and antidote, Stendhal advised his friend, against the prevailing malady of resorting to an inflated rhetoric and of neglecting those little concrete details—gestures, words, expressions, attitudes—which capture individual character far more effectively than elevated, abstract generalizations.

To Mme Gaulthier's credit, it must be pointed out that in her good-natured reply to Stendhal's frank criticism, she showed not the slightest sign of hurt vanity and readily admitted that she would always remain a dabbler in literary matters.[5] If anything, the friendly bond between the aging and unsuccessful writer and diplomat and the amateur-novelist was strengthened by this exchange.

Mme Gaulthier's literary effort having provided Stendhal with the basic canvas on which to paint his own gallery of contemporary types, he set about writing at his customary rapid pace. And as is always the case with Stendhal's works of fiction, *Lucien Leuwen* is both novel and autobiography. That it remained unfinished is probably due to the author's realization that its bold, satiric depiction of politics under Louis-Philippe made publication a chancy business for his already compromised career as a diplomat. Another factor was his boredom with life at Civitavecchia and his eagerness to drop everything to order to obtain a leave of absence and return to Paris.

What probably triggered Stendhal's initial interest in *The*

Lieutenant as a subject for a novel of his own was the fact that its hero had been a student expelled from the Ecole Polytechnique. Stendhal himself, after all, had left Grenoble for Paris in 1799 with the intention of pursuing his studies at the famous school but had rather inexplicably never carried out this plan. Furthermore, Leuwen had obtained an officer's commission in the army and had promptly fallen in love. No wonder, therefore, that Stendhal had paid Mme Gaulthier the compliment that there was "truth" in *The Lieutenant*. [6]

Following his own advice on how to go about writing a novel on this theme, Stendhal elaborated his story around Lucien Leuwen. The only son of a wealthy banker, Lucien is at first an idealistic youth whose republican convictions and activities had caused his expulsion from the Ecole Polytechnique. What is unusual in the opening chapters of the novel is the warm, close relationship between M. Leuwen *père* and *fils*, Stendhal's way of imagining, in fictional terms, the kind of supportive paternal role of which he himself had been deprived. Lucien's major adventure as a second lieutenant in the 27th Lancers stationed in the provincial town of Nancy is his passionate but unfulfilled love for the beautiful, unattainable young royalist, Mme de Chasteller. The poetic, compelling figure of Mme de Chasteller is doubtless one of the most memorable features of *Lucien Leuwen*, and it has been suggested that she is the fictional counterpart of the haunting memory of Métilde Dembowski. [7] Be that as it may, the poignant, unhappy love affair between the ardent young second lieutenant and the proud, chaste Mme de Chasteller endows the novel with a delicate aura of lyricism and nostalgia which counterbalances its realistic portrayal of worldly society and behavior. Thus memory, invention, and observation combine in a complex and subtle interplay, which is further illuminated for the reader by the author's copious marginal notes and comments that have fortunately been preserved. [8]

Experimental and improvisatory novelist that he was, Stendhal was especially vulnerable to the impact on his creative powers of his current moods and states of mind. His inspiration and enthusiasm in writing *Lucien Leuwen* flagged as he faced the task of bringing his original plan to a final conclusion. The structure of the book was supposed to be tripartite, with Nancy, Paris, and Rome as the three successive settings in which Lucien's political and sentimental education is depicted. Unlike Stendhal's other novels and short stories, it was to end happily with the reunion and marriage of the two lovers. The novel stops short of the third part, and the manuscript is interrupted as Lucien, having left Paris for Italy in order to assume his post as secretary in the French embassy in Rome, stops off in Geneva and, like the young Henri Beyle in 1800 on his way to Milan, reverently visits the locations on Lake Geneva immortalized by Rousseau's *La Nouvelle Héloïse*.[9] Thus, quite appropriately, one of Stendhal's uncompleted but most intriguing works of fiction comes to a standstill with a touching personal homage to Jean-Jacques the dreamer, artist, and lover.

It has been said that *Lucien Leuwen* remained an unfinished work and is essentially an interesting failure because in this novel Stendhal departed from fictional techniques he had established in *The Red and the Black* and that were most congruent with his own temperament and esthetics.[10] According to this interpretation, Stendhal had been sufficiently impressed by Balzac's achievements to conceive the idea of writing a Balzacian novel: a work of fiction in which the sociological framework would be meticulously detailed, where concrete particulars concerning locations, the external appearance of characters, including their wearing apparel, would be itemized in lengthy descriptions. That Stendhal made a conscious and deliberate effort to correct what he considered to be the excessive abruptness and elliptic quality of *The Red and the Black* in composing *Lucien Leuwen* is undeniable from his comments and manuscript notations. That at the same time he wished to remain faithful to his basic understanding of human destiny as an unpredictable unfolding of events and actions in which accident, caprice, and chance play a great part is also made clear by several features in *Lucien Leuwen*, and especially by his highly individualistic, even idiosyncratic concept of the hero. To Mme

Gaulthier he had written that a hero, even more than the ordinary man, is subject to ludicrous, awkward impulses and actions.[11] A concrete application of this idea is the scene in Nancy where Lucien clumsily falls from his horse while Mme de Chasteller observes him from her window. This admixture of the comic as well as the quixotic element is a typical Stendhal novelistic contrivance. It is the author's own tribute to those eighteenth-century fictional types, from Lesage's Gil Blas to Fielding's Tom Jones, who perpetuated the picaresque tradition of the sharp-witted yet fumbling hero. It is also an integral part of Stendhal's own *Weltanschauung*, his own view of life and human behavior, derived both from his personal experience and his observation of others. Try as he might, therefore, to look upon the world in a Balzacian way, he remained loyal to his intuitive perception of how men and women act, especially when they are driven by strong passions.

Furthermore, the exhaustive cataloguing of external peculiarities of a character or a social setting always bored Stendhal, both as a reader and an author. He had little patience with material descriptions. Realism in a novel was not achieved, in his view, through a faithful recreation of certain specific locales and predetermined sociological types. He was far more concerned with capturing moral truths, and these do not depend upon fixed, predictable data. As a modern critic has aptly pointed out, Stendhal's heroes have this distinguishing characteristic that "they discover themselves existentially, through their reactions; and they even discover their reactions as a surprise."[12] Nothing is fixed, static, or foreordained in Stendhal's fictional world; unlike the protagonists in a novel by Balzac or even Flaubert, his heroes and heroines achieve self-knowledge not through a logical, stable process, but rather through a set of chance happenings, fortuitous events or catastrophes, followed by moments of insight and self-revelation.

There are revealing differences as well as points of contact between Julien Sorel and Lucien Leuwen. Both are typical Stendhalian heroes in that they combine passionate, impulsive temperaments with a high degree of self-awareness. Their main dissimilarity is due to their widely divergent social positions. While

Lucien Leuwen is a rich man's pampered son, Julien Sorel, the carpenter's scorned offspring, remains painfully conscious of the chasm that separates his deepest aspirations from his actual position in the world. Because of this fundamental conflict between Julien's fierce pride and low station, he is, from the outset, destined to a tragic fate. Lucien Leuwen's clash with the social realities of his time is more complicated and ambiguous. Lucien Leuwen is as ambitious as Julien Sorel, and neither hesitates to resort to unscrupulous means in order to advance himself in the world. Both Julien Sorel and Lucien Leuwen take themselves very seriously, but Julien is far more guarded, cautious, and calculating, for as a youth bereft of status and money he cannot afford to make mistakes. The chinks in Lucien's pride and vanity are generally treated in a rather light-hearted, comical vein. A far tenser climate marks the moral progression of Julien Sorel.

Both *The Red and the Black* and *Lucien Leuwen* present unflattering pictures of French society. In *The Red and the Black*, the drabness, conformism, and hypocrisy fostered by the Bourbon regime are sharply contrasted with the ambition, energy, and passion of the low-born Julien Sorel. In *Lucien Leuwen*, Louis-Philippe's government is shown in an equally harsh light, and here we get a more detailed panorama of political types, their intrigues, their readiness to sacrifice principle for personal gain, and their total lack of idealism and sincerity. The message is crystal-clear: the France of Louis-Philippe, dominated by a crassly materialistic bourgeoisie, represented no significant improvement over the rigid legitimism and reactionary politics of the France of Charles X. But unlike the somber and perpetually tense Julien Sorel, Lucien Leuwen already prefigures the amiable Fabrice del Dongo, the hero of the *Charterhouse of Parma*.

Whether with *Lucien Leuwen* Stendhal came nearest to writing a fictional autobiography, as has been suggested, remains a debatable point.[13] But autobiography weighed heavily on Stendhal's mind, for in September of 1835 he abruptly gave up his novel and, in November of the same year, embarked upon the *Life of Henry Brulard*, which was to retrace his spiritual development more fully than the *Souvenirs d'égotisme* and furnish some sort of an answer to a question which, now more than ever before, haunted him: "What kind of man have I been?" [14]

Stendhal had reached his fifties and faced his own mortality without having resolved the problem of his true identity, and this had become a growing source of inner anguish. The question now loomed so large in his intimate preoccupations that all other projects were relegated to the background as he set out on this adventure of self-exploration and self-discovery.

The *Life of Henry Brulard* opens with a striking tableau. Stendhal, seated on the steps of the Janiculum Hill in Rome, embraces in one long, lingering gaze the majestic panorama of the Eternal City:

> The sunshine was magnificent. A hardly perceptible sirocco wind caused a few small white clouds to rise above mount Albano, a delightful warmth was in the air, I felt happy to be alive. . . . The whole of ancient and modern Rome, from the old Appian Way with the ruins of its tombs and aqueducts to the magnificent garden of the Pincia built by the French, spreads out before me. [15]

Stendhal's insight into his strengths and weaknesses, sharpened by years of self-analysis, came into full play when, sensing that time was growing short, he resolved to take final stock of his accomplishments and failures. He was keenly aware that his real self profoundly differed from his social persona: "I am supposed to be, I think, the most cheerful and least sensitive of men." All his casual acquaintances and even his friends would have been greatly surprised, he mused, to learn that his habitual state had been that of the unhappy lover and daydreamer. Even his taste for travel had been the manifestation of a deeply felt spiritual need. The quest for new, exotic sites was an integral part of his lifelong voyage of self-discovery, of his search for a sharper awareness of his own identity. A picturesque natural setting had meaning for him only insofar as it struck a responsive chord of his sensibility: "Landscapes have been like a *bow* playing upon my soul." [16]

Strongly felt emotions, however, had a way of blotting out conscious thought, so that Stendhal's most meaningful experiences were those he found the most difficult to record, since his memory had retained of them only hazy, blurred images, too indistinct to be of significant help to the autobiographer.[17] Rather than fill in these gaps by resorting to the writer's creative imagination, a practice he considered a gross abuse of the memorialist's art and a dangerous confusion of what should remain two distinct genres—fiction and non-fiction—Stendhal decided from the outset that he would consistently try to follow the dictates of objective truth. Narrative appeal would have to be sacrificed in the process, for otherwise he would be merely emulating Rousseau who, in his famous *Confessions,* had no compunction, as he himself blithely stated, about supplying fictional details in order to enhance the reader's interest and who felt that such minor embellishments in no way affected the fundamental value and veracity of his testimony.[18]

Stendhal's standards of truth are indeed more rigorous than those not only of Rousseau, but also of Chateaubriand and most autobiographical writers, especially those whose romantic temperament and imagination inevitably led them to indulge their personal fantasies and subconscious urges. Assuredly, Stendhal's capacity to fantasize was equal to that of even a Rousseau, but unlike Jean-Jacques he kept a tight rein on his emotions and impulses. More self-critical and skeptical, less consumed by an overriding desire to play upon the reader's sympathies, he determined to tell only what had happened as he recalled it, respecting the gaps and uncertainties in dates and facts. Where only fragmentary episodes offered themselves, he would honestly present them as such. His autobiography would in some ways resemble those ancient frescoes partly eroded by time, with whole segments missing. At least the reader could be assured of confronting a forthright, if undramatized and at times disjointed, account of a man's life.

In his *Confessions,* Rousseau had endeavored to underscore the continuity and consistency of his moral being, for he was convinced that, despite the complexities and contradictions of the human heart and the twists and turns of fate, there is a basic unity and harmony in every existence which can be detected by prophetic signs and unalterable symbols. By retracing and reliving his past he hoped to discover those essential signposts that would help him understand the meaning of his life beyond the disorder of exterior events and the baffling mystery of some of his most portentous decisions.

While boldly presenting himself as an exceptional being, Rousseau nevertheless confidently expected to leave a message useful to others by revealing some universal truths concerning human nature. At the same time, he was anxious to exonerate himself from the damaging charges that had been leveled against him by his enemies and former friends turned adversaries. His *Confessions* were written with a twofold purpose: it would be an inward journey into the successive stages of his evolving self through time, and it would, by disclosing his faults and misdeeds, show him as a fallible and imperfect man, but not a criminal or monster. His *Confessions* would be both an essay in self-justification and an appeal to posterity. Hence Rousseau's eagerness to engage the reader's empathy and interest. Hence his tendency, despite repeated avowals to seek only the truth, to dramatize events, to place himself in the center of the stage. Rousseau was anxious to present a continuous and compelling narrative, with no missing piece.

Stendhal, on the other hand, had no such clear purpose in mind when he conceived the idea of writing *The Life of Henry Brulard*. He would relate the story of his life primarily for his own enjoyment and to pass the time that weighed so heavily in his dull and obscure consulate at Civitavecchia: "Being good for nothing, not even for my job of writing official letters, I have had a fire lighted and I write this, without lying I hope, without deceiving myself, with pleasure, like a letter to a friend." The *Life of Henry Brulard* is replete with admonitions all aimed at preserving simple, factual, unromanticized truth: "To tell the *truth*, and nothing but the *truth*, this is the only thing that matters." [19] But what precautions one had to resort to in order not to lie unconsciously! The most appropriate homage the aging Stendhal felt he could offer these enchanting memories of his youth was to touch upon them ever so discreetly and gently so as to preserve their pristine state: "Tender feelings are spoiled when described in detail" is the final message of *The Life of Henry Brulard*.[20]

When the news reached Stendhal, on March 26, 1836, that the leave of absence he had been asking for had at last been granted, he felt so elated that, abandoning his autobiography at the point where he had made the discovery of Milan and Italy in 1800, he eagerly set off for Paris. In spite of the accumulated burden of his advancing years, Stendhal was as ready as ever to welcome adventure. He had not yet written off his own future and the wonder and unpredictability of life.

The Life of Henry Brulard was never finished. But if it does not go beyond Stendhal's seventeenth year, it offers us a wealth of intimate details revealing not only the circumstances of the writer's early life, but, more importantly, his reaction to the big and small events that contributed to shaping his mental and emotional outlook. When, in *The Life of Henry Brulard*, Stendhal gives us an account of his childhood experiences which combines tenderness and humor, when he relates, with a mixture of reticence and defiance, those apparently trivial anecdotes clustered around his family and birthplace, he delineates a literary pattern that was to be followed by such diverse writers as Gide, Joyce, and Proust. Stendhal, no less than Rousseau, was in this respect, as in several others, an initiator and a trailblazer. *The Life of Henry Brulard* evokes with a sensitivity and nostalgia reminiscent of the *Confessions* the joys and anxieties of childhood and adolescence and the slow, painful path to freedom.

XVIII

Escape from Civitavecchia: The Diplomat on Leave (*Italian Chronicles, Memoirs of a Tourist,* and Other Works)

FOR THE LAST two years, the hope that had sustained Stendhal through his fits of spleen, bouts of ill health, and recurrent feeling of loneliness was that he would soon be allowed to escape from Civitavecchia and return to Paris. When at last an official missive informed him, in March 1836, that he had been granted a leave of absence for reasons of health, he hastened to put his affairs in order and, by May 11, he was on his way, having embarked on the *Pharamond* destined for Marseilles via Livorno and Genoa. The sea voyage had been swift and "magnificent," as Stendhal happily reported from Marseilles on May 16.[1]

Arriving in Paris on May 24, Stendhal, thinking that his stay there would be of relatively short duration, set himself up in the Hôtel de la Paix, on the rue du Mont-Blanc, near the Chaussée d'Antin, on the Right Bank. As things turned out, however, he would remain in the French capital for a full three-year period.

Eagerly he resumed his intellectual, social, and personal rela-

248

tionships. Upon his arrival, however, he had found the Department of Foreign Affairs, and particularly its Minister, Adolphe Thiers, rather ill-disposed toward him. No doubt Stendhal's chronic absenteeism while in Civitavecchia, his unorthodox opinions and behavior had a great deal to do with the cool reception accorded him upon his return to Paris. As for Thiers himself, statesman and historian, he and Stendhal had never been able to hit it off, as the latter's correspondence and personal writings clearly show.[2] Fortunately for Stendhal, Thiers was soon replaced by Count Louis-Mathieu Molé in the Foreign Ministry, and it was thanks to the latter's good will that the consul's leave was so generously prolonged. Molé had been kindly disposed toward Stendhal from the outset of the July Monarchy.[3]

Paris and its animated social and cultural life had a tonic effect on Stendhal's spirit and health. Although still in his early fifties at the beginning of his three-year leave, he had recently been plagued by the discomforts and ailments portending physical decline. These somewhat premature symptoms of old age were doubtless caused partly by his bouts with venereal disease and by his excessive corpulence. What is even more probable is that finding himself once more confined to the wearisome routine and atmosphere of Civitavecchia, he had, as always when he felt unhappy, bored, or depressed, developed various symptoms of ill health. Once in Paris, however, he rebounded quickly and, sensing that time was growing short, he tackled with equal zest both literary projects and travels throughout France. An almost feverish quality marks these activities and also accounts for his successive changes of residence in Paris during this period.[4]

A characteristic of Stendhal was the intellectual and emotional youthfulness he retained despite his growing infirmities. With his short, portly body and visible signs of advancing years, Stendhal was nevertheless not yet ready to resign himself to old age and perpetual bachelorhood. Like many men facing their climacteric who feel that they have yet to achieve happiness through a lasting attachment, Stendhal turned his thoughts once more to a long-cherished dream of finding the perfect companion of his life.

Rousseau tells us in his *Confessions* that, as he contemplated his imminent senescence, he experienced with particular poignancy a longing to know the ecstasy of requited love.[5] A similar mood must have overtaken Stendhal as he impulsively "crystallized" on the charming person of Baroness Eulalie-Françoise Lacuée de Saint-Just, recently widowed and seven years his junior. Through Pierre Daru, Stendhal had long been acquainted with her family, and especially with her father, Count François de Réal, who had played a significant role in the Napoleonic regime. As is made clear by Stendhal's *Souvenirs d'égotisme*, as well as by his formal letter of proposal to the Baroness Lacuée, what he admired most in her character and what probably caused him to fall in love with her in the first place was her "heroism." [6] In 1815, she had played a daring role in helping her father escape from France to the United States, and when the political climate had sufficiently changed to make his return safe, she had traveled by herself to the New World in order to bring him back.

Stendhal had always admired women of courage and boldness. Hence his lifelong reverence for Madame Roland, the Egeria of the Girondists during the Revolution.[7] Perhaps he hoped to find in the Baroness Lacuée another Métilde Dembowski. Those spiritual qualities he especially prized—selflessness, capacity for self-sacrifice, idealism, and dedication to a higher cause—he particularly valued when he thought they were embodied in a member of the opposite sex.

Stendhal's formal letter of proposal to the Baroness was written in October 1836.[8] It was turned down and, a few weeks later, she married Léonor-François Fresnel, an engineer and a first cousin of Mérimée, the writer and friend of Stendhal.

Rejected by the Baroness Lacuée, Stendhal turned to another woman of intellect and charm, Mme Gaulthier, none other than the author of *The Lieutenant*, the unpublished manuscript which had served as the basis of his own unfinished novel *Lucien Leuwen*. Ever since his return to Paris, Stendhal had renewed his relationship with her. His letters and notes to her during this period reflect his growing attachment and tenderness.[9] That she was able to repulse his amorous advances without offending his sensibilities and losing his friendship is all to her credit as a woman of tact and resourcefulness. In an affectionate and playful letter to him dated December 25, 1836, she reveals her good judgment and her understanding of his complex, sometimes contradictory nature. With skill and finesse, she expresses her admiration and fondness for him and makes it nevertheless plain that the best way to preserve their mutually satisfying relationship is to leave things as they are:

> Don't have any regrets about this day; it must count among one of the best in your life and for me it was the most glorious! . . . You will not deny it; there is in your heart a satisfaction which is bound up to what we strange people call conscience. As for me, I am happy and yet I love you and loving is to wish what your friend would want for you; therefore, you don't really want what you want; my instinct has guessed right. . . . Beyle, call me a dumb, frigid, silly, cowardly, stupid female, everything you want, the insults will not erase the happiness of our divine conversation. . . . Beyle, believe me, you are worth a hundred thousand times more than is believed and than you believe yourself. . . .[10]

Mme Gaulthier's perception of Stendhal's real feelings about her must have been correct, for, if anything, their friendship was strengthened after this crisis. Stendhal had enough respect and consideration for women as persons to value their companionship even when sexual conquest was out of the question.

Among the women of some note or influence and social hostesses in whom Stendhal had an interest during these years was the beautiful Countess de Montijo de Guzmán, the wife of a Spanish nobleman and the mother of two lovely little girls, Maria Francisca, familiarly called Paca, and Maria Eugenia, who was to rise to a position of great eminence by marrying Napoleon III in 1853 and becoming Empress Eugénie.

Ever since his childhood, Stendhal had felt a strong affinity with the Spanish character and liked to refer to certain traits of his own nature—pride, idealism, passion—as his *espagnolisme*. He soon became a regular habitué of the Countess de Montijo and her two charming daughters, and after dinner, he liked to regale Paca and Eugenia, then in their early teens, with stories of Napoleon, his army, and his great battles and victories. He had been introduced to the Montijos by Mérimée, himself a great admirer of all things Spanish and a friend of the countess, whom he regarded as a "perfect type" of Andalusian beauty.[11] After Stendhal's return to Civitavecchia in 1839, he kept up his correspondence with the Montijos, who had by then gone back to Madrid, especially with the younger daughter, Eugenia, who seems to have grown genuinely fond of him, as her affectionate letters and later reminiscences demonstrate. The aging and lonely bachelor found in the company of the Montijo women the kind of warm, tender atmosphere he might have known as husband and father. This is the most likely explanation for his attachment and for the spiritual and moral advice he lavished on his favorite, Eugenia.[12] Stendhal was not averse to playing the role of mentor with a young girl in whom he sensed interesting potentialities, and many years earlier he had played a similar role with his sister Pauline.

Literary ideas, unfinished projects still awaiting completion, and plans for new writings kept Stendhal busy during his three-year stay in Paris. In November 1836, he was working once more on his twenty-year-old biographical study of Napoleon, this time retitled *Memoirs on Napoleon*.[13] The lengthy preface which precedes the *Memoirs* gives a clear indication of Stendhal's growing admiration for what Napoleon had come to embody as a symbol of daring, energy, and genius to Romantic writers and artists alike. Interestingly, for the Stendhal of 1836 and 1837, Napoleon was the modern French equivalent of the Italian *condottiere*, the bold and self-reliant leader of a small army of mercenaries in the fourteenth and fifteenth centuries. That such prominent Italian families as the Sforzas had *condottieri* as their founding members added to the piquancy of the parallel.

By April 1837, however, Stendhal had given up the *Memoirs on Napoleon* and returned to the writing of fiction. His new project was to be a novel entitled *The Pink and the Green*. It occupied him until June of 1837 and never went beyond nine well-developed chapters and an outline of what was to follow.[14] *The Pink and the Green* represents essentially a second, more detailed version of another unfinished novel, *Mina de Vanghel*, begun in 1830, right after the completion of *The Red and the Black*.

The two aborted works have several interesting features in common. In both cases Parisian social and cultural life is observed through the eyes of a foreigner, a novelistic device going back to Montesquieu's famous *Persian Letters*. What is more noteworthy is Stendhal's choice of a young woman of social position, wealth, intellect, and strong will as his principal character. A German heiress named Mina, whose father has recently died, arrives in France where she seeks culture as well as true love. She simultaneously yearns for a great passion yet is fearful of being ensnared by a fortune hunter more interested in her money than in her person.

Once more, Stendhal has created the kind of psychological tension which recurs in his heroes and heroines and which consists of opposing and equally powerful emotional drives. These inner conflicts also enable the novelist to set almost insurmountable obstacles in the path of love. Stendhalian lovers, whether they be men or women, born into wealth and social position or struggling to overcome their lowly status, are star-crossed not so much by external factors as by rules and duties of their own making.

Admirer though he was of Laclos's *Liaisons dangereuses*, the famous eighteenth-century novel where passion is reduced to sexual conquest and subjugation, his own ideal is obviously the Rousseauistic and Romantic view of love, which demands the sublimation of one's instinctual impulses. What is clearly implied in all of Stendhal's works of fiction as well as in his treatise *De l'amour* is that the highest and noblest form of love is the unconsummated kind, or that which is pitted against nearly impossible odds and finds its fulfilment in brief encounters fraught with danger and secrecy. Mina is no different from most Stendhalian heroines in that she is proud, passionate, and unpredictable. That she ends by rejecting the lover she idolizes is by now a familiar feature going back to Vanina Vanini, the heroine of the first of the *Italian Chronicles.*

Stendhal's return to the French capital made it possible for him to renew or establish personal contact with editors and publishers; this in turn led to an agreement with the influential and prestigious *Revue des Deux-Mondes* for a series of stories freely adapted from the Italian manuscripts he had unearthed and which after his death were grouped in one collection and brought out under the title of *Italian Chronicles.* With one exception, *Vanina Vanini,* published in 1829 in the *Revue de Paris,* these stories appeared in the *Revue des Deux-Mondes* between 1837 and 1839. [15]

Stendhal had long been fascinated by the literary possibilities he detected in these old manuscripts. Although always short of funds, he had gone to the expense of buying the rights to this material, and to the influential critic Sainte-Beuve he had confided, at the end of 1834, his intention of translating "faithfully" these ancient accounts. [16]

What particularly attracted Stendhal to these anonymous chronicles was the simple, direct, and rather naïve manner in which they related tales of love, jealousy, revenge, and violence in which he recognized his favorite theme of the man or woman of exceptional daring and energy whose actions defy the laws and customs of their time. What the stories lacked in stylistic elegance and sophistication they amply made up with the dramatic interest generated by their exotic settings, mysterious and suspenseful ambience, and scenes of horror, pain, and ferocity reminiscent of the Gothic novel, popularized by Ann Radcliffe. Stendhal was familiar with the genre, which had influenced Walter Scott and Byron. Here were the castles, convents, tortures, executions dear to the practitioners of the novel that combines terror with sexuality. Yet what attracted Stendhal to the genre was not the external paraphernalia and decor, but rather, as his letter to Sainte-Beuve clearly suggests, an opportunity to be the interpreter of pseudo-historical folk narratives whose principal merit was their artless portrayal of human passions ranging from generous self-sacrifice to extreme cruelty. In the process of adapting these accounts he sometimes added a great deal of his own, as in the *Abbess of Castro*, notwithstanding his assurance to the reader that the story is merely a faithful translation of sixteenth-century manuscript material. The *Abbess of Castro* exalts an age in Italy when passions were at their most intense. The implications of this view are obvious: such lawlessness and violence may be contrary to morality as it was understood in nineteenth-century France, but it was precisely this fierce climate that produced the Leonardos, the Michelangelos, and the Raphaels.[17]

Some of the episodes recounted in the *Italian Chronicles* may seem excessively melodramatic and even grotesque in their depiction of lust, jealousy, incest, and ferocity. But they bear the Stendhalian stamp in the form of swift-moving narratives and lively, witty asides and digressions by the author-translator. Working on these stories of a bygone age, Stendhal was honing a literary technique which was to find its most felicitous expression in *The Charterhouse of Parma*.

In the meantime, however, he had undertaken systematic travels throughout France. In 1836, 1837, and 1838, sometimes alone or else in the company of Mérimée, he had made extensive journeys through the major provinces and towns of France, following itineraries that took him successively to the center and west, notably Bourges, Tours, Le Havre, Rouen, to the southwest and southeast, particularly Bordeaux, Toulouse, Carcassonne, Montpellier, Marseilles, Toulon, and Valence, and even beyond the French frontiers, to Bern, Basel, Baden, Mainz, Frankfurt, Rotterdam, Amsterdam, The Hague, and Brussels.[18] On his leisurely journey back to Paris, he had stopped off in Grenoble in June of 1838. It was to be the last time he would see his native city, which all his life he had hated so intensely and maligned so consistently. His impressions of the town and its surroundings, as set down in the forthcoming *Memoirs of a Tourist*, testify to a certain mellowing on the part of the aging writer. He was at last able to look upon Grenoble and its inhabitants with a measure of objectivity and even sympathy.

Stendhal's *Memoirs of a Tourist,* published in two volumes at the end of June 1838, perpetuates a tradition brilliantly exemplified by the eighteenth century. Stendhal had long been an avid reader and great admirer of travel accounts and one of his favorite works was the *Letters from Italy,* by Charles de Brosses, friend of Buffon and contributor to the *Encyclopedia.*[19] Stendhal's *Memoirs of a Tourist,* however, confine themselves to France. Significantly, the title page of the original edition does not bear Stendhal's name, but specifies that it is by "the author of *The Red and the Black.*" Ironically, this was hardly a recommendation for critics and readers alike, who had largely failed to appreciate the novel. Similarly, the *Memoirs of a Tourist,* with its outspoken criticism of French customs and manners, could not easily please its intended audience. Stendhal's outlook and style are too close to eighteenth-century cosmopolitanism, skepticism, and irreverence to make him acceptable to the contemporary reading public. Yet the book has an enduring interest and charm, not only through the barely disguised expression of the author's unorthodox opinions, but also through his skilful use of a fictional device, that of a narrator: in this case, rather ironically, the unexpected personage of a middle-aged commercial traveler in hardware. But the salesman-tourist has this in common with the artist, that he is a seeker of truth. He has already traveled extensively, and as a widower he has discovered a thing that at first made him feel terribly guilty: he is quite happy to be alone.

What is it that attracted Stendhal so strongly and consistently to the travel journal or travel account as a literary genre? His own restlessness and love of travel, the delight he took in comparing cultures and civilizations, and the personal pleasure he derived from discovering new places and customs certainly had a great deal to do with this fascination. But Stendhal was not a mere hedonist seeking novel sensations and pleasurable impressions. His quest was of a more profound nature. He sensed intuitively that one of the deepest yearnings of the human spirit is for the unknown, the strange, and the exotic. Travel satisfies this need for change, for to move from city to city, to discover new places and behold unaccustomed sights is to experience one's own freedom.

The *Memoirs of a Tourist* and its companion piece, *Travels in the South of France,*[20] like Stendhal's previous travelogues, are more than incidental works. They contain striking sketches of French towns, knowledgeable comments on local traditions, customs, and cultural activities, perspicuous observations on political and social institutions, and they are generously sprinkled with the personal views of a highly independent and irreverent mind. The tone is genial and informal and is further enlivened by well-placed dialogues and anecdotes; the descriptions are pithy and pungent, the overall pace is brisk. Here again Stendhal's style and manner are closer to eighteenth-century travelers and touristic guides than to the high-flown prose and lyrical outbursts of Chateaubriand's travel accounts. Humor, nimbleness of thought, lightness of touch, and wariness of any kind of posturing characterize the *Memoirs of a Tourist.*

Despite the less than ideal state of his health and the inconveniences and discomforts of travel, Stendhal had thoroughly enjoyed his journeys in the French provinces. His insatiable curiosity, his love of adventure, his good-natured willingness to cope with, even welcome, the unexpected, his affability and sociability with both travel companions and strangers, his perceptiveness as a political observer, his exceptional competence as an amateur of the arts, his skill as a narrator and story-teller, all these qualities endow the *Memoirs of a Tourist* and the *Travels in the South of France* with an enduring charm and appeal. And in these lively, unselfconscious pages, the twentieth-century reader can glimpse, through the vignettes, sketches, and descriptions, what French towns and provinces were like at the time of Louis-Philippe. Here are picturesque little scenes revealing a kind of leisurely life that has by now all but vanished. In this largely rural and pastoral France Stendhal moved tirelessly from town to town, making the most of the opportunities of meeting and chatting with people in coaches and inns, and in the evening disregarding his fatigue in order to set down his impressions and thoughts.

Stendhal was a true son of the Age of Enlightenment in the enthusiasm and zest with which he explored new places or set about rediscovering familiar locales. His cosmopolitism, skepticism, and cultural relativism were eminently eighteenth-century traits. And despite earnest efforts, he was never able to grow enthusiastic before a Gothic church or sculpture. The *Memoirs of a Tourist* and the *Travels in the South of France* did not pretend to appeal to the reader through a depiction of exotic sites and people. But the passing of time has endowed these two works with another, more subtle kind of exoticism. Thanks to a highly alert and sharply observant guide, we can evoke towns and landscapes the contours of which have since been metamorphosed through modern industrialization and technology. The French provinces of the late 1830s had changed little since the Old Regime, and Stendhal, ever the acute student of human nature, eagerly welcomed this opportunity to investigate for himself the traditions, customs, and cultural heritage of his native land. The resulting two travelogues are eminently Stendhalian: they show us pictures of a France of a bygone age, and they give us a sprightly portrait of the author as the eternal tourist and voyager.

XIX

The Charterhouse
of Parma

IT WAS DURING his prolonged leave in France that Stendhal conjured up subjective and ideal pictures of Italy which lend their vividness and color to the *Italian Chronicles*. Ever since he had given up for good his old dream of becoming a successful playwright and had turned to the novel as the most suitable genre for the modern writer, he had been contemplating the project of creating a truly great work of fiction with Italy as its main theme and framework.

Working on the *Italian Chronicles* had set him, he believed, on the right track for this ambitious novel dealing with the passions, intrigues, and characters he favored as the raw material with which to construct a story that would grip the reader's interest. *The Charterhouse of Parma* started out, modestly enough, as yet another short story in the manner of the *Italian Chronicles*. It was to depict the powerful Farnese family, especially the colorful and adventurous youthful years of the notorious Alessandro Farnese, who was eventually to rise to the exalted position of Pope as Paul III, in 1534.[1] Once more, the historical materials which form the basis of the chronicle are of a dubious and wholly unreliable nature. But as with the other accounts that Stendhal found in his Italian manuscripts, he was not looking for historical accuracy, but rather for a deeper kind of truth about human nature and human passions in a political and social climate conducive to the clash of strong, ruthless personalities hardly encumbered by moral scruples or petty considerations of propriety.

The title of the original manuscript was *Origine delle grandezze della famiglia Farnese* and it related the lustful, lawless, and violent ways of the twenty-year-old Alessandro Farnese who, in his endeavors and enterprises, was greatly aided by a politically influential and beautiful aunt, Vandozza Farnese. An able scholar, the young Farnese nevertheless became increasingly bold and insolent and when he went so far as to kidnap and rape a young noblewoman, he was imprisoned in the Castle of Sant' Angelo by orders of the Pope, but managed to escape. Eventually, he came out of hiding and disgrace, rose to the rank of a cardinal at the youthful age of twenty-four, became wealthy and for many years enjoyed the favors of a lady of rank named Cleria. In his mature years, he changed his ways, grew wise and high-minded, but continued his illicit relationship with Cleria, which remained such a well-kept secret that it never caused a scandal and did not hinder his progress toward the papacy.

Such is the raw material upon which Stendhal based what is considered by many as his greatest novel. It was in September of 1838 that Stendhal struck upon the idea of giving this story a nineteenth-century setting. Fired by this idea, he proceeded with extraordinary speed and facility. Injecting into the story his own personal experience, his novelistic imagination, and his profound and enduring love of Italy, he in turn dictated or wrote *The Charterhouse of Parma* in fifty-two days. He had begun his novel on November 4; the completed manuscript was forwarded to Romain Colomb, Stendhal's cousin and literary executor, on December 25.[2] By the beginning of April 1839 the novel was printed and put on sale; the title page identified it as being by the author of *The Red and the Black*, and once more the setting was a contemporary one, but the characters were of course Italian, not French. In his Foreword to the novel, Stendhal briefly warned his readers that Italians behave differently from Frenchmen and that this may be a cause of some dismay: "Italians are sincere, good-natured, and being rather bold, say what they think; it is only by fits that they have vanity; then it becomes a passion. . . . Finally, poverty is not ridiculous among them. . . . I admit that I have had the daring of allowing the protagonists to keep their sharpness of character." [3]

And in good eighteenth-century tradition, he disclaimed, somewhat tongue in cheek, any responsibility for the ethics of his characters: "I state unequivocally that I heap the greatest moral blame upon many of their actions. Why give them the high morality and graciousness of French characters, who love money above everything else and hardly ever sin out of hatred or love? The Italians of this story are just about the opposite." [4]

The message of this warning, so typically Stendhalian in its irony, is clear. The characters in the novel, unlike most of those in *The Red and the Black*, are moved by the sort of passions Stendhal associated with the Italian temperament. In other words, the reader should not expect from them hypocrisy, dissimulation, or false pride. Whether good or evil, his characters are on an epic scale and are wholly natural, that is, true to their powerful impulses and uninhibited by social conventions and codes.

This Stendhalian vision—or rather myth—of sixteenth-century Italian society transposed to the nineteenth century is not only entirely consistent with the author's views on human nature at its most compelling, it is also expressed with a lyricism and a brio that faithfully reflect the inspired verve and élan with which he had dashed off the novel. All the youthful impetuousness of Stendhal's own nature, miraculously preserved through the years, illuminate the pages of the novel and confer on its principal characters a generosity, audacity, and recklessness that make them so appealing and delightful.

Also in contrast to the brooding, somber atmosphere of *The Red and the Black*, *The Charterhouse of Parma* is bathed in the lovely, sunlit landscapes of Lombardy.[5] Similarly, while Julien Sorel was the ambitious, calculating, and suspicious plebeian fighting by every ruthless means to rise in a society that recognizes only privileges of birth and wealth, Fabrice del Dongo, the hero of

The Charterhouse of Parma, is doubtless closer to what Stendhal himself had been in his youth: idealistic, impulsive, spirited, and much more open than Julien Sorel to the tender, gentle feelings that a beautiful natural setting or a charming woman's face and form can inspire in a sensitive, loving soul. It is as though in Fabrice del Dongo Stendhal was trying to recapture his own youthful dreams, adventures, and high hopes.

In *The Charterhouse of Parma* Stendhal's lyrical, poetic vision of life asserts itself brilliantly. Here the deterministic materialist and atheist, the loyal disciple of Helvétius and the Ideologists, is superseded by the believer in the unpredictability and miraculous wonderment of life. The almost constant presence of danger, whether on the battlefield of Waterloo or in a prison cell in the great Farnese tower—a fictional structure reminiscent of the Castel Sant' Angelo in Rome—only serves to sharpen Fabrice's sensibilities and heighten his zest for life. Stendhal's hero is of course a far cry from the crude brigand of the original short story. His youthful enthusiasm and eagerness, his heedlessness to his own safety, his joyful acceptance of the unexpected in human events, his appealing unselfconsciousness, his inexperience and child-like curiosity make him an ideal participant and witness in the Battle of Waterloo scenes. It is obvious that Stendhal had only to recall his own experiences as a soldier to depict with a truthfulness and immediacy never before achieved in fiction young Fabrice's thoughts, emotions, and sense of bewilderment while the battle is in progress. Also evoked, through Fabrice's exuberant admiration for Napoleon—which is what causes him to desert secretly his family and the sunny surroundings of Lake Como for the grim battlefield of Waterloo—is Stendhal's own lifelong fascination with the Napoleonic legend and what it embodied for the members of his generation.

Like all Stendhalian heroes and heroines, Fabrice is both the reflection and magnification of certain psychological and temperamental traits which Stendhal himself either admired or associated with his own natural inclinations. Whereas Julien Sorel partially represented the darker side of his vision of human nature, Fabrice del Dongo is the incarnation of what Stendhal was fond of calling his *espagnolisme*, the chivalous and rather quixotic ideal of generosity, in the classical sense of the term: greatness of soul and stoutness of heart, nobility of spirit as well as daring and initiative in the heat of action. That young, unworldly Fabrice is Italian born and bred is meant to bring into sharper relief this generosity (for Stendhal viewed Italians as naturally generous, as we have seen), and that he is suddenly brought into contact with sophisticated Frenchmen at Waterloo is, of course, intentional on the part of the author. This enables Stendhal to focus, as he had already done in *The Pink and the Green* (where the heroine, Mina de Vanghel, a German heiress, finds herself facing for the first time the conventions and traditions of Parisian society) on a theme dear to his heart: the artificiality of French manners and mores and the exaggerated importance accorded in France, and especially in Paris, to those social values that pertain to that supremely egotistical emotional disposition, *amour-propre*. And in this respect, as in so many others, Stendhal was giving renewed expression to a typical eighteenth-century notion, one that Rousseau in particular had stated repeatedly and with his distinctive eloquence and conviction.[6]

That the Italian background and setting endow *The Charterhouse of Parma* with an exotic aura is undeniable, and critics have made much of this aspect of the novel. One distinguished Stendhalian even went so far as to state: "There exists doubtless no other major work of fiction, in French or any other literature, so purely exotic as *La Chartreuse de Parme*."[7] This is perhaps overstating the case, for exoticism for its own sake was never Stendhal's esthetic goal. If *The Charterhouse of Parma* is exotic, it is not in the usual sense of the term. It certainly does not reside principally in its decor, which is more symbolic than picturesque. The presence of mountains, lakes, and high towers is not meant merely to add color to the narrative. These external features are, rather, visible symbols of Stendhal's inner landscape and subconscious obsessions. The prison theme, for instance, also present in *The Red and the Black*, is an integral part of that spiritualized reality which enables Stendhal's young heroes to find fulfillment in love while facing imminent death. As has already been shown, love, for Stendhal, achieves its greatest emotional intensity when it encounters its most insuperable obstacles.

In *The Charterhouse of Parma*, these intertwined themes of love and death, set against an enchanting Italian decor, are endowed with a lyricism and luminosity, a tenderness and delicacy of tone which, faithful to his esthetics of conciseness and allusion rather than fulsome description, Stendhal has masterfully perfected and orchestrated. Thus, the very sparseness of descriptions alerts the reader to the significance of those details that are singled out; but the function of these selected concrete elements is not to enhance the illusion of reality, external or psychological. All the components of the novel are subordinated to what has aptly been called "the poetic perspective." [8] And it is indeed one of those paradoxes typical of Stendhal that he who so consistently steered clear of poetic rhetoric should have written the Romantic novel which, by its vision, movement, and sheer understated lyricism, achieves the kind of poetry that affects us all the more because of its authenticity and its rejection of the conventional and obvious devices.

If Fabrice is Stendhal's fictional projection of his young, idealistic self, Count Mosca, minister and man of experience and of the world, is Fabrice's dramatic counterpart. He might well be, as has been suggested, a recreation of Stendhal, the mature, disillusioned, yet still generous man, capable of understanding the excesses and rashness of conduct of Fabrice.[9] If Count Mosca is "corrupt" in the sense that he relishes court intrigues and eagerly takes an active part in political games, he nevertheless retains the ability to view life as an adventure; and in this respect, he is Fabrice's older, chastened, more cynical brother. Yet both share a common taste for risk and both are at heart gamblers.

As in *The Red and the Black*, two dissimilar yet complementary feminine figures vie for the hero's affections. The touching young Clelia Conti is somewhat reminiscent of both Mme de Rênal in *The Red and the Black* and of Mme de Chasteller in *Lucien Leuwen* and belongs to that class of high-principled, yet passionate women whose model in Stendhal's own experience had been most memorably exemplified by Métilde Dembowski. Clelia Conti's counterpart is the fiery but worldly-wise Duchess Sanseverina, who has been said to evoke Stendhal's Italian mistress, Angela Pietragrua, in her knowledgeable seductiveness and sensuous ardor, and who stands out as a singularly vivid embodiment of the intrepid, self-reliant Stendhalian heroine, disdainful of conventional morality, shrewd and politically astute, as well as swift and decisive in thought and action. The Duchess Sanseverina is the Italian version of the proud, wilful Mathilde de La Mole in *The Red and the Black*; but she has more dash and color—as well as less arrogant hauteur—than the demanding mistress of Julien Sorel. Another parallel with *The Red and the Black* can be traced on the basis of the respective careers and ambitions of the two heroes, Julien Sorel and Fabrice del Dongo. Both young men aspire to make their mark in the military, mainly as a result of their fascination with Napoleon; yet both opt for the priesthood out of necessity rather than religious conviction. Both Julien and Fabrice, furthermore, have that in common with Stendhal himself that they have unsympathetic and ungenerous fathers. The Marquis del Dongo, Fabrice's father, is a political reactionary and a religious fanatic who hates everything his son admires, particularly the French and Napoleon. Stendhal's relentless father-hatred is once more transposed in fictional terms.

It is not only the Italian locale that lends *The Charterhouse of Parma* a picturesqueness that is readily associated with Romanticism and that singles it out for preference among many Stendhal devotees. More perhaps than any other work of fiction by Stendhal, it testifies to an important and distinctive feature of his originality as a writer and literary personality: his uncanny capacity for retaining that freshness of outlook and enthusiasm associated with youth. Especially illustrative of this ability is the opening chapter of the novel, which depicts the first triumphant entrance of Bonaparte's ill-equipped army in Milan in 1796 that, in its essential features, foreshadowed the 1800 French re-occupation young Beyle had personally witnessed as an eager participant.

Stendhal is intent on portraying the French troops as the

representatives of Enlightenment and progress, greeted as liberators by a Milanese population profoundly weary of the repressive Austrian rule, especially in 1800. This is brought into sharp focus by a number of concrete examples illustrating the political feelings and sympathies of the common people as well as of the enlightened elements among the Italians, despite all the efforts of the political and religious authorities to discredit and denounce the message of "the *Encyclopedia* and Voltaire." [10]

The Charterhouse of Parma is both a political and a poetic novel, and its main originality as well as its attraction to modern readers may indeed lie in its happy marriage of these two generally mutually exclusive ingredients. Its political message is of course congruent with Stendhal's liberal and enlightened Romanticism and with his more personal and subversive suggestion that political games should not be taken too seriously. Its poetic message is of a more elusive and complex nature, and it has a great deal to do with Stendhal's essentially lyrical concept of youth, love, and beauty. It has none of the bitterness and somberness of *The Red and the Black*, and it forcefully affirms Stendhal's lifelong belief in the fundamental freedom of the individual, in his aptitude for choice and for overcoming the sociological or psychological forces that would constrict him.

The literary characteristics that made *The Chaterhouse of Parma* such an exceptional novel elude the traditional critical methods and conventions. More than ever, Stendhal resorts here to the elliptical shorthand style dear to his heart, especially in those tender, intimate scenes involving love: the prison scene of fulfilled passion between Fabrice and Clelia Conti is a famous example. As a noted Stendhalian so aptly put it: "Reading Stendhal is an exercise in agility." [11] But it is precisely this demand made on the reader's intelligence and critical faculties, this steadfast refusal to indulge in the then prevalent and popular Romantic clichés, which caused Stendhal to remain such a puzzling case for the readers of his time.

One contemporary reader of *The Charterhouse of Parma*, however, who had already achieved the kind of fame and status by 1840 to which Stendhal still aspired, although sixteen years his junior, was sufficiently moved by the novel to devote to it a lengthy and remarkable article published in the *Revue Parisienne* of September 25, 1840. The author of this article, to his everlasting glory, is no less than Honoré de Balzac.[12]

What is it that made Balzac, who in his own novels differed so markedly from Stendhal in his philosophical, religious, and social outlook, as well as in his literary style, react with such acumen and penetration to *The Charterhouse of Parma?* It is probably because Balzac, endowed as he was with the kind of generosity and intuition characteristic of only truly creative geniuses, recognized in Stendhal an equal. His praise was unstinting when he spoke of Stendhal's contribution to what he called "the literature of ideas," but was less generous when it came to Stendhal's style.

Stendhal's response to Balzac's article was one of overwhelming and delighted surprise. By the time Balzac's article had appeared, Stendhal was back in Civitavecchia, and it is from there that he wrote him a lengthy and appreciative letter in which he poured out his heart and set forth his basic esthetic beliefs.[13] Balzac's article had reached Stendhal on October 14; Stendhal immediately began composing his letter. But not satisfied with his first draft, dated October 16, he rewrote it two more times and made as well a rather large number of more minor changes in wording until, on October 29, he decided he had done his best and at last mailed it the following day. As for Balzac's criticisms of *The Charterhouse of Parma*, which concerned mainly its style, deemed too careless by the author of *The Human Comedy*, Stendhal paid such close attention to them and heeded them in such a spirit of humility and docility that he forthwith undertook to rewrite and "improve" his novel in light of Balzac's suggestions and remarks. Fortunately, Stendhal had never been any good at minute, careful stylistic polishing and revising, and he soon gave up on this effort to recast *The Charterhouse of Parma* according to Balzac's specifications. From what we have of the reworked passages and fragments, we can see that the original version was more congruent with Stendhal's own esthetics of a natural, elliptic, improvisatory style.[14]

Contrary to Balzac's impression, it was not negligence or

carelessness that caused Stendhal to write the way he did. Conditioned as he was, like his contemporaries, by a novelistic tradition that demanded leisurely, detailed descriptions and lengthy explanations and commentaries on the actions of the protagonists, a tradition that owed a great deal to Walter Scott (Balzac's acknowledged master), Balzac was understandably put off by Stendhal's unadorned, understated style. For his part, Stendhal endeavored, with touching modesty and sincerity, to enlighten Balzac on this aspect of his writing; and the reasons why he had deliberately rejected an inflated rhetoric form the innermost core of his remarkable letter. He could have been content to write a courteous note of thanks, with the usual phrases and clichés, in order to express his appreciation to Balzac for his laudatory article. But the reservations expressed with regard to the style of *The Charterhouse of Parma* obviously stirred him deeply, less in his vanity and *amour-propre* as an author than in what probably constituted the very heart of his esthetic belief as a writer. As he explained, with his customary brevity and subtlety, and with here and there an inevitable Stendhalian touch of humor and irony, his paramount rule was *truthfulness*. And to be truthful, whether writing a novel or an autobiography, meant to set down one's thoughts and feelings straightforwardly, without embellishment or dramatization. The most dangerous and constant threat to truthfulness and authenticity was the temptation—so flattering to one's ego, or to use the language of the time, vanity and *amour-propre*—to dramatize, overstate, and beautify needlessly. The prime culprit of this type of literary mendacity was, of course, Chateaubriand, Stendhal's lifelong *bête noire*. With characteristic lack of diplomacy and discretion, Stendhal did not hesitate to name the author of *The Genius of Christianity* in his letter to Balzac as the major contributor to a veritable literary malady that had assumed epidemic proportions.[15]

That his own refusal to give into the popular demand for such high-flown, bombastic rhetoric had been the main reason why he had remained an obscure, little-read author was something, he assured Balzac, to which he had reconciled himself long ago. At least, he found comfort and hope in the firm belief that, by the end of the nineteenth century and all the more so by the middle of the twentieth, the practitioners of the inflated style would be forgotten and that his own works, with their total lack of affectation and artificial eloquence, had a better chance of survival. And finally, he proudly professed his loyalty to the writers of prerevolutionary France, notably Montesquieu, as his supreme masters of the French language.[16] It was not out of mere nostalgia that Stendhal looked back upon the writers of the Enlightenment as his models, not only in his ideological and political outlook, but also in his esthetics. His deeply-felt and lifelong conviction that these were essentially more forward-looking and progressive than most of his own contemporaries, is clearly implied, if not directly expressed, throughout the letter to Balzac. Thus, by an interesting and somewhat paradoxical effect of his very personal optics, Stendhal held the view that it was by casting and keeping his gaze firmly upon the great men of letters and *philosophes* of prerevolutionary France that he would have the best chances of obtaining his own passport to posterity.

An important corollary of the basic principle of truthfulness was the desirability for a writer to compose rapidly, on the spur of the moment, and to avoid too much planning and organizing.[17] Hence his own manner of dashing off his works, especially *The Charterhouse of Parma*, by penning or dictating from twenty to thirty pages at a sitting. By rejecting the usual preparatory stages, by trusting his own instincts and his resourcefulness, he hoped to achieve the kind of artistic veracity that transcends all forms of pretentions. For words, used too cunningly, can easily become a beautiful and imposing way for the writer to conceal his true self. And it is obvious that one of Stendhal's main objections to the Romantics—and one of the reasons why he felt estranged in their midst—was his sharp awareness that his way of approaching a literary work, both as a reader and a creator, differed markedly from theirs. He sought above all qualities of naturalness, clarity, simplicity, directness, and truth, and he noted, with a mixture of sadness and irritation, that these were greatly neglected by authors who, with almost no exception, evinced uncritical self-indulgence and long-windedness, a convenient screen behind which they could hide the pathetic paucity and unoriginality of their ideas!

Thus Stendhal, in his letter to Balzac, expressed his basic agreement with what had been said about *The Charterhouse of Parma* by his famous contemporary, but then proceeded to demonstrate what moral and esthetic priorities had dictated the content and form of the novel. Having revised his letter three times, without however modifying its central message in any significant way, Stendhal felt sufficiently satisfied and vindicated to call it quits. And he concluded his missive to Balzac in a manner somewhat reminiscent of Rousseau writing to Voltaire, for he, too, was in the position of the more obscure of the two writers, yet determined to maintain his independence and dignity.[18] Like Rousseau, Stendhal boldly told his distinguished correspondent that the latter was more worthy of a *sincere* and thoughtful letter than of the customary platitudes and flatteries. Unlike Rousseau, however, Stendhal derived no special personal gratification or psychological release from polemics. Too skeptical, too detached, too distrustful also of literary controversies of which he had had his share with his notorious *Racine and Shakespeare,* he breathed a deep sigh of relief after completing his letter to Balzac and turned his thoughts to other matters.

As for Stendhal's personal relations with the famous novelist; they had been cordial from the outset. They had most likely met one another in one of the Parisian salons that they both frequented during Stendhal's leaves of absence in the French capital.[19] And despite their profound differences, ideologically and esthetically, each had the good judgment to hold the other in great esteem and admiration. That no undue flattery or petty vanity and envy marred the relationship between these two great men of letters is a tribute to their generous readiness to recognize talent and originality among their peers.

XX

Lamiel: An Unfinished Masterpiece

IT WAS WITH a heavy heart that Stendhal had returned to the loneliness and boredom of his Civitavecchia post. He had left Paris on June 24, 1839, but, as usual, had proceeded in the most indirect way possible, with detours and stops along the way, to Zurich, Lucerne, Lake Maggiore, Turin, and Genoa, among other places. By August 10, however, he had resumed his consulate, but had also resumed his absenteeism in order to relieve the tedium of Civitavecchia; once more there were frequent and prolonged stays in Rome, as well as more occasional journeys to less conveniently accessible Florence.

In the meantime, Stendhal had embarked upon a new literary project. It was to be a novel, entitled *Lamiel,* but it remained unfinished. Obviously still in the creative, euphoric mood that had presided over the inspiration and composition of *The Charterhouse of Parma,* Stendhal confidently launched what was to be another full-fledged novel with all the typically Stendhalian features: a satiric portrayal of contemporary French society and, pitted against the false values, artifices, and constricting world, a bold, exceptional individual, endowed with both strong passions and a keen, penetrating intellect. What makes *Lamiel* such a remarkable yet logical work in the slow and roundabout evolution of Stendhal as a writer and as a novelist is the fact that its main protagonist is a young woman.

271

Of all the major French men of letters Stendhal can unhesitatingly be viewed as one of those most truly sympathetic to the difficult lot of women in society in general, and particularly to the tragic fate that awaits those women of superior intellect and forceful character who do not hesitate to play an aggressive part in a society which is ruled and dominated by men. This explains, in large part, his lifelong reverence for Madame Roland and the role she soon assumed in his mind as the symbol, the archetype of emancipated womanhood. A highly controversial figure during the Revolution, admired by some and hated by others, she doubtless appealed to Stendhal's imagination and sensibilities not only as a political martyr (she was guillotined in 1793), but also as the ideal lover and companion he had so persistently sought among the women he had known. Her *Memoirs*, feverishly composed in prison and in the very shadow of the guillotine, which as a youth he had read in a state of exaltation comparable to that experienced when he had first come upon Rousseau's novel of passion and self-sacrifice, *La Nouvelle Héloïse*, had a profound impact upon him. Henceforth, whenever Madame Roland's name was mentioned, it was a shorthand way of designating a select category of women who were especially dear to his heart.[1] These were the feminine counterparts of the Julien Sorels and the Fabrice del Dongos, and that Stendhal even envisaged women as the equals of men, as worthy of playing the parts of heroines—not merely the victims or crafty manipulators—is the clearest proof of his enlightened outlook on what Simone de Beauvoir so aptly and ironically called "the second sex."

This liberal, sympathetic outlook is also forcefully demonstrated by Stendhal's unforgettable gallery of women, so finely individualized, so different from Balzac's stereotyped heroines. For Stendhal's female protagonists have the capacity, traditionally reserved for heroes only, to seek and define their own identity and to assert their will and freedom of choice as individuals. And here again, the eighteenth century, more than his own, was Stendhal's frame of reference, for in the novels of Marivaux, Prévost, Diderot, Rousseau, Laclos, and others, women had been the focus of attention, and it had been through their adventures and misadventures that the deceptions, shams, cruelties, and absurdities of contemporary society had been held up for ridicule or eloquently denounced.

Most of these eighteenth-century heroines had this in common that they were, for a variety of reasons, alienated from society. One of the most remarkable, and perhaps the most direct forerunner of Lamiel, is the Marquise de Merteuil, the ruthless and masterfully cynical and scheming heroine of Choderlos de Laclos's *Liaisons dangereuses,* who manages to retain her social respectability through a strategy of total hypocrisy and sexual seduction and manipulation. She is the female Tartuffe. And Tartuffe had long held a special fascination for Stendhal, not merely as the most consummate religious hypocrite, but, more importantly, as the symbol of the supreme individualist and rebel who, in the face of the evils and pressures of society, assumed duplicity and hypocrisy as his most effective weapons to protect his inner freedom while insuring his personal survival.[2] The theme of concealment, of the necessity to wear a mask in society, had greatly preoccupied Stendhal, especially since the fall of Napoleon, which for him meant specifically the end of the progress accomplished in the wake of the Revolution and the triumph of all those obscurantist and retrograde social and religious values he profoundly abhorred. No wonder that, after his return from Russia and upon witnessing the invasion of Paris by the allied armies, he had jotted down this thought in his diary, on July 4, 1814: "I am brought back by painful experience to this axiom: *conceal your life.*"[3]

If Stendhal's novels, especially *The Red and the Black,* illustrate the idea that the exceptional man, in order to survive in a world where hypocrisy is at the basis of all values, where conformism, uniformity, observance of rules, and religious orthodoxy are prerequisites for social acceptance, *Lamiel* in turn focuses on the even more ambiguous and precarious position of the superior woman. Stendhal's strong feminist sympathies manifest themselves most clearly in this compelling but unfortunately incomplete novel. His lifelong empathy and admiration for women who, like

Métilde Dembowski, proudly defied social conventions and with exemplary courage devoted themselves to hazardous political causes found its most forceful expression in *Lamiel*.

Yet Stendhal was determined to couch his ideas and feelings on the subject not in philosophical terms which would mar the narrative, but within a novelistic framework. *Lamiel* was to be the logical culmination of Stendhal's evolution and accumulated experience as a writer and social critic. And of all his fictional heroes and heroines, Lamiel would be the most radical exponent of his philosophy of individualism and enlightened, self-avowed egoism. The fact that he selected a woman as the main protagonist in order to illustrate his thesis has troubled many a reader and even puzzled some of the most penetrating Stendhalians, who cannot help but feel disturbed by a work that tells the story of a country girl who, early in life, achieves an unexpected, startling emancipation from conventional, and especially sexual, taboos.[4]

That it is a young woman, rather than a young man, who sets out to undermine the foundations of society and to subvert its moral fabric is of course rather disturbing for readers conditioned by a novelistic tradition in which the heroine is presented, from the outset, as a noble and touching victim. Lamiel is a more complex and intriguing character, and in many ways she is a forerunner of the twentieth-century liberated woman. In some ways, however, she is reminiscent of Mélanie Guilbert, Stendhal's youthful mistress, for she, like Mélanie, hails from Normandy and soon finds herself in a state of rebellion against her straitlaced milieu.[5] The fact that Lamiel is an adopted child reinforces the ambiguity and precariousness of her social position. Interestingly, there are also in the early chapters describing Lamiel's Norman background little vignettes of provincial life reminiscent of Balzac in their picturesque realism. It is as though Stendhal, in answer to Balzac's criticism of his *Charterhouse of Parma*, wanted to demonstrate that he, too, could excel in the technique of storytelling.

Like Julien Sorel, Lamiel escapes a mediocre fate through her impressive intellectual promise. She becomes the protégée of the local chatelaine, the Duchess of Miossens. Lamiel, however, continues to be dissatisfied with her lot, and her contact with provincial aristocracy only confirms her in her desire to escape from this constricting environment. She falls ill, mainly as a result of her mental depression, and at last a curious figure of a doctor is summoned to treat her, Dr. Sansfin. He is a hunchback, an object of local ridicule, yet a man with a penetrating, corrosive intelligence and a completely cynical outlook on life. He soon becomes Lamiel's adviser and guide, and the philosophy he teaches her is essentially one of subversion and subterfuge.

Fortified with these principles, Lamiel sets out, as her first endeavor, to rid herself of her virginity with a local rustic, whose approach to this business is entirely matter-of-fact, an experience that confirms her in her determination to seek happiness in her own way and to avoid being deceived by the illusion of love. She had read so much about this great passion in books that she had expected something extraordinary. Her disappointment was, of course, quite understandable under the circumstances.

In the course of her lengthy "educational" sessions with Dr. Sansfin, Lamiel had moreover become highly aware of the inferior social status of women and of their legal subservience to their husbands. She was told about the innumerable inequities between the sexes, about the double moral standard that prevailed, especially where a married woman's conduct is concerned. And Dr. Sansfin, an unbeliever in the eighteenth-century tradition, took delight in pointing out to his young pupil the important role the Catholic Church played in reinforcing these codes through religious doctrine and education. Thus, while a man notorious for his infidelities could derive glory from his reputation as a seducer and Don Juan, his unfortunate spouse, if found to be adulterous, was looked upon with loathing by her peers and, her reputation as well as her position irreparably damaged, she had to end her days in isolation and poverty with nothing to look forward to, save an eternity in hell for her misdeed. Hypocrisy and duplicity were the only weapons available to an intelligent young woman aspiring to realize fully her potential as a human being in a society that denied her this fundamental right. Like the superiorly crafty and cunning

Marquise de Merteuil of the *Liaisons dangereuses,* Lamiel soon
learned that her primary duty in life was to do exactly as she
pleased, to have lovers and to pursue sexual and other gratifications while maintaining an irreproachable exterior.[6]

Such a strategy required, of course, boldness and force of
character, a strong intellect and a sure knowledge of society and
contemporary mores, and sufficient personal charm as well as psychological acumen to manipulate the emotions and feelings of
others. But if Lamiel endeavors to be as scheming and ruthless as a
Marquise de Merteuil, if she sets out to emulate this notorious
eighteenth-century fictional model, she ends up acting in a way
that is more congruent with Stendhal's other heroines. Despite Dr.
Sansfin's training, despite her self-avowed "principles," Lamiel is
too free, impulsive, and quixotic a spirit to practice methodically a
system requiring perpetual duplicity and deceit.

If Lamiel succeeds in enticing the aristocratic Duc de Miossens, a rather sympathetic and appealing character in the
Stendhalian tradition of the liberal-minded but somewhat weak-
willed young nobleman reminiscent in particular of the heroes of
Armance and *The Pink and the Green,* she soon tires of him and
his effete ways and leaves him. Running away to the French capital, she leads an existence that openly flouts the traditional social
conventions concerning women. Believing love, as depicted in poetry and fiction, is but a creation of the feverish imagination of
writers, Lamiel at last experiences, to her own surprise, dismay,
and delight, real love. The object of her affections happens to be a
criminal. But this does not unduly disturb her, since one of her
favorite books had been a popularization of the daring exploits of Car-
touche, a notorious eighteenth-century malefactor. Lamiel's lover,
moreover, is no ordinary criminal; he is well-educated and well-
read, and he proudly professes his own brand of social philosophy
in the name of which he has declared war upon a society he considers unjust and unfair to the individual, especially the individual
who, like himself, is over-qualified for a menial type of job: "I
wage war against a society which wages war against me. I read
Corneille and Molière. I have too much schooling to work with

my hands and earn three francs a day for ten hours of work." [7]
Such reasoning is reminiscent of the arguments invoked by the
cynical, volatile, and eloquent self-proclaimed social parasite and
immoralist in Diderot's brilliant satirical dialogue, *Rameau's
Nephew.*

Lamiel is not only impressed by her lover's radical ideology;
she is completely won over by his dash, his audacity, and his
willingness to take chances with the police for her sake. Thus
when he flouts the authorities openly by taking her to the theater,
her passion for him knows no bounds. All major Stendhalian protagonists exhibit such boldness and impetuosity of spirit. It is this
readiness, even eagerness, to defy death or to risk personal disgrace by challenging the powers that be that makes Stendhal's
heroes and heroines such compelling creations. And this capacity
to commit impulsive, rash acts, to *"faire des folies,"* as Stendhal
liked to put it, was, of course, the novelistic expression of his
espagnolisme, of his fundamentally individualistic, quixotic outlook on life, of his lifelong cult of those human qualities that transcend mere intellectual brilliance or conventional morality. Even
in the novels that were left in an unfinished or even fragmentary
state, these characteristics stand out very clearly.

There is another eighteenth-century work of fiction that *Lamiel* brings to mind, and which Stendhal himself mentions as a
major source of inspiration of his novel. It is Lesage's *Gil Blas,* a
work Stendhal had long admired. A lively and deliberately rambling story in the picaresque manner, *Gil Blas* recounts the adventures of a young Spaniard who, during his journey from Oviedo to
Salamanca, where he is to pursue his studies, is captured by
brigands, escapes, is employed by many masters and, after a
number of setbacks and mishaps, eventually makes good and becomes a respectable member of society. What Stendhal doubtless
appreciated in *Gil Blas* was its broadly satirical panorama of a wide
assortment of social types, classes, and professions.

Lesage's principal purpose, in writing *Gil Blas* and his other
works, was to point up the basic human vices: foolishness, greed,
envy. As a novelistic hero, Gil Blas was a highly original creation

for the period, since he is far from "morally" admirable. He can
be hypocritical, cowardly, mendacious, and cynical. But his basic
instincts are decent, and he is capable of acts of generosity. Above
all, he is unpretentious, good-natured, adaptable, and willing to
learn from his experiences; and he has a sense of humor and
irony, which he exercises at his own expense with the kind of self-
knowledge that Stendhal could not fail to value.

Lamiel would be a modern, female reincarnation of Lesage's
hero, a carefree and none too scrupulous adventuress who nevertheless remains loyal to her own integrity as an individual. She
may lie to the world and dissemble in order to further her own interests; but she is truthful with herself, and in the final analysis it is
this fundamental honesty that alienates her irrevocably from a society she had set out to deceive. In this respect, of course, Lamiel,
who ends up, according to Stendhal's sketchy draft, as a radical
revolutionist and urban guerrilla and who, in order to avenge the
death of her lover at the hands of French justice, sets fire to the
Paris courthouse and is herself burned to death in the process,
acquires a tragic dimension entirely lacking in the more pliable
and opportunistic Gil Blas.

Stendhal had begun work on *Lamiel* in October of 1839.[8]
But in the sluggish, lethargic atmosphere of Civitavecchia the creative élan that had sustained him through his extraordinarily swift
composition of *The Charterhouse of Parma* and through other
projected works soon deserted him. One of these was a novel in
diary form, of which only a brief but suggestive sketch remains,
entitled *Earline*. The enigmatic heroine of this draft is supposed,
according to most Stendhal critics, to have been inspired by an actual woman, the last love of Stendhal's life. Her identity, however,
remains somewhat shrouded in mystery, although the tendency is
to consider her real-life model as a beautiful Roman lady,
Countess Giulia Cini.[9] What is certain is that Stendhal's amorous
feelings had lost none of their customary intensity and that they
were probably even heightened by the realization that this was his
ultimate fling with passion, one of the great preoccupations of his
life. What Stendhal himself designated as "the last romance" was

intense but short-lived, lasting from mid-February until the end of March 1840.

By then, Stendhal had begun experiencing such alarming physical symptoms as temporary losses of balance and bouts of dizziness. In vain he tried to find comfort and relief in work and in cherished memories. On March 15, 1841, he sustained an attack of apoplexy which left him physically weakened and mentally debilitated. His customary lucidity, however, had not deserted him, and it is with a remarkable degree of objectivity and detachment that he observed the progress of his illness and its impact on his faculties. As soon as he was well enough to hold pen in hand, he reported in one of his letters: "I have grappled with the abyss; it is the transition which is unpleasant, and this feeling of horror comes from all the nonsense one's head has been stuffed with at the age of three." [10] And he noted that his verbal memory was particularly affected. He would, for instance, have to make extraordinary efforts in order to remember such ordinary words as *glass.* He decided, however, to ignore his malady as best he could, and his official diplomatic reports testify to his determination to carry on with his duties as though nothing had happened. Before long, however, he had to request a leave of absence, and on October 21, 1841, he was on his way to France by steamship bound for Marseilles.

Stendhal's friends in Paris were struck by his obviously diminished intellectual capacities and physical strength. Bravely, Stendhal plunged into a round of social and intellectual activities, for had not these generally proved to be a tonic, both mentally and physically, in times of depression and illness? For a while, Stendhal's health and spirits seemed to rebound. As the spring of 1842 approached, he felt sufficiently recovered and confident to begin thinking again of his projects and unfinished manuscripts. Against the advice of his doctor, he resumed writing and dictating, and there was even a contract with the *Revue des Deux Mondes* for the publication of short stories.

On March 22, 1842, at around seven o'clock in the evening, as he was walking on the rue Neuve-des-Capucines, he suddenly collapsed on the pavement. He had been felled by another stroke, this time a deadly one. By a coincidence, he was only a few steps away from the Ministry of Foreign Affairs and from the room he had rented in the Hôtel de Nantes, on the rue Neuve-des-Petits-Champs. Passers-by carried him to a nearby shop, where efforts to revive him proved futile. Still unconscious, he was brought to his nearby lodging where, according to the testimony of his cousin and loyal friend, Romain Colomb, who had been summoned to his side, he remained in a coma until the end. When death came on March 23, which was a Wednesday, at two in the morning, Stendhal, mercifully, felt nothing.[11]

This was precisely the kind of death Stendhal had wished for himself. Shortly after his first stroke in March of 1841, he had written: "I think there is nothing ridiculous about dying in the street, when one does not do it on purpose." [12] This statement turned out to be prophetic. Stendhal had always regarded death as a rather unsightly event, less to be feared than to be disposed of as discreetly as possible, like an unavoidable yet unseemly bodily function. Unbeliever that he was, he had consistently stripped death of all its terrifying and mystical trappings and religious symbolism. The overwhelming feelings of dread and horror he had experienced, as a boy of seven, upon being made to witness the full panoply of the Catholic rituals at the passing of his beloved mother had left an indelible mark upon his psyche. Death, he was convinced, was a sordid business; the swifter and more private, therefore, the better.

Stendhal had faced his final malady and approaching end in the same spirit he had endured the hardships of a Russian winter as a soldier in Napoleon's army: with gallantry and a defiant willingness to confront the unknown head-on, and with contempt for those measures of prudence that might improve his personal chances of survival. Death held no real terror for Stendhal; it was merely the "passage" that made him apprehensive. That passage turned out to be as swift and painless as he had hoped for.

The obsequies of Stendhal were simple and private. A religious service was held on March 24, and on the same day Stendhal was interred in the Montmartre Cemetery. The funeral cortege was, at least according to contemporary reports, a rather paltry one: it consisted of about three or four persons, one of whom was Mérimée. No oration was pronounced at Stendhal's graveside. Meager notices and obituaries appeared in the newspapers. The kind of tribute Stendhal deserved had to await the judgment of posterity.

Epilogue

THAT STENDHAL STUBBORNLY remained, until the end of his life, a disciple of the eighteenth-century *philosophes*, a skeptic and unbeliever, a political libertarian and a dauntless opponent of all forms of sham and hypocrisy in a period of history when the tenets dear to his heart had become unfashionable, made his own position all the more isolated and misunderstood among his contemporaries. And that he stubbornly clung to a style of writing which, in its directness, clarity, and understated suggestiveness, remained unappreciated by a reading public weaned on the fulsome rhetoric of the Romantics further set him apart even from those who might have responded to the ideals contained in his works. He was simply too subtle, too wary of high-sounding phrases and noble, self-proclaimed principles and sentiments to be understood by his own age.

It is only in the late nineteenth and in the twentieth centuries that Stendhal came into his own as a man of letters and, perhaps more importantly, as a penetrating analyst of the human heart, as a *moraliste* in the great French tradition founded by Montaigne and brilliantly exemplified by a score of authors of the seventeenth and eighteenth centuries, such as La Rochefoucauld, La Bruyère, Pascal, Vauvenargues, and Chamfort. But it was especially as a self-avowed heir to the Enlightenment, to its spirit of intellectual curiosity, to its confidence in the individual's capacity to shape his own destiny that Stendhal stands out from among his contemporaries, who thought him old-fashioned because of his loyal admiration for such writers as Montesquieu, Helvétius, and the Ideologists.

Because he steadfastly refused to compromise his esthetic ideals of veracity, simplicity, and clarity, he was looked upon as a *cœur sec*, as a man of wit and indeed some talent, but bereft of real sensitivity and depth. Both in his writings and in his personal behavior, Stendhal had succeeded only too well in the art of eluding the great clichés of his time, and especially the cherished one of unabashed self-revelation. For uncritical sincerity, Stendhal had soon discovered through a careful study of Rousseau, can easily turn into the most deceptive form of self-delusion. It is, at heart, this caution in the face of all the seductive manifestations of Romanticism that made Stendhal appear so curiously anachronistic in his age, so excessively rational and intellectual. And the Romantics, on the whole, viewed intelligence with suspicion—as a limited faculty which easily leads to smugness and which cannot reveal the most profound truths about man and his destiny on earth. Stendhal, for his part, was too clear-minded to subscribe to unverified myths, to beliefs accepted on faith. And in this respect, of course, as in so many others, he was a man of the eighteenth century who frequently expressed his dismay and disappointment in the face of the prevailing ideologies of his time.

Stendhal, who admired the spirit of adventure, the willingness to take risks, to gamble on uncertain stakes, would doubtless have been gratified to see his one act of faith—that in the correct judgment of future readers—so brilliantly vindicated in the form of the overwhelming endorsement, indeed cult, that posterity has bestowed upon his works, his thought, and even his personality. His unique and privileged position has been widely acknowledged and his every scrap of manuscript is treasured and lovingly scrutinized by a devoted team of scholars and critics.

Incorrigible individualist, non-conformist, and loner that he was, Stendhal might well have looked upon this tardy vindication with a pleased but slightly bemused smile. To be sure, he had repeatedly invoked the *happy few* as his ideal and posthumous readers. His tentative hope and belief were fulfilled beyond any expectation.

Notes

ABBREVIATIONS

C.—   *Correspondance,* ed. Henri Martineau and Victor Del Litto (Paris: Bibliothèque de la Pléiade, 1962–68), 3 vols.

E.A.—*Essais d'autobiographie,* in *Œuvres intimes,* ed. Henri Martineau and Victor Del Litto (Paris: Bibliothèque de la Pléiade, 1961), 1 vol.

H.B.—*Vie de Henry Brulard,* in *Œuvres intimes,* ed. Henri Martineau and Victor Del Litto (Paris: Bibliothèque de la Pléiade, 1961), 1 vol.

J.—   *Journal,* in *Œuvres intimes,* ed. Henri Martineau and Victor Del Litto (Paris: Bibliothèque de la Pléiade, 1961), 1 vol.

P.D.—*Petit Dictionnaire stendhalien,* Henri Martineau (Paris: Le Divan, 1948).

R.—   *Romans et Nouvelles,* ed. Henri Martineau (Paris: Bibliothèque de la Pléiade, 1963–64), 2 vols.

S.E. —*Souvenirs d'égotisme,* in *Œuvres intimes,* ed. Henri Martineau and Victor Del Litto (Paris: Bibliothèque de la Pléiade, 1961), 1 vol.

All translated quotations appearing in this book are my own.

PROLOGUE

1. See V. Del Litto, *La Vie intellectuelle de Stendhal: Genèse et évolution de ses idées, 1802–1821* (Paris: Presses Universitaires de France,

1962): Jules C. Alciatore, "Stendhal lecteur de *La Pucelle,*" *Stendhal Club* (July 15, 1960), pp. 325–34; Jules C. Alciatore, "Stendhal et les romans de Voltaire," *Stendhal Club* (Jan. 15, 1961), pp. 15–23.

2. See Henri Peyre, *Les Générations littéraires* (Paris: Boivin, 1948), pp. 129–34.

3. Peyre, p. 134.

4. See Victor Brombert, "Stendhal lecteur de Rousseau," *Revue des Sciences Humaines* (Oct.–Dec. 1958), pp. 463–82; Gita May, "Préromantisme rousseauiste et égotisme stendhalien: Convergence et divergences," *L'Esprit Créateur* (Summer 1966), pp. 97–107.

5. Georg Lukács aptly stresses this affinity. See *Studies in European Realism,* Introd. Alfred Kazin (New York: Grosset and Dunlap, 1964), p. 68.

6. *Vie de Henry Brulard,* in *Œuvres intimes,* ed. H. Martineau and V. Del Litto (Paris: Bibliothèque de la Pléiade, 1961), p. 14 (hereafter referred to as *H.B.*).

CHAPTER I. BEGINNINGS

1. *H.B.,* p. 14.

2. *H.B.,* p. 81.

3. See Libero Solaroli, "Stendhal et la clef des *Liaisons dangereuses,*" *Stendhal Club* (Oct. 15, 1958), pp. 109–13.

4. *H.B.,* pp. 58–59.

5. *H.B.,* p. 76.

6. See Henri Martineau, "Chérubin Beyle," in *Petit Dictionnaire stendhalien* (Paris: Le Divan, 1948), pp. 71–77 (hereafter referred to as *P.D.*).

7. *H.B.,* p. 25.

8. *H.B.,* p. 149.

9. For further details on the Beyles and Gagnons, see *P.D.,* pp. 67–77, and pp. 225–31). Also Paul Arbelet, *La Jeunesse de Stendhal* (Paris: Champion, 1919), I, 3–63.

10. See Henri Martineau, *Le Cœur de Stendhal* (Paris: Albin Michel, 1952), I, 29–54.

11. *H.B.*, p. 61.

12. *H.B.*, pp. 61, 62.

13. *P.D.*, pp. 72, 73.

14. *H.B.*, pp. 99–100.

15. *P.D.*, p. 73.

16. *H.B.*, pp. 99–100.

17. *H.B.*, pp. 99–100.

18. *H.B.*, p. 67.

19. *H.B.*, p. 67. Paul Arbelet, in his *Jeunesse de Stendhal*, has attempted, without completely positive results, to trace the genealogical tree of the Gagnons (ii, 201–03).

20. *H.B.*, p. 67.

21. See Paul Arbelet, *La Jeunesse de Stendhal*, i, 43. Also "Antoine Gagnon," in *P.D.*, p. 225.

22. *H.B.*, p. 60.

23. *H.B.*, p. 37.

24. *H.B.*, p. 23.

CHAPTER II. FIRST TRAUMAS AND CONFLICTS

1. *H.B.*, pp. 26–35.

2. *H.B.*, p. 26.

3. Stendhalians, as one might expect, differ in the emphasis they place upon young Beyle's Oedipal relationship with his mother. Whereas the French philosopher and critic Alain minimizes it (see his *Stendhal*, Paris: Rieder, 1935, p. 31), Georges Blin, in *Stendhal et les problèmes du roman* (Paris: Corti, 1954), p. 203, and Gilbert Durand, in *Le Décor mythique de "La Chartreuse de Parme"* (Paris: Corti, 1961), p. 28, both view it in contemporary Freudian terms.

4. *H.B.*, p. 27.

5. Lester Crocker, *Jean-Jacques Rousseau; The Quest, 1712–1758* (New York: Macmillan, 1968), p. 11.

6. *H.B.*, p. 31; also p. 27: "She died at the height of her youth and beauty. . . . That was when the life of my mind began."

7. *H.B.*, pp. 29, 32.

8. *H.B.*, pp. 27–29.

9. *H.B.*, p. 27.

10. *H.B.*, pp. 35, 32.

11. *H.B.*, p. 57.

12. *H.B.*, p. 63. For further details on the abbé Raillane, see *P.D.*, pp. 400–03.

13. *P.D.*, pp. 401–02. Also Henri Martineau, *Le Cœur de Stendhal*, I, 64–66.

14. *H.B.*, p. 63.

15. *H.B.*, p. 64.

16. *H.B.*, p. 75.

17. *P.D.*, pp. 401–03.

18. *H.B.*, p. 85.

19. *H.B.*, pp. 126, 130.

20. *H.B.*, p. 127.

21. *H.B.*, p. 130.

22. *Romans et Nouvelles*, ed. H. Martineau, I, 697 (hereafter referred to as *R.*)

23. *H.B.*, p. 158.

24. *H.B.*, pp. 21, 22.

25. *Confessions*, Book I, ed. J. Voisine (Paris: Garnier, 1964), p. 19.

26. *H.B.*, p. 22.

27. *H.B.*, pp. 4, 6.

28. *H.B.*, p. 6.

29. *H.B.*, p. 6.

CHAPTER III. REVOLUTIONARY FERVOR

1. *P.D.*, p. 73.

2. *H.B.*, p. 98.

3. *H.B.*, pp. 48, 50.

4. *H.B.*, p. 100.

5. *H.B.*, pp. 145–46.

6. *H.B.*, pp. 104, 108.

7. *H.B.*, p. 66.

8. For more details on this question, see Gita May, *Madame Roland and the Age of Revolution* (New York and London: Columbia University Press, 1970), especially ch. 9, "1789 and Soaring Hopes."

9. *H.B.*, p. 139. Also see Lucien Jansse, "Stendhal et les classes sociales," *Stendhal Club* (Oct. 15, 1963), pp. 35–45.

CHAPTER IV. WIDENING HORIZONS

1. *P.D.*, pp. 300–01.

2. *H.B.*, p. 137.

3. *H.B.*, p. 142.

4. See Stendhal, *Du Romantisme dans les arts*, ed. J. Starzynski (Paris: Hermann, 1966), and Gita May, *Diderot et Baudelaire, critiques d'art* (Geneva: Droz, 1957), especially ch. 2, "Les Figures intermédiaires: Stendhal, Delacroix."

5. See Jean Roussel, *Jean-Jacques Rousseau en France après la Révolution: 1795–1830* (Paris: Librairie A. Colin, 1972).

6. *H.B.*, p. 168.

7. See Gita May, "Stendhal and the Age of Ideas," in *Literature and History in the Age of Ideas*, ed. Charles G. S. Williams (Columbus: Ohio State University Press, 1975), pp. 343–57.

8. See V. Del Litto, *La Vie intellectuelle de Stendhal*, pp. 249–51, 450–54. Also Gita May, "Molière and Stendhal," in *Molière and the Commonwealth of Letters*, ed. Roger Johnson, Jr., Editha S. Neumann,

and Guy T. Trail (Jackson: University Press of Mississippi, 1975), pp. 125–32.

9. *H.B.*, p. 81.

10. *H.B.*, p. 81. Also see Jean Prévost, "Les Tentatives théâtrales en 1801" and "Le Théâtre manqué," in his fine study, *La Création chez Stendhal* (Paris: Mercure de France, 1951), pp. 44–65. Prévost writes very perceptively about Stendhal's youthful ambition and abortive career as a playwright. Paulette Trout, in *La Vocation romanesque de Stendhal* (Paris: Editions Universitaires, 1970), also devotes a lengthy and useful analysis to this subject.

11. See Jules C. Alciatore, *Stendhal et Helvétius; Les Sources de la philosophie de Stendhal* (Geneva: Droz, 1952), and V. Del Litto, *La Vie intellectuelle de Stendhal.*

12. See Jules Alciatore, *Stendhal et Helvétius,* and V. Del Litto, *La Vie intellectuelle de Stendhal,* for further details concerning Stendhal's indebtedness to Destutt de Tracy.

13. See François Michel, "Stendhal mathématicien," in *Etudes stendhaliennes,* ed. V. Del Litto (Paris: Mercure de France, 1972), pp. 386–400.

14. *H.B.*, p. 202.

15. *H.B.*, pp. 189, 191–93, 242. Also *P.D.*, pp. 237–38.

16. *H.B.*, pp. 91, 189, 222, 254–59, 262–63. Also *P.D.*, pp. 188–90.

17. *H.B.*, pp. 189, 193, 198–99, 201–02, 264–66, 272. Also *P.D.*, pp. 266–68.

18. Although Jay himself, as Stendhal points out in his *Vie de Henry Brulard,* lacked talent as an artist, he was an outstanding teacher and knew how to fire the imagination of his students (*H.B.*, pp. 189, 198, 201).

19. See *H.B.* and the *Correspondance* (hereafter referred to as *C.,*) for more details on Félix Faure. Also *P.D.*, 216–17.

20. Plana and Barral appear frequently in *H.B.* and *C.* And see *P.D.*, 391–92, for Plana and *P.D.*, 40–41, for Barral.

21. Mante, like the other friends from the Central School, is often mentioned in *H.B.*, and *C.* Also see *P.D.*, pp. 313–14.

22. See *H.B.* and *C.* for further information. Also *P.D.*, pp. 145–47.

23. As we shall see, and as is amply demonstrated in *H.B.* and *C.*, the role of Romain Colomb as a dedicated friend and trusted confidant was to grow with time. Also see *P.D.*, pp. 132–33, and Henri Martineau, *Le Cœur de Stendhal*, I, 262–65, 353–56, 364–66.

24. See *H.B.* and Vol. I of *C.* for further information; also *P.D.*, pp. 78–79.

25. *H.B.*, p. 322.

26. *H.B.*, p. 233.

27. For further details on Virginie Kubly, see *P.D.*, pp. 277–80.

28. *H.B.*, p. 208.

29. *H.B.*, p. 212.

30. *H.B.*, p. 310.

CHAPTER V. PARIS AND LONELINESS

1. *H.B.*, pp. 310–11.

2. *H.B.*, p. 311.

3. *H.B.*, p. 311.

4. *H.B.*, p. 315.

5. *H.B.*, p. 317.

6. *H.B.*, p. 319.

7. *H.B.*, p. 315.

8. *H.B.*, p. 349; and *R.*, I, 450.

9. *H.B.*, p. 348.

CHAPTER VI. THE DISCOVERY OF ITALY

1. *H.B.*, pp. 370–71.

2. *H.B.*, p. 373.

3. See Georges Lefebvre, *Napoleon; From 18 Brumaire to Tilsit, 1799–1807*, tr. Henry F. Stockhold (New York: Columbia University Press, 1969), p. 98.

4. *H.B.*, p. 77.

5. *H.B.*, p. 379.

6. *H.B.*, p. 383.

7. *H.B.*, p. 384.

8. *H.B.*, p. 387.

9. See Paul Arbelet, *La Jeunesse de Stendhal* (Paris: Champion, 1919), II, 74.

10. *H.B.*, pp. 391–92.

11. See *H.B.*, p. 392: "This city became the most beautiful place on earth for me. My homeland has no charm at all for me, and I feel for the place where I was born a revulsion amounting to physical nausea (to seasickness). Milan has been for me from 1800 to 1821 the place where I constantly longed to live." Also see *Essais d'autobiographie* (hereafter referred to as *E.A.*), p. 1,500. For further details on Stendhal's epitaph, see Henri Martineau, *Le Cœur de Stendhal*, II, 414–15, V. Del Litto, *Album Stendhal* (Paris: Gallimard, 1966), pp. 309–11.

12. See Georges Lefebvre, *Napoleon; From 18 Brumaire to Tilsit, 1799–1807*, pp. 96–104.

13. In his *History of Painting in Italy* (1817), Stendhal would write about this masterpiece at greater length than about any other work by an Italian painter.

14. See Gilbert Durand, *Le Décor mythique de "La Chartreuse de Parme,"* for a penetrating analysis of Stendhal's artistic recreation of his favorite natural settings in his novels.

15. *C.*, I, 8–9 and 11–19.

16. *H.B.*, p. 394.

17. For further details on Louis Joinville and Angela Pietragrua, see *P.D.*, pp. 269–70 and 384–86. Also see *H.B.* and the *Journal* (hereafter referred to as *J.*) for numerous references to Angela Pietragrua.

18. *H.B.*, p. 393.

19. *H.B.*, p. 380.

20. It is, of course, impossible to track down specific medical information on Stendhal's bout with syphilis. Authoritative biographers agree,

however, that it was most probably during his first stay in Milan that Stendhal contracted a venereal disease (see Paul Arbelet, *La Jeunesse de Stendhal*, II, 77–79, Henri Martineau, *Le Cœur de Stendhal*, I, 138). There are, furthermore, in Stendhal's diary and letters discreet but unmistakable references to his ailment and its recurrent flare-ups. In a diary entry of October 2, 1801 (*J.*, p. 424), Stendhal unequivocally refers to his illness and its unpleasant consequences as "la vérole," which was the name then commonly given to syphilis.

21. See *J.*, pp. 405–08, 424.

22. *J.*, pp. 412, 414, 420, 425–27.

23. *C.*, I, 13–19.

24. For further details on these campaigns, see Georges Lefebvre, *Napoleon; From 18 Brumaire to Tilsit, 1799–1807*, p. 102.

25. *C.*, I, XIX.

26. The full text of Pierre Daru's letter to Dr. Gagnon has been reproduced in Paul Arbelet, *La Jeunesse de Stendhal*, II, 206–07.

27. *Souvenirs d'égotisme* (Hereafter referred to as *S.E.*), p. 1,478.

28. *C.*, I, XIX.

CHAPTER VII. FIRST LITERARY EFFORTS

1. *C.*, I, XIX.

2. See V. Del Litto, *La Vie intellectuelle de Stendhal*, for a detailed analysis of the early stages in Stendhal's intellectual evolution.

3. See Pierre Moreau, "Les Stendhaliens avant Stendhal," *Revue des Cours et Conférences* (Jan. 30, 1927), pp. 301–09 (March 15, 1927), pp. 656–64 (March 30, 1927), pp. 734–46, and Gita May, "Stendhal et les moralistes classiques," *L'Esprit Créateur* (Spring–Summer 1975), pp. 263–70.

4. See Marcel Heisler, *Stendhal et Napoléon* (Paris: Nizet, 1969) and Dennis Porter, "Stendhal and the Lesson of Napoleon," *PMLA*, 85 (1970), 456–62.

5. See *H.B.*, pp. 7, 54, 56, 272; *S.E.*, pp. 1,497, 1,500; *P.D.*, pp. 351–55.

6. See J., pp. 429, 474, 486, 498.

7. See J., p. 459.

8. See H.B., p. 272. Also E.A., p. 1,497.

9. See J., p. 429.

10. For the text of Beyle's letter of resignation, see C., I, 37.

11. C., I, 34–35.

12. C., I, 41.

13. C., I, 31–73.

14. See Paulette Trout, "Stendhal et l'optique théâtrale," in La Vocation romanesque de Stendhal (Paris: Editions Universitaires, 1970), pp. 105–08.

15. See Jean Prévost, La Création chez Stendhal (Paris: Mercure de France, 1951), pp. 44–65, for a fine analysis of Stendhal's aborted, yet eventually fruitful, endeavors as a playwright.

16. See V. Del Litto, La Vie intellectuelle de Stendhal, pp. 249–51, 450–54; Gita May, "Molière and Stendhal," pp. 125–32, and Henri Peyre, "Stendhal and Balzac as Admirers and Followers of Molière," pp. 133–44, both in Molière and the Commonwealth of Letters, ed. Roger Johnson, Guy T. Trail, and Editha Neumann (Jackson: University Press of Mississippi, 1975).

17. Jean Prévost, La Création chez Stendhal, pp. 44–65.

18. See C., I, 267, 278–79, 281, 658.

19. See H.B., pp. 13, 20, 312, 346, 367, 369; J., pp. 430–32, 450, 474, 477, 497. Also P.D., pp. 408–10.

20. J., pp. 430–32, 434, 474.

21. H.B., p. 254; J., pp. 435, 439, 452, 454, 455–60, 462–64, 466, 484, 500, 535, 539, 554, 573.

22. C., I, 58–59, 69–71.

23. C., I, xx, 75–91.

24. J., pp. 444–47; C., I, 89–91.

25. C., I, 90 (letter dated March 29, 1804).

CHAPTER VIII. MARSEILLES INTERLUDE

1. *P.D.*, pp. 197, 252–54. Also see Paul Arbelet, *Stendhal épicier ou les infortunes de Mélanie* (Paris: Plon, 1926) and, by the same critic, *Louason, ou les perplexités amoureuses de Stendhal* (Grenoble: B. Arthaud, 1937).

2. *J.*, p. 540.

3. *J.*, pp. 589, 596, 598, 601, 603–05, 608, 610–11, 614–16, 621, 623, 625, 631, 643, 645–46, 648–49, 653, 659, 678, 681, 584.

4. *J.*, p. 685–87.

5. *J.*, p. 708.

6. *C.*, I, 211, 214–15, 219–20, 228, 233, 241, 244–45, 255–56, 262, 220, 226, 234, 241, 255.

7. *C.*, I, 221–22.

8. See Georges Lefebvre, *Napoleon from 18 Brumaire to Tilsit; 1799–1807*, p. 193.

9. See chapter 4, above, for a discussion of the importance of the early art lessons with Le Roy and, at the Grenoble Central School, with Jay.

10. See Gita May, "Stendhal and Madame Roland," *Romanic Review*, 53 (1962), 16–31.

11. *J.*, p. 797.

12. See *H.B.*, pp. 8, 13, 15, 20, 56, 104; *E.A.*, pp. 1,489, 1,498, 1,500.

13. *J.*, p. 797.

14. *C.*, I, 1,211, 1,226–28.

15. *H.B.*, pp. 8, 15, 104.

16. *C.*, I, 290–91, 308, 320, 323, 266–67, 325–26.

17. *C.*, I, 1,177–79, 1,200–02.

18. *J.*, p. 799.

CHAPTER IX. ADVENTURES IN GERMANY AND AUSTRIA

1. Mme de Barcoff lived in Moscow until 1812, and Beyle saw her again in Paris in 1813 and 1814, when their intimacy as lovers was resumed, as the *Journal* testifies (*J.*, pp. 1,222, 1,259). After this, however, their paths parted for good (also see *P.D.*, p. 253).

2. *J.*, pp. 815, 819–20.

3. *P.D.*, pp. 161–62.

4. *J.*, p. 827. See also *C.*, I, 328.

5. See Stendhal's letter of Aug. 10, 1840, in which he reminisces about his entry into Berlin in 1806 (*C.*, III, 379).

6. See *C.*, I, 335–36, 381–400.

7. *J.*, p. 850.

8. *C.*, I, 376, 349, 344.

9. *C.*, I, 482, 441–43.

10. *C.*, I, 482, 334.

11. *C.*, I, 442, 440, 496.

12. *C.*, I, 513–14.

13. *C.*, I, 366, 441, 536, 601–02, 625.

14. See *R.*, I, 965–66, II, 1,077–78.

15. *C.*, I, 339–41, 355–56, 362–66, 379–80.

16. *C.*, I, 480.

17. *C.*, I, 346, 353; *J.*, pp. 830–31, 829.

18. *C.*, I, 374.

19. *C.*, I, 522–53; *J.*, pp. 881–82, 884, 887–88.

20. *C.*, I, 536.

21. *C.*, I, 534, 539, 558; *J.*, pp. 919, 950, 953; *H.B.*, pp. 213–14, 270.

22. *J.*, pp. 898–99.

CHAPTER X. THE TASTE OF SUCCESS

1. For further information on this question, see Felix Markham, *Napoleon* (New York: New American Library, 1966), pp. 98–99.

2. *J.*, p. 959.

3. *C.*, I, XXII. For the fascinating story of how Napoleon rapaciously plundered the museums and collections of occupied Europe in order to enrich the Louvre, see Francis Henry Taylor, *The Taste of Angels; A History of Art Collecting from Rameses to Napoleon* (Boston: Little, Brown, 1948), pp. 548–70.

4. The flat was at number 3, rue Neuve-du-Luxembourg, today 5, rue Cambon. See Beyle's letter to his sister dated Oct. 22, 1810 (*C.*, I, 593). See also the letter to his sister dated Oct. 9, 1810 (*C.*, I, 591).

5. *C.*, I, 592.

6. *C.*, I, 584–86, 592.

7. For more information on Angélina Bereyter, her background and her career as a singer, see *P.D.*, pp. 52–54. Also see *J.*, p. 1,004.

8. *H.B.*, p. 13.

9. See *J.*, p. 1,029.

10. *C.*, I, 606 (letter dated Sept. 10, 1811).

11. *J.*, p. 1,084.

12. *J.*, p. 1,118.

13. See Paul Arbelet, *L'Histoire de la peinture en Italie et les plagiats de Stendhal* (Paris: Calmann-Lévy, 1913). Also Margaret Tillett, *Stendhal: The Background to the Novels* (London: Oxford University Press, 1971), p. 33.

14. *J.*, pp. 1,142–60.

15. *J.*, pp. 1,166–68.

16. See Georges Lefebvre, *Napoleon from Tilsit to Waterloo; 1807–1815*, tr. J. E. Anderson (New York: Columbia University Press, 1969), pp. 311–12.

17. See Stendhal's letter of July 23, 1812, to his sister Pauline (*C.*, I, 650.

18. Georges Lefebvre, *Napoleon from Tilsit to Waterloo, 1807–1815*, p. 312.

CHAPTER XI. THE RUSSIAN CAMPAIGN

1. *C.*, I, 654–55.

2. For further details on the Russian campaign, see Georges Lefebvre, *Napoleon from Tilsit to Waterloo, 1807–1815*, pp. 311–18.

3. Stendhal himself believed that Rostopchine was responsible for the Moscow fire (see *J.*, p. 1,193).

4. See *J.*, pp. 1,191, 1,195.

5. *C.*, I, 667, 672.

6. *C.*, I, 678–88.

7. The wounded officer in question later recounted the episode to the writer Prosper Mérimée, who in turn related the anecdote in his biographical sketch of Stendhal entitled *H.B.* and published in 1850 (See Prosper Mérimée, *Portraits historiques et littéraires*, Paris: Calmann Lévy, 1892).

8. *C.*, I, 688–89.

9. *J.*, p. 1,197.

10. *J.*, p. 1,202.

11. *J.*, pp. 1,199–1,201.

12. *J.*, pp. 1,227–29.

13. *C.*, I, 698–99. Mérimée, in his *H.B.*, also refers to this incident, which Stendhal later liked to relate in tragicomical terms.

14. See Henri Martineau, *Le Cœur de Stendhal*, I, 301.

15. *C.*, I, 699.

16. *J.*, p. 1,229.

17. *C.*, I, 700.

18. *J.*, p. 1,238.

19. *J.*, p. 1,241.

CHAPTER XII. FROM SOLDIER TO WRITER

1. See Henri Martineau, *Le Cœur de Stendhal*, ɪ, 311. For further details on Stendhal's mission in Grenoble, see his diary and what he called "Journal de mon triste séjour à Genoble" (*J.*, pp. 1,253–56).

2. *C.*, ɪ, 766; *J.*, p. 1,256; *C.*, ɪ, 766 (letters dated April 1 and 4, 1814).

3. *J.*, p. 1,256.

4. *J.*, p. 1,258.

5. *H.B.*, p. 11.

6. *J.*, p. 1,259 (July 4, 1814: "I have been sleeping for *eight days with the old passion*" [in English].

7. *J.*, p. 1,259.

8. For a perceptive analysis of this work, see Jean Prévost's chapter "Les Vies de Haydn, Mozart et Métastase," in *La Création chez Stendhal*, pp. 107–19.

9. *J.*, p. 1,270.

10. The only two letters from Angela Pietragrua to Beyle that have come down to us, dated Dec. 1 and 28, 1815 (*C.*, ɪ, 1,241), show that, until the end of their relationship, she tried to have him assume the sole responsibility and full guilt for their breakup.

11. *C.*, ɪ, 800.

12. *C.*, ɪ, 802.

13. See Paul Arbelet's critical edition in the Champion series and his *Histoire de la peinture en Italie et les plagiats de Stendhal*. Also helpful for an understanding of the work are Jean Prévost's chapter, *"L'Histoire de la peinture en Italie,"* in *La Création chez Stendhal*, pp. 120–41, and H.-F. Imbert's remarks in *Les Métamorphoses de la liberté; Ou Stendhal devant la Restauration et le Risorgimento* (Paris: Corti, 1967), pp. 127–43.

14. For perceptive comments, see Margaret Tillett, *Stendhal: The Background to the Novels*, pp. 33–45.

15. *C.*, ɪ, 832 (letter to Louis Crozet dated Oct. 20, 1816; it was on the evening of Oct. 16 that Beyle dined with Byron).

16. See *Mélanges de littérature*, ed. H. Martineau (Paris: Le Divan, 1933), III, 255–99, esp. 276–77.

17. *C.*, II, 16–18.

18. See H.-F. Imbert, *Les Métamorphoses de la liberté*, for more details on this aspect of Stendhal's life and career.

19. The *Memoirs on Napoleon* appeared in 1876 and the *Life of Napoleon* in 1897. See Stendhal, *Vie de Napoléon*, ed. M. Wassiltchikov (Paris: Payot, 1969). Also Marcel Heisler, *Stendhal et Napoléon* (Paris: Nizet, 1969) and Dennis Porter, "Stendhal and the Lesson of Napoleon," *PMLA*, 85 (1970), 456–62.

20. *J.*, pp. 1,378–89.

21. *J.*, p. 1,275.

22. *J.*, p. 1,288.

23. For a perceptive analysis of this aspect of Stendhal's character, see Georges Blin, *Stendhal et les problèmes de la personnalité* (Paris: Corti, 1958).

CHAPTER XIII. MÉTILDE AND *DE L'AMOUR*

1. See *H.B.*, p. 11; *S.E.*, pp. 1,395–96.

2. For further details on Métilde's origins, see *P.D.*, pp. 174–79.

3. *H.B.*, p. 10; *S.E.*, p. 1,404.

4. See *C.*, I, 965–81.

5. *C.*, I, 974–82.

6. See Stendhal's letter to Pierre Daru from Genoble (dated Aug. 30, 1819): "My father leaves enormous debts" (*C.*, I, 988).

7. *C.*, I, 988.

8. *C.*, I, 1,055.

9. *C.*, I, 1,000.

10. Letter of July 23, 1820 (*C.*, I, 1,030–31). Also see H.-F. Imbert, *Les Métamorphoses de la liberté*, p. 268.

11. *S.E.*, pp. 1,403, 1,409.

12. *S.E.*, p. 1,395.

13. *S.E.*, p. 1,396, 1,395.

14. *H.B.*, p. 5.

15. *H.B.*, pp. 12, 14–16, 132–33, 353.

16. See *De l'amour*, ed. H. Martineau (Paris: Garnier, 1959), pp. 8–9.

17. *De l'amour*, pp. 5–6.

18. *De l'amour*, p. 25.

CHAPTER XIV. PARIS UNDER THE RESTORATION

1. *S.E.*, pp. 1395–96.

2. See André Strauss, *La Fortune de Stendhal en Angleterre* (Paris: Didier, 1966), for Stendhal's impact on English letters.

3. See Charles Baudelaire, "Qu'est-ce que le romantisme?" ("What is Romanticism?") in his *Salon de 1846, Œuvres complètes*, ed. Y.-G. le Dantec (Paris: Bibliothèque de la Pléiade, 1961), p. 879. Also see Gita May, "Les Figures intermédiaires: Stendhal, Delacroix," in *Diderot et Baudelaire, critiques d'art* (Geneva: Droz, 1973, 3d ed.), pp. 17–27.

4. For a recent translation and critical presentation of this work, see *Life of Rossini*, ed. Richard N. Coe (Seattle: University of Washington Press, 1970).

5. See *H.B.*, p. 17 and *passim*.

6. *H.B.*, pp. 101, 181–82, 228, 261. Also *S.E.*, p. 1,430.

7. *S.E.*, p. 1,429.

8. In his essay, *H.B.*, already mentioned, in which he endeavored to reveal to the public Stendhal's qualities of mind and heart which had been so little appreciated during his lifetime.

9. The letters exchanged by the two friends attest to the familiar and open nature of their relationship (see *C.*, II, 96–99, 152–54, 181–83, 204, 800–01, 829–30, 858–64, 866–68, 875–77, 879–85, 886–88, 893–95, 897–904, 919, 924; III, 31, 529–34, 538–39, 595).

10. See René Dollot, *Stendhal journaliste* (Paris: Mercure de France, 1948).

11. *H.B.*, p. 69.

12. *J.*, pp. 903–05 and *passim*.

13. *E.A.*, p. 1,499.

14. *H.B.*, p. 15.

15. *C.*, II, 792, 800.

16. *E.A.*, p. 1,499.

17. *H.B.*, p. 15.

18. *H.B.*, p. 5.

19. *C.*, III, 535.

20. *H.B.*, p. 5.

21. For more comments on Stendhal's reactions to the eighteenth-century novelists, see Gita May, "Stendhal and the Age of Ideas," *Literature and History in the Age of Ideas; Essays on the French Enlightenment presented to George R. Havens*, ed. Charles G. S. Williams (Columbus: Ohio State University Press, 1975), pp. 343–57.

22. For further details on the genesis and composition of *Armance*, see *R.*, I, 11–22. Also Jean Prévost, "Armance," in *La Création chez Stendhal*, pp. 225–36, and F. W. J. Hemmings, "Narcissus," in *Stendhal: A Study of His Novels* (Oxford: Clarendon Press, 1964), pp. 60–94.

23. See *R.*, I, 12–13.

24. *De l'amour*, pp. 335–39.

25. See F. W. J. Hemmings, *Stendhal*, p. 92.

26. See Stendhal, *Du Romantisme dans les arts*, ed. J. Starzynski (Paris: Hermann, 1966).

27. *H.B.*, pp. 13, 15–16, 56.

28. *C.*, II, 193–94.

CHAPTER XV. *THE RED AND THE BLACK*

1. These manuscripts were eventually acquired by the Bibliothèque Nationale in Paris (see *R.*, II, 532–33).

2. See Stendhal's witty and deliberately provocative preface to his *Italian Chronicles*.

3. For further details on the composition and publication of the *Italian Chronicles*, see R., II, 529–52. Also Jean Prévost, "*Les Chroniques italiennes*," in *La Création chez Stendhal*, pp. 221–24, 320–31, and F. W. J. Hemmings, *Stendhal*, p. 33, n. 1, and p. 164, n. 2. Finally, see the prefatory essays in *Chroniques italiennes*, ed. Roland Beyer (Paris: Julliard, 1964), and the same work, ed. Michel Mohrt (Paris: Editions Gallimard et Librairie Générale Française, 1964).

4. For a recent, although measured, expression of this point of view, see F. W. J. Hemmings, *Stendhal*, p. 71 (Hemmings is nonetheless more nuanced than most other commentators in stating this reservation). Also see Joanna Richardson, *Stendhal* (New York: Coward, McCann and Geoghegan, 1974), p. 223.

5. For further distinctions between the two writers, see Georg Lukács, *Studies in European Realism*, "Balzac and Stendhal," pp. 65–84, and *Stendhal et Balzac; Actes du VIIᵉ Congrès international stendhalien*, ed. V. Del Litto (Aran: Editions du Grand Chêne, 1972).

6. Notably Charles Lalo (see F. W. J. Hemmings, *Stendhal*, p. 84).

7. For Stendhal's comments on Diderot as thinker, esthetic theorist, art critic, and novelist, see Gita May, "Stendhal and the Age of Ideas," pp. 349–51.

8. This aspect of Stendhal's art as a novelist is perceptively analyzed by Victor Brombert, in his *Stendhal: Fiction and the Themes of Freedom* (New York: Random House, 1968). Also see Michael Wood, *Stendhal* (Ithaca: Cornell University Press, 1971), pp. 28–30.

9. See Georges Blin, *Stendhal et les problèmes du roman*, "Les Intrusions d'auteur" (Paris: Corti, 1954), pp. 179–321.

10. See Robert M. Adams, *Stendhal: Notes on a Novelist* (New York: Noonday Press, 1959), pp. 198–220.

11. See in particular "*Le Rouge et le Noir*," in *La Création chez Stendhal*, by Jean Prévost, pp. 239–80; "Le Rouge et le Noir," by Martin Turnell, and "In the Hôtel de La Mole," by Erich Auerbach, in *Stendhal; A Collection of Critical Essays*, ed. Victor Brombert (Englewood Cliffs, N.J.: Prentice-Hall, 1962), pp. 15–33, 34–46; "*Le Rouge et le Noir*: The Ambiguities of Freedom," in *Stendhal: Fiction and the Themes of Freedom*, by Victor Brombert, pp. 61–99; "The Dreamer," in *Stendhal*, by F. W. J. Hemmings, pp. 95–131.

12. Stendhal was fond of such symbolic, allegorical uses of colors, as is also shown by the way in which he used them as tentative titles or subtitles for other works of fiction. See *R.*, I, 198.

13. See F. W. J. Hemmings, *Stendhal*, p. 117, n. 2, for some examples of this type of reaction.

14. See *H.B.*, pp. 13–14.

15. Margaret Tillett, in her *Stendhal*, pp. 1–21.

16. See *R.*, I, 703.

17. For a more detailed examination of this aspect of Stendhal's esthetics, see Francine Marill-Albérès, *Le Naturel chez Stendhal* (Paris: Nizet, 1956).

18. *R.*, I, 704.

19. *R.*, I, 713.

20. See Jean-Pierre Richard, "Connaissance et tendresse chez Stendhal," *Littérature et sensation* (Paris: Editions du Seuil, 1954), pp. 17–116.

21. *E.A.*, p. 1,499.

22. *C.*, II, 187.

CHAPTER XVI. AN UNCONVENTIONAL DIPLOMAT

1. *C.*, II, 186–87.

2. *C.*, II, 188.

3. *C.*, II, 189–90 (his salary, as he delightedly informed his friend Adolphe de Mareste, was to be fifteen thousand francs a year; *C.*, II, 190).

4. *C.*, II, 191–92.

5. *C.*, II, 194–200.

6. *C.*, II, 201. Also see *E.A.*, p. 1,499.

7. *C.*, II, 201–02, 198–99, 201–03.

8. *C.*, II, 201.

9. *C.*, II, 250–51.

10. *C.*, ii, 277.

11. *C.*, ii, 278–80.

12. *C.*, ii, 294.

13. *C.*, ii, 298, 302, 306, 308.

14. *E.A.*, p. 1,499.

15. *C.*, ii, 285, 376.

16. *C.*, ii, 488, 491, 500, 509, 512–13, 599.

17. *C.*, ii, 484–85. And see Diderot's critical essays on the theater, notably his influential *Entretiens sur le fils naturel, De la poésie dramatique,* and *Paradoxe sur le comédien.*

18. *C.*, ii, 172.

19. See *R.*, i, 470, n. 2; *H.B.*, p. 194.

20. *C.*, ii, 485.

21. See Georges May, *Le Dilemme du roman au XVIIIe siècle* (New Haven: Yale University Press, 1963).

22. See *Mélanges de littérature*, ed. H. Martineau (Paris: Le Divan, 1933), iii, 415–44.

23. *Mélanges*, iii, 305–06.

24. *Mélanges*, ii, 342–76. The projected article has also been reproduced at the end of the handy Garnier edition of *The Red and the Black*, ed. H. Martineau (Paris: Garnier, 1957), pp. 509–27.

25. *C.*, ii, 487.

26. Victor Brombert, *Stendhal: Fiction and the Themes of Freedom*, p. 184.

27. See Lionel Trilling's fine essay on this problem in Western culture, *Sincerity and Authenticity* (Cambridge: Harvard University Press, 1971).

28. *H.B.*, pp. 13–14.

29. *S.E.*, p. 1,393.

30. The sketches are reproduced in *La Vie de Stendhal*, by V. Del Litto (Paris: Editions du Sud, 1965).

CHAPTER XVII. TWO UNFINISHED WORKS:
LUCIEN LEUWEN AND *THE LIFE OF HENRY BRULARD*

1. *H.B..*, p. 192; *J.*, pp. 1,189, 1,235; *S.E.*, p. 1,421; *C.*, III, 12.

2. See *J.*, pp. 985, 992, 994; *C.*, I, 1,133, 1,139–40, 1,148–50, 1,203, 1,212, 1,214, 1,233; *C.*, II, 88–89, 147–48, 154–55, 157–59, 167–68, 176, 183–84, 515–16, 559–61.

3. *C.*, II, 643–44.

4. *R.*, I, 737.

5. *C.*, II, 644, 724, 916–17.

6. *C.*, II, 644.

7. See Victor Brombert, *Stendhal: Fiction and the Themes of Freedom*, p. 111.

8. *R.*, I, 1,387–1,413.

9. *R.*, I, 1,384.

10. See Maurice Bardèche, *Stendhal romancier* (Paris: Editions de la Table Ronde, 1947), p. 246; Harry Levin, "Stendhal," in *The Gates of Horn: A Study of Five French Realists* (New York: Oxford University Press, 1963), p. 133; Michael Wood, *Stendhal*, pp. 118–23.

11. *C.*, II, 724.

12. Victor Brombert, *Stendhal: Fiction and the Themes of Freedom*, p. 95.

13. See F. W. J. Hemmings, *Stendhal*, p. 143.

14. *H.B.*, p. 5.

15. *H.B.*, p. 3.

16. *H.B.*, pp. 12, 14.

17. *H.B.*, p. 387.

18. See Jean-Jacques Rousseau, *Confessions*, ed. J. Voisine (Paris: Garnier, 1964), p. 4.

19. *H.B.*, p. 9.

20. *H.B.*, p. 395.

CHAPTER XVIII. ESCAPE FROM CIVITAVECCHIA:
THE DIPLOMAT ON LEAVE (*ITALIAN CHRONICLES*,
MEMOIRS OF A TOURIST, AND OTHER WORKS)

1. C., III, 201–02, 531, 216.

2. C., III, 188–89, 197, 201–02; *H.B.*, p. 366; *S.E.*, p. 1,472.

3. C., II, 188, 190–91, 386, 1,025, n. 8, 444, 468, 718; III, 111, 141.

4. See Henri Martineau, *Le Cœur de Stendhal*, II, 317–18, for further details concerning Stendhal's lodgings during his three-year leave of absence.

5. *Confessions*, ed. J. Voisine, pp. 504–05.

6. C., III, 221; *S.E.*, p. 1,414.

7. See Gita May, "Stendhal and Madame Roland," *Romanic Review*, 53 (1962), 16–31.

8. C., III, 221.

9. C., III, 218–19, 222–23, 225–26, 250–51.

10. C., III, 536–37.

11. C., III, 533.

12. C., III, 378–80, 572, 583. Also Pierre Jourda, *Stendhal raconté par ceux qui l'ont vu* (Paris: Stock, 1931), pp. 120–22.

13. See Marcel Heisler, *Stendhal et Napoléon* (Paris: Nizet, 1969), pp. 101–15.

14. See *R.*, II, 1,053–60.

15. See *R.*, II, 532–33. It was Stendhal's cousin, loyal friend, and literary executor, Romain Colomb, who assembled the collection in 1855. For more details on *Vanina Vanini*, see chapter 15, above.

16. C., II, 762–63.

17. *Chroniques italiennes*, ed. Michel Mohrt, pp. 22, 29.

18. For more details on these peregrinations, see Stendhal's *Memoirs of a Tourist*, reproduced in the comprehensive edition published by Le Divan. It was also translated by Allan Seager (Evanston, Ill.: Northwestern University Press, 1962).

19. See *Mélanges de littérature*, III, 415–16.

20. Tr. Elisabeth Abbott, Introd. Victor Brombert (New York: Orion Press, 1970).

CHAPTER XIX. *THE CHARTERHOUSE OF PARMA*

1. For further details on the sources of *The Charterhouse of Parma*, see R., II, 11–14; F. W. J. Hemmings, *Stendhal*, pp. 170–72.

2. R., II, 15.

3. R., II, 23–24.

4. R., II, 24.

5. See Gilbert Durand, *Le Décor mythique de "La Chartreuse de Parme."*

6. See Georges May, "Rousseau and France," *Yale French Studies,* Fall–Winter 1961–62, pp. 122–35.

7. F. W. J. Hemmings, *Stendhal,* p. 164.

8. Victor Brombert, *Stendhal: Fiction and the Themes of Freedom,* p. 167.

9. Margaret Tillett, "The Dilemma of Count Mosca," in *Stendhal,* pp. 124–42.

10. R., II, 26.

11. Victor Brombert, *Stendhal: Fiction and the Themes of Freedom,* p. 69.

12. In a letter to Stendhal dated April 5, 1839, Balzac had already expressed the basic ideas he was to amplify in his article (see C., III, 557); and, no doubt, the laudatory letter must have pleased Stendhal. But when Balzac publicly proclaimed his admiration in the *Revue Parisienne,* Stendhal was understandably overcome with gratitude.

13. C., III, 393–405 (letter begun Oct. 16 and completed Oct. 29, 1840).

14. See R., II, Appendix II, 510–25, for these revised fragments and additions.

15. C., III, 394–95.

16. C., III, 396.

17. C., III, 394, 398, 401.

18. See Rousseau's famous letter to Voltaire of Aug. 18, 1756 (generally referred to as the Letter on Providence).

19. *P.D.*, pp. 32–33.

CHAPTER XX. *LAMIEL:* AN UNFINISHED MASTERPIECE

1. For a full account of Madame Roland's life and works, see Gita May, *Madame Roland and the Age of Revolution* (New York: Columbia University Press, 1970).

2. For enlightening remarks on the Tartuffe myth in Stendhal's novels, particularly in *The Red and the Black*, see Victor Brombert, *Stendhal: Fiction and the Themes of Freedom*, p. 98. Also Gita May, "Molière and Stendhal," pp. 125–32.

3. *J.*, p. 1,258.

4. F. W. J. Hemmings, in his otherwise excellent *Stendhal*, betrays this characteristic unease in his discussion of *Lamiel* (see pp. 195, 206).

5. See André Doyon and Yves du Parc, *De Mélanie à Lamiel* (Aran: Editions du Grand Chêne, 1972).

6. *R.*, II, 940–41.

7. *R.*, II, 905, 1,031.

8. *R.*, II, 862.

9. See *Œuvres intimes*, pp. 1,503–22, 1,619–20.

10. C., III, 434 (letter to Domenico Fiore dated April 5, 1841).

11. See André Doyon, "Le Dossier de la mort de Stendhal," *Stendhal Club* (Oct. 15, 1966), pp. 13–17.

12. C., III, 435.

Selective Bibliography

I. Works by Stendhal

The standard and most comprehensive edition of Stendhal's works is edited by Henri Martineau (Paris: Le Divan, 1927–37), 79 small volumes.

There is also the recent, well-documented, and more accessible Bibliothèque de la Pléiade edition (published by Gallimard), presenting the works listed below.

The fictional writings in two volumes, ed. Henri Martineau:
Romans et Nouvelles, Vol. I, containing *Armance, Le Rouge et le Noir, Lucien Leuwen*. Paris: Gallimard, 1952.
Romans et Nouvelles, Vol. II, containing *La Chartreuse de Parme, Chroniques italiennes, Lamiel, Le Rose et le Vert, Mina de Vanghel, Souvenirs d'un gentilhomme italien, Le Juif, Le Coffre et le revenant. Le Philtre, Le Chevalier de Saint-Ismier, Philibert Lescale, Féder*. Paris: Gallimard, 1952.
The personal and autobiographical essays in one volume, ed. Henri Martineau and Victor Del Litto, *Œuvres intimes*, containing *Vie de Henry Brulard, Journal, Souvenirs d'égotisme, Essais d'autobiographie, Earline, Les Privilèges*. Paris: Gallimard, 1955.
The correspondence in three volumes, ed. Henri Martineau and Victor Del Litto:
Correspondance, Vol., I, 1800–21. Paris: Gallimard, 1962.
Correspondance, Vol. II, 1821–34. Paris: Gallimard, 1967.
Correspondance, Vol. III, 1835–42. Paris: Gallimard, 1968.

Whenever possible, I have made use of the Pléiade edition, and all translations are my own.

The following are also useful editions of individual works by Stendhal:

Vie de Henry Brulard. Ed. Henri Martineau. Paris: Garnier, 1953.
Du Romantisme dans les arts. Ed. J. Starzynski. Paris: Hermann, 1966.
Chroniques italiennes. Ed. Michel Mohrt. Paris: Editions Gallimard et Librairie Générale Française, 1964.
Chroniques italiennes. Ed. Roland Beyer. Paris: Julliard, 1964.
Le Rouge et le Noir. Ed. Roger Nimier. Paris: Edition Gallimard, 1960.
Le Rouge et le Noir. Ed. Henri Martineau. Paris: Garnier, 1957.
La Chartreuse de Parme. Ed. Henri Martineau. Paris: Garnier, 1942.
Armance. Ed. Henri Martineau. Paris: Garnier, 1950.
De l'amour. Ed. Henri Martineau. Paris: Garnier, 1959.
Lucien Leuwen. Ed. Claude Roy. Paris: Librairie Générale Française, 1960.
Lamiel, suivi de *Armance*. Ed. Roger Nimier. Paris: Librairie Générale Française, 1961.
Rome, Naples et Florence en 1817. Ed. Roland Beyer. Paris: Julliard, 1964.
Vie de Napoléon. Ed. Michel Wassiltchikov. Paris: Payot, 1969.
Napoléon. Ed. Victor Del Litto. Lausanne: Editions Rencontre, 1961.
Romans. Ed. Samuel S. de Sacy. Paris: Editions du Seuil, 1969. 2 vols.
English translations include:
The Abbess of Castro, and other Tales. C. K. Scott Moncrieff, trans. New York: Boni and Liveright, 1926.
Armance. C. K. Scott Moncrieff, trans. New York: Boni and Liveright, 1926.
The Charterhouse of Parma. C. K. Scott Moncrieff, trans. New York: Modern Library, 1925; American Library, 1962.
The Life of Henry Brulard. Jean Stewart and B. C. J. G. Knight, trans. New York: Funk and Wagnalls, 1958.
Life of Rossini. Richard N. Coe, trans. Seattle: University of Washington Press, 1970.
Memoirs of a Tourist. Allan Seager, trans. Evanston, Ill.: Northwestern University Press, 1962.
Memoirs of Egotism. Hannah and Matthew Josephson, trans. New York: Lear, 1949.

Memoirs of an Egotist. T. W. Earp, trans. New York: Noonday Press, 1958.

The Private Diaries of Stendhal. Robert Sage, trans. New York: Doubleday, 1954; Norton, 1962.

On Love. Philip Sidney Woolf and Cecil N. Sidney Woolf, trans. Mount Vernon, N.Y.: Peter Pauper Press, n.d.

On Love. H. B. V., trans., under the direction of C. K. Scottt Moncrieff. New York: Boni and Liveright, 1927.

Racine and Shakespeare. Guy Daniels, trans.; Foreword, André Maurois. New York: Crowell-Collier Press, 1962.

Travels in the South of France. Elisabeth Abbott, trans.; Introd. Victor Brombert. New York: Orion Press, 1970.

Selected Journalism. Geoffrey Strickland, ed. and trans. New York: Grove Press, 1959.

A Roman Journal. Haakon Chevalier, trans. New York: Orion Press, 1957.

Rome, Naples, and Florence. Richard N. Coe, trans. New York: Braziller, 1960.

The Shorter Novels of Stendhal. C. K. Scott Moncrieff, trans. New York: Liveright, 1946.

Lamiel. T. W. Earp, trans. New York: New Directions, 1952.

The Red and the Black. C. K. Scott Moncrieff, trans. New York: Modern Library, 1953.

Scarlet and Black. Margaret R. B. Shaw, trans. London: Penguin Books, 1965.

Lucien Leuwen. Louise Varèse, trans. New York: New Directions, 1950, 2 vols.

II. Studies on Stendhal, General Critical and Historical Works, and Other Relevant Sources

Abrams, M. H. *The Mirror and the Lamp; Romantic Theory and the Critical Tradition.* New York: Norton, 1958.

Adams, Robert M. *Stendhal: Notes on a Novelist.* New York: Noonday Press, 1959.

Alain, Auguste Chartier, pseud. *Stendhal.* Paris: Rieder, 1935.

Alciatore, Jules C. *Stendhal et Helvétius: Les Sources de la philosophie de Stendhal*. Geneva: Droz, 1952.

—— "Stendhal et *La Princesse de Clèves*." *Stendhal Club*, July 15, 1959, pp. 281–94.

—— "Stendhal lecteur de *La Pucelle*." *Stendhal Club*, July 15, 1960, pp. 325–34.

—— "Stendhal et les romans de Voltaire." *Stendhal Club*, Jan. 15, 1961, pp. 15–23.

Allem, Maurice. *L'Epopée napoléonienne dans la poésie française*. Paris: Librairie des Annales, 1912.

Aragon, Louis. *La Lumière de Stendhal*. Paris: Denoël, 1954.

Arbelet, Paul. *L'Histoire de la peinture en Italie et les plagiats de Stendhal*. Paris: Calmann Lévy, 1913.

—— *La Jeunesse de Stendhal*. Paris: Champion, 1919. 2 vols.

—— *Stendhal épicier, ou les infortunes de Mélanie*. Paris: Plon, 1926.

—— *Louason, ou les perplexités amoureuses de Stendhal*. Grenoble: B. Arthaud, 1937.

Artz, Frederick B. *Reaction and Revolution, 1814–32*. New York: Harper & Row, 1934.

Atherton, John. *Stendhal*. London: Bowes and Bowes, 1965.

Auerbach, Erich. "In the Hôtel de La Mole." In *Mimesis*, tr. from the German, Willard Trask. New York: Doubleday Anchor, 1957, pp. 400–34.

Balzac, Honoré de. *Etudes sur M. Beyle; Analyse de La Chartreuse de Parme*. Geneva: Editons d'Art Skira, 1943; rpt. of Balzac's famous article on *The Charterhouse of Parma*, first pub. in *La Revue parisienne*, Sept. 25, 1840.

Bardèche, Maurice. *Stendhal romancier*. Paris: Editions de la Table Ronde, 1947.

Bardos, J.-P., ed. *Stendhal*. Paris: Didier, 1970.

Barzun, Jacques. *Berlioz and His Century; An Introduction to the Age of Romanticism*. New York, Meridian Books, 1956; rpt. from *Berlioz and the Romantic Century*, revised by author.

—— *Classic, Romantic, and Modern*. New York: Doubleday, Anchor Books, 1961.

—— "Stendhal on Love." *The Energies of Art; Studies of Authors Classic and Modern*. New York: Vintage Books, 1962. Pp. 104–33.

Blin, Georges. *Stendhal et les problèmes du roman*. Paris: Corti, 1954.

—— *Stendhal et les problèmes de la personnalité*. Paris: Corti, 1958.

Blum, Léon. *Stendhal et le beylisme.* Paris: Albin Michel, 1930.

Boyer, Ferdinand. *Les Lectures de Stendhal.* Paris: Editions du Stendhal Club, 1925.

—— *Stendhal et les historiens de Napoléon.* Paris: Editions du Stendhal Club, 1926.

Brinton, Crane. *The Jacobins: An Essay in the New History.* New York: Macmillan, 1930.

—— *A Decade of Revolution; 1789–1799.* New York: Harper, 1934.

Brombert, Victor. *Stendhal et la voie oblique.* Paris: Presses Universitaires de France, 1954.

—— "Stendhal lecteur de Rousseau," *Revue des Sciences Humaines* (Oct.–Dec. 1958), pp. 46382.

—— ed. *Stendhal: A Collection of Critical Essays.* Englewood Cliffs, N.J.: Prentice Hall, 1962.

—— *Stendhal: Fiction and the Themes of Freedom.* New York: Random House, 1968.

—— "Esquisse de la prison heureuse." *Revue d'Histoire Littéraire de la France,* March–April 1971, pp. 247–61.

Brooks, Peter. "Stendhal and the Styles of Worldliness." *The Novel of Worldliness.* Princeton: Princeton University Press, 1969. Pp. 219–78.

Bruun, Geoffrey. *Europe and the French Imperium; 1799–1814.* New York: Harper & Row, 1963.

Caraccio, Armand. *Stendhal.* Paris: Hatier, 1963.

—— *Stendhal.* Tr. Dolores Bagley. New York: New York University Press, 1965.

Carlyle, Thomas. *The French Revolution.* New York: Modern Library, 1934.

—— *On Heroes and Hero-Worship and the Heroic in History.* London: Oxford University Press, 1965.

Carné, L. de. "De la popularité de Napoléon." *Revue des Deux Mondes,* 22 (1840), 857–69.

Chabrun, Elisabeth. *Stendhal, écrivain du XXᵉ siècle.* Paris: La Table Ronde, 1973.

Chassé, Charles. *Napoléon par les écrivains.* Paris: Librairie Hachette, 1921.

Chauteaubriand, François-René de. *Mémoires d'Outre-tombe.* Paris: Bibliothèque de la Pléiade, 1951. 2 vols.

Chuquet, Arthur. *Stendhal-Beyle.* Paris: Plon, 1902.

Cobban, Alfred. *A History of Modern France*. Baltimore: Penguin, 1961. 2 vols.

Cordier, Henri. *Bibliographie stendhalienne*. Paris: Champion, 1914.

Crouzet, Michel. "Misanthropie et vertu: Stendhal et le problème républicain." *Revue des Sciences Humaines*, Jan.–March 1967, pp. 29–52.

Daumas, Georges. "Félix-Romain Gagnon, oncle de Stendhal." *Stendhal Club*, July 15, 1959, pp. 281–94.

Debraye, Henry. *Stendhal: Documents iconographiques*. Geneva: Pierre Cailler, 1950.

Dédéyan, Charles. *L'Italie dans l'œuvre romanesque de Stendhal*. Paris: Société d'édition d'enseignement supérieur, 1963. 2 vols.

Delacroix, Eugène. *Correspondance générale*. Ed. André Joubin. Paris: Plon, 1936–38. 5 vols.

——— *Journal*. Ed. André Joubin. Paris: Plon, 1932. 3 vols.

——— *The Journal of Eugène Delacroix*. Tr. Walter Pach. New York: Crown, 1948; Viking Press, 1972.

Del Litto, Victor. *La Vie intellectuelle de Stendhal: Genèse et Evolution de ses idées, 1802–1821*. Paris: Presses Universitaires de France, 1962.

——— *La Vie de Stendhal*. Paris: Editions du Sud, 1965.

——— *Album Stendhal*. Paris: Gallimard, 1966.

——— *Stendhal en Dauphiné*. Paris: Hachette, 1968.

Del Litto, ed. *Première Journée du Stendhal Club*. Lausanne: Editions du Grand Chêne, 1965.

——— *Stendhal et Balzac: Actes du VIIe Congrès international stendhalien*. Aran, Switzerland: Editions du Grand Chêne, 1972.

Denommé, Robert T. "Changing Perspectives in Stendhal's *Vie de Henry Brulard* and *La Chartreuse de Parme*." *Romanic Review*, 67 (1976), 28–37.

Dollot, René. *Stendhal journaliste*. Paris: Mercure de France, 1948.

Doyon, André. "Le Dossier de la mort de Stendhal." *Stendhal Club*, Oct. 15, 1966, pp. 13–17.

Doyon, André and Yves du Parc. *De Mélanie à Lamiel*. Aran, Switzerland: Editions du Grand Chêne, 1972.

Durand, Gilbert. *Le Décor mythique de "La Chartreuse de Parme."* Paris: Corti, 1961.

Dutourd, Jean. *L'Ame sensible*. Paris: Gallimard, 1959.

——— *The Man of Sensibility*. Tran. Robin Chancellor. New York: Simon & Schuster, 1961.

Felman, Shoshana. *La Folie dans l'œuvre romanesque de Stendhal.* Paris: Corti, 1971.

Fowlie, Wallace. *Stendhal.* London: Macmillan, 1969.

Gay, Peter. *The Enlightenment: An Interpretation.* New York: Knopf, 1966–69. 2 vols.

Genette, Gérard. "Stendhal." *Figures II.* Paris: Editions du Seuil, 1969. Pp. 155–93.

Gilman, Stephen. *The Tower as Emblem.* Frankfurt: Klostermann, 1967.

Goimard, Jacques, ed. *L'Italie au temps de Stendhal.* Paris: Hachette, 1966.

Green, Frederick C. *Stendhal.* Cambridge: Cambridge University Press, 1939.

Gutwirth, Marcel. *Stendhal.* New York: Twayne, World Author Series, 1971.

Hazard, Paul. *La Vie de Stendhal.* Paris: Gallimard, 1928.

—— *Stendhal.* Tr. Eleanor Hard. New York: Ungar, 1965.

Heisler, Marcel. *Stendhal et Napoléon.* Paris: Nizet, 1969.

Hemmings, F. W. J. *Stendhal: A Study of his Novels.* Oxford: Clarendon Press, 1964.

—— "Baudelaire, Stendhal, Michel-Ange et Lady Macbeth." *Stendhal Club,* April 15, 1961, pp. 85–98.

Herold, J. Christopher, ed. *The Mind of Napoleon; A Selection from his Written and Spoken Words.* New York: Columbia University Press, 1955.

Hobsbawm, E. J. *The Age of Revolution; 1789–1848.* New York: New American Library, 1962.

Houssaye, Henry. "Napoléon dans la littérature du XIXe siècle." *La Revue Hebdomadaire,* May 25, 1907, pp. 401–27.

Imbert, Henri-François. *Les Métamorphoses de la liberté; Ou Stendhal devant la Restauration et le Risorgimento.* Paris: Corti, 1967.

—— *Stendhal et la tentation janséniste.* Geneva: Droz, 1970.

Jansse, Lucien. "Stendhal et les classes sociales." *Stendhal Club,* Oct. 15, 1963, pp. 35–45.

Jones, Grahame C. *L'Ironie dans les romans de Stendhal.* Lausanne: Editions du Grand Chêne, 1966.

Jones, Howard Mumford. *Revolution and Romanticism.* Cambridge: Harvard University Press, 1974.

Josephson, Matthew. *Stendhal; Or The Pursuit of Happiness.* New York: Doubleday, 1946.

Jourda, Pierre. *Stendhal raconté par ceux qui l'ont vu.* Paris: Stock, 1931.

Krutch, Joseph Wood. "Stendhal," *Five Masters; A Study in the Mutations of the Novel*. Bloomington: Indiana University Press, 1959. Pp. 177–249.

Lefebvre, Georges. *The French Revolution from its Origins to 1793*. Tr. E. M. Evanson. New York: Columbia University Press, 1962.

—— *The French Revolution from 1793 to 1799*. Tr. J. H. Stewart and J. Friguglietti. New York: Columbia University Press, 1964.

—— *Napoleon; From 18 Brumaire to Tilsit, 1799–1807*. Tr. H. F. Stockhold. New York: Columbia University Press, 1969.

—— *Napoleon; From Tilsit to Waterloo, 1807–1815*. Tr. J. E. Anderson. New York: Columbia University Press, 1969.

Levin, Harry. "Stendhal," *The Gates of Horn: A Study of Five French Realists*. New York: Oxford University Press, 1963. Pp. 84–144.

Lukács, Georg. "Balzac and Stendhal." *Studies in European Realism*. Introd. Alfred Kazin. New York: Grosset and Dunlap, 1964. Pp. 65–84.

Madelin, Louis. "Napoléon à travers le siècle 1821–1921." *Revue des Deux Mondes*, May 1, 1921, pp. 73–93.

McWatters, K. G. "La Présence de Napoléon dans *La Chartreuse de Parme*." *Stendhal Club*, April 15, 1970, pp. 213–8.

Marill-Albérès, Francine. *Le Naturel chez Stendhal*. Paris: Nizet, 1956.

—— *Stendhal*. Paris: Editions Universitaires, 1970.

Markham, Felix. *Napoleon*. New York: New American Library, 1966.

Martineau, Henri. *Le Cœur de Stendhal; Histoire de sa vie et de ses sentiments*. Paris: Albin Michel, 1952–53. 2 vols.

—— *Petit Dictionnaire stendhalien*. Paris: Le Divan, 1948.

—— *L'Œuvre de Stendhal; Histoire de ses livres et de sa pensée*. Paris: Albin Michel, 1951.

Martino, Pierre. *Stendhal*. Paris: Boivin, 1934.

Mason, Haydn T. "Condorcet et Stendhal." *Stendhal Club*, April 15, 1967, pp. 255–58.

May, Georges. *Le Dilemme du roman au xviiie Siècle*. New Haven: Yale University Press, 1963.

May, Gita. "Les Figures intermédiaires: Stendhal, Delacroix." *Diderot et Baudelaire, critiques d'art*. Geneva: Droz, 1957. Pp. 17–42.

—— "Stendhal and Madame Roland." *Romanic Review*, 53 (1962), 16–31.

—— "Préromantisme rousseauiste et égotisme stendhalien." *L'Esprit Créateur*, Summer 1966, pp. 97–107.

—— "Aspects de la sensibilité stendhalienne." *Symposium*, 23 (1969), 303–18.

—— "Stendhal et les moralistes classiques." *L'Esprit Créateur*, Spring–Summer 1975, pp. 263–70.

—— "Molière and Stendhal." *Molière and the Commonwealth of Letters: Patrimony and Posterity*, ed. Roger Johnson, Jr., Editha S. Neumann, and Guy T. Trail. Jackson: University Press of Mississippi, 1975. Pp. 125–32.

—— "Stendhal and the Age of Ideas." *Literature and History in the Age of Ideas*, ed. Charles G. S. Williams. Columbus: Ohio State University Press, 1975. Pp. 343–57.

Mérimée, Prosper. "H.B.: Notes et souvenirs." *Portraits historiques et littéraires*. Paris: Calmann Lévy, 1892.

Michel, François. *Etudes stendhaliennes*. Paris: Mercure de France, 1972.

Moreau, Pierre. "Les Stendhaliens avant Stendhal." *Revue des Cours et Conférences*, Jan. 30, 1927, pp. 301–09; March 15, 1927, pp. 656–64; March 30, 1927, pp. 734–46.

Mylne, Vivienne. *The Eighteenth-Century French Novel; Techniques of Illusion*. New York: Barnes and Noble, 1965.

Paupe, Adolphe. *Histoire des œuvres de Stendhal*. Paris: Dujarric, 1903.

Peyre, Henri. *Les Générations littéraires*. Paris: Boivin, 1948.

—— *Literature and Sincerity*. New Haven: Yale University Press, 1963.

—— *Qu'est-ce que le romantisme?* Paris: Presses Universitaires de France, 1971.

—— "Stendhal and Balzac as Admirers and Followers of Molière." *Molière and the Commonwealth of Letters: Patrimony and Posterity*, ed. Roger Johnson, Jr., Editha Neumann, and Guy T. Trail. Jackson: University Press of Mississippi, 1975. Pp. 133–44.

Porter, Dennis, "Stendhal and the Lesson of Napoleon." *PMLA*, 85 (1970), 456–62.

—— "Politics, Happiness and the Arts: A Commentary on Stendhal's *Rome, Naples et Florence en 1817*," *French Studies*, 24 (1970), 254–61.

Prévost, Jean. *La Création chez Stendhal*. Paris: Mercure de France, 1951.

Proust, Marcel. "Notes sur Stendhal." *Contre Sainte-Beuve*. Paris: Gallimard, 1954. Pp. 413–16.

Richard, Jean-Pierre. "Connaissance et tendresse chez Stendhal." *Lit-*

térature et sensation. Paris: Editions du Seuil, 1954. Pp. 17–116.

Richardson, Joanna. *Stendhal*. New York: Coward, McCann & Geoghegan, 1974.

Roussel, Jean. *Jean-Jacques Rousseau en France après la Révolution, 1795–1830; Lectures et Légende*. Paris: Colin, 1972.

Roy, Claude. *Stendhal par lui-même*. Paris: Editions du Seuil, 1960.

Royer, Louis. *Bibliographie stendhalienne*. Paris: Editions du Stendhal Club, 1930–67. 8 vols.

Rudé, Fernand. *Stendhal et la pensée sociale de son temps*. Paris: Plon, 1967.

Rudé, George. *Revolutionary Europe; 1783–1815*. New York: Harper Torchbooks, 1964.

Seznec, Jean. "Stendhal et les peintres bolonais." *Gazette des Beaux-Arts*, 53 (1959), 167–78.

Showalter, English. *The Evolution of the French Novel, 1641–1782*. Princeton: Princeton University Press, 1972.

Solaroli, Libero. "Stendhal et la clef des *Liaisons dangereuses*." *Stendhal Club*, Oct. 15, 1958, pp. 109–13.

Staël-Holstein, Anne-Louise Germaine Necker, Baronne de. *Lettres sur les ouvrages et le caractère de J.-J. Rousseau*. Paris: n.p., 1788.

—— *De L'Influence des passions sur le bonheur des individus et des nations*. Paris: Maradan, 1818.

—— *Considérations sur les principaux événements de la Révolution française*. Paris: Delaunay, 1820.

—— *De La Littérature considérée dans ses rapports avec les institutions sociales*. Ed. Paul Van Tieghem. Geneva: Droz, 1959. 2 vols.

—— *Ten Years of Exile*. Tr. Dorothy Beik. New York: Saturday Review Press, 1972.

Starobinski, Jean. "Stendhal pseudonyme." *L'Œil vivant*. Paris: Gallimard, 1961. Pp. 193–257.

Strachey, Lytton. "Henri Beyle." *Books and Characters French and English*. New York: Harcourt, Brace, 1922. Pp. 267–93.

Strauss, André. *La Fortune de Stendhal en Angleterre*. Paris: Didier, 1966.

Strickland, Geoffrey. *Stendhal: The Education of a Novelist*. Cambridge: Cambridge University Press, 1974.

Thibaudet, Albert. "Stendhal et Molière." *La Nouvelle Revue Française*, Nov. 1, 1924, pp. 593–606.

Thompson, J. M. *Napoleon Bonaparte; His Rise and Fall.* New York: Oxford University Press, 1951.

Thomson, David. *Democracy in France.* London: Oxford University Press, 1958.

Tillett, Margaret. *Stendhal: The Background to the Novels.* London: Oxford University Press, 1971.

Trahard, Pierre. *La Sensibilité révolutionnaire; 1789–1794.* Paris: Boivin, 1936.

Trilling, Lionel. *Sincerity and Authenticity.* Cambridge: Harvard University Press, 1974.

Trout, Paulette. *La Vocation romanesque de Stendhal.* Paris: Editions Universitaires, 1970.

Turnell, Martin. "Stendhal." *The Novel in France.* New York: Vintage Books, 1958. Pp. 127–216.

Vaillant, Pierre. "Stendhal à la bibliothèque de Grenoble." *Stendhal Club*, Oct. 15, 1965, pp. 17–24.

Valéry, Paul. "Stendhal," *Variété, Œuvres*, ed. Jean Hytier. Paris: Bibliothèque de la Pléiade, 1957. I, 553–82.

Weber, Jean-Paul. *Stendhal: Les Structures thématiques de l'œuvre et du destin.* Paris: Société d'édition d'enseignement supérieur, 1969.

Wood, Michael. *Stendhal.* Ithaca: Cornell University Press, 1971.

Index